Inhalt

W0205620

Vorwort vii

A Society 1

1 Health and Wellbeing
The cost of marital breakdown 2
Health care in the UK 4
Adolescence and body image 6
Radio interview: advice to parents 8
Recognizing addiction 10
Recognizing addiction, cont'd 12

2 Education
Schools in the United Kingdom 14
Gender bias in education 16
German Department, University of Camford 18

3 Race and Religion
A Colorblind Society? 20
Operation Athena 22
"Cults" in the USA 24

4 Law and Order
Is it time to amend the Second Amendment? 26
Readers' Forum 28

B The Environment 31

1 The Living World
How our countryside has changed 32
North America – Natural Vegetation 34
North America – Natural Vegetation, cont'd 36

2 Environmental Problems – First World
Climate Change 38
Greenpeace Toxics Campaign 40
Marine pollution in the North Sea 42
Wild Britain is under threat 44

3 Environmental Problems – Third World
Desertification 46
Tropical Deforestation 48

4 **Sustainable Development**

Radio interview: sustainable development 50
Grow organic, buy organic 52
Is recycling wasteful? 54
Re: Is recycling wasteful? 56

C The Economy 59

1 **National and Global Economy**

The Industrial Revolution 60
The United States of America 62
Radio debate: globalization 64
Poverty, First World lending and Third World debt . . . 66

2 **The World of Business**

New man at the top 68

3 **Employment**

The glass ceiling 70
Getting it right ... recruitment and selection 72
Going freelance 74

4 **Money Matters**

What is Economic and Monetary Union? 76

D Literature 79

1 **General**

Figurative language 80
Discussion: reading preferences 82

2 **Prose**

Radio interview: the role of the narrator 84
The British novel post-1945 86
The novels of Patrick O'Brian 88

3 **Poetry**

Discussion: what is poetry 90
Ted Hughes and the Poetry of Violence 92

4 **Drama**

Comedy 94
Tragedy 96
Discussion: *Death of a Salesman* 98

E The Media 101

1 **Broadcasting**

Question Time: the future of the BBC 102
The best and worst of TV 104

2 The Press
The British press 106
The Newspaper 108

3 Online
Discussion: Websites 110
An educ@tional experience 112

4 Censorship and Control
Interview: regulating the Internet 114
Interview: regulating the Internet, cont'd 116
Is there too much violence on our screens? 118
A gross intrusion / Fair game 120
Internet piracy is not a victimless crime 122

F Politics 125

1 Systems and Institutions
Dialogue: elections in the United States 126
The United Kingdom: Central Government 128
Main institutions of the European Union 130
The UN in brief 132

2 Policies and Issues
Time to close the door? 134
Discussion: role of the armed forces 136
Enlargement of the EU 138
Scandal – does it matter? 140
Which way now? 142
Is the death penalty a just and humane punishment? 144

3 Campaigning and Protest
Greenpeace 146
Eyewitness reports from the demonstrations 148

4 Conflict and Oppression
The crisis in Kosovo 150
Dialogue: human rights 152

G Science and Technology 155

1 Information Technology
Are we too dependent on computers? 156
Interview: artificial intelligence 158

2 Energy Technology
Renewable energy – options for the UK 160
Renewable energy – options for the UK, cont'd 162

3 Space Exploration
Space – a distraction from more important issues? . 164
There's gold (and water) in them there asteroids . . . 166

4 Biotechnology and Medicine
Benefits of Genetic Modification 168
GM agriculture – good or bad? 170
Laboratory tests on animals 172

Useful Expressions for Essay Writing 175

Index 178

Vorwort

Focus on Vocabulary richtet sich an Englisch Lernende, die das Abitur anstreben. Doch auch für fortgeschrittene Lernende aus anderen Bereichen, die ihre Englischkenntnisse vertiefen wollen, ist es ein ebenso sinnvoller wie nützlicher Begleiter.

Focus on Vocabulary ist kein „Wörterbuch" im tradierten Sinne, sondern geht von einem kontextbezogenen Lernansatz aus. Demnach ist es weitaus effektiver, Wörter in einem zusammenhängenden, eingängigen und interessanten Text zu lernen oder zu wiederholen, statt sich lange Wortlisten einzuprägen. Darüber hinaus vermittelt kontextbezogenes Wörterlernen nicht nur den grammatisch richtigen Gebrauch, sondern auch den Sinnzusammenhang, in dem ein Wort üblicherweise erscheint. Ein einzelnes Wort in einer Liste steht immer für sich, dagegen ist der Kontext für die Erinnerung eines Wortes eine Eselsbrücke, die in Prüfungen, beim Verfassen von Aufsätzen und beim Lesen von englischen Texten hilfreich ist. Das Lesen in einer fremden Sprache hilft den Lernenden wiederum, ihre Gedanken gleich in dieser Sprache zu formulieren, statt den Umweg über das Deutsche und die Übersetzung zu nehmen.

Eine weitere sinnvolle Lernmethode ist, sich verwandte Wörter, also Wörter aus Wortfamilien, einzuprägen. Deshalb werden in *Focus on Vocabulary* Antonyme, Synonyme und Wortfamilien in einer separaten Spalte aufgeführt. Kennt man ein Wort aus der Familie, lässt sich ein weiteres oder eine Wortkombination leichter herleiten.

Focus on Vocabulary ist in sieben thematische Einheiten untergliedert, von denen jede einen Bereich der englischsprachigen Welt betrachtet:

- Society (Gesellschaft)
- The Environment (Umwelt)
- The Economy (Wirtschaft und Handel)
- Literature (Literatur)
- The Media (Medien)
- Politics (Politik)
- Science and Technology (Wissenschaft und Technik)

Jede dieser thematischen Einheiten ist in vier Unterkapitel gegliedert, in denen die facettenreichen Aspekte eines Themas aus unterschiedlichen Perspektiven beleuchtet werden. Die Themen, um die es auf den 80 Textseiten geht, stammen aus den für die Oberstufe typischen Themengebieten. Somit bieten die Texte auch ausgezeichnete Anregungen für Diskussionen und Aufsätze.

Focus on Vocabulary eröffnet vielfältige Möglichkeiten, Wörter zu lernen und zu wiederholen. Hier nur einige Anregungen für die Handhabung des Buches:

- als Wiederholungshilfe für eine Klausur
- als Anregung für Aufsätze, Textaufgaben und Diskussionen
- als Anregung für die Wortbildung
- um den Gebrauch eines bestimmten Wortes nachzuschlagen

Das Buch hat einen Index, der die Worte und deren Fundstellen enthält. So können alle Worte rasch kontextbezogen im Buch gefunden werden.

Wir hoffen, dass Ihnen *Focus on Vocabulary* ein ebenso interessanter wie auch nützlicher Begleiter ist und wünschen Ihnen viel Freude und Erfolg.

Abkürzungen und Symbole

ABK	Abkürzung
ADJ	Adjektiv
ADV	Adverb
N	Nomen
s.o.	someone
s.th.	something
UGS	Umgangssprache
UK	britische Variante
US	amerikanische Variante
VI	intransitives Verb
VT	transitives Verb
VTI	transitives u. intransitives Verb
≈	Synonym
<>	Antonym (Gegensatz)
!	Achtung, Falle!

A Society

1 Health and Wellbeing

2 Education

3 Race and Religion

4 Law and Order

relationship-counselling.org.uk

The cost of marital breakdown

Modern marriages and cohabitations are under a lot of strain. People now have higher expectations of their relationships in terms of happiness and personal fulfilment, and think less about familial responsibilities. Gender-defined roles are changing, leading to tensions. In a 1994 survey only 24 per cent of respondents agreed that a husband's role is to provide for his family and a wife's to manage the household, compared with 43 per cent in 1948. Yet on average women still do more household chores – leaving them with 10 hours less leisure time than their partners every week. Experts agree that stable relationships are vital to a healthy society. Yet 4 out of 10 first marriages, and 7 out of 10 second marriages end in divorce.

Some examples of the impact of relationship breakdown:

- ***on health***

Individuals experiencing divorce or separation are more likely to suffer from mental health problems than their happily married peers. Men are nine times more likely to experience depression.

- ***on children***

Separation and divorce, and the marital conflict which precedes them, are extremely damaging to young children. Children from 'broken homes' are more likely to suffer behavioural and educational problems.

- ***on the nation***

The cost of divorce to the public is over £4 billion a year – largely through legal aid. The cost to British companies is over £5000 a year for each divorcing employee, through absenteeism and lost productivity.

It is important to acknowledge and resolve problems early. Three quarters of divorcees consider that their problems started in the first five years. Yet British couples are still reluctant to seek professional help in the early stages. Professional intervention can help couples to identify problems and reevaluate attitudes before dissatisfaction becomes crisis.

If breakup is inevitable, counselling can help individuals to come to terms with the process and find the confidence and self-esteem to make a new start.

marital breakdown	das Scheitern von Ehen	VI	*to break down*
marriage	Ehe	VTI	*to marry*
cohabitation	eheähnliche Gemeinschaften	VI	*to cohabit*
to be under strain	Belastungen ausgesetzt sein	VT	*to strain*
expectations of	Erwartungen an	VT	*to expect s.th. of s.th.*
personal fulfilment	Selbstverwirklichung	VT	*to fulfil*
familial	familiär		
gender-defined	geschlechtsspezifisch		
tensions	Spannungen	ADJ	*tense*
survey ['sɜːveɪ]	Umfrage	VT	*to survey [sɜː'veɪ]*
respondent	Befragte/r	VI	*to respond (to)*
to provide for	sorgen für	N	*provision*
to manage the household	den Haushalt führen	≈	*to run the household*
household chores	Hausarbeit	≈	*housework*
stable	stabil	N	*stability*
divorce	Scheidung	VTI	*to divorce*
impact	Auswirkung	VI	*to impact (on)*
separation	Trennung	VTI	*to separate*
mental health problems	seelische Probleme	vgl.	*mental health* – seelische Gesundheit
marital conflict	Ehekonflikt		
to precede [prɪ'siːd]	vorausgehen		
damaging to	schädigend für	<>	*beneficial to*
broken home	zerrüttete Familienverhältnisse		
behavioural	Verhaltens-	VI	*to behave*
educational	Erziehungs-		
legal aid	Rechtshilfe		
absenteeism [ˌæbsən'tiːɪzm]	Nichterscheinen am Arbeitsplatz	vgl.	*absentee* – Abwesende/r
productivity	Produktivität	ADJ	*productive*
resolve	lösen	N	*resolution*
divorcee	Geschiedene/r		
to be reluctant to do s.th.	etw. ungern tun	<>	*to be keen to do s.th.*
in the early stages	im Anfangsstadium		
to reevaluate	neu beurteilen	≈	*to reappraise*
dissatisfaction	Unzufriedenheit	ADJ	*dissatisfied (with)*
crisis	Krise		
inevitable	unvermeidlich	≈	*unavoidable*
counselling	soziale Beratung	VT	*to counsel*
to come to terms with	sich abfinden mit	≈	*to accept*
confidence	Zuversicht	ADJ	*confident*
self-esteem	Selbstachtung	≈	*self-respect*

Health care in the UK

The National Health Service (NHS) was founded in 1948. It is the largest single organization in Europe, directly employing one million people to provide medical care and treatment for all UK citizens. It is a fair and cost-effective solution to meeting the health needs of a nation.

Primary care

Primary care is concerned with people's everyday health needs. Professionals working in this area include general practitioners, specialist therapists, dentists, ophthamologists and pharmacists.

The first point of call for NHS patients is the general practitioner (GP). GPs usually work together in groups, called 'practices', to provide health care to a particular neighbourhood. Everyone is entitled to register with a GP, and consultations are free. GPs diagnose common health problems and prescribe treatment and medication, but refer serious or complex cases to hospitals and specialists.

The services of NHS dentists and ophthalmologists are not free, although they are subsidized by the state, and individuals on low incomes may be exempt from charges. The introduction of charges for eye tests and dental check-ups in the 1980s and early 1990s was controversial; many felt that these charges might discourage individuals from consulting a dentist or ophthalmologist until they require treatment, rather than having routine preventative check-ups. There is a shortage of NHS dentists, which means that many people have to resort to expensive private practices.

Hospitals

All hospital treatment under the NHS is free, including consultations, medication, nursing and intensive care. NHS hospitals are considered quite good by international standards, but there are long waiting lists for many non-urgent operations, due to shortages of staff and equipment. There are chronic problems with the recruitment of doctors and nurses, due to low pay and poor working conditions in comparison with the private sector. Hospitals take up more than 60 per cent of the NHS budget, and it is difficult to see where additional funding can come from whilst respecting the principle of free health care for all and avoiding the need for private medical insurance.

1 Health and Wellbeing

health care	Gesundheitswesen	VT	*to care for*
medical care	medizinische Versorgung		
medical treatment	medizinische Behandlung	VT	*to treat*
cost-effective	kosteneffizient	N	*cost-effectiveness*
to meet needs	Bedürfnissen gerecht werden		
general practitioner (GP)	praktischer Arzt/ praktische Ärztin	≈	*family doctor*
specialist therapist	Fachtherapeut/in	vgl.	*therapy – Therapie*
dentist	Zahnarzt/Zahnärztin	ADJ	*dental*
ophthalmologist [ɒfθæl'mɒlədʒɪst]	Augenarzt/ Augenärztin	vgl.	*optician – Optiker/in*
pharmacist	Apotheker/in	vgl.	*pharmacy* – Apotheke
first point of call	erste Anlaufstelle		
practice	Praxis	VI	*to practise*
to be entitled to	Anspruch haben auf	N	*entitlement*
to register with	sich anmelden bei	N	*registration*
consultation	Konsultation	vgl.	*consultant – Facharzt/ärztin*
to diagnose	diagnostizieren	N	*diagnosis*
to prescribe	verschreiben	N	*prescription*
medication	Medikamente		
to refer to	überweisen an	N	*referral*
to subsidize	subventionieren	N	*subsidy*
exempt from	befreit von	N	*exemption*
charge	Gebühr	VTI	*to charge*
eye test	Augenuntersuchung		
dental check-up	Zahnkontroll- untersuchung		
controversial [ˌkɒntrə'vɜːʃl]	umstritten	N	*controversy*
to discourage from	abhalten von	<>	*to encourage to*
to consult	konsultieren		
preventative	vorbeugend	N	*prevention*
shortage of	Mangel an	vgl.	*to be short of*
to resort to	sich wenden an	vgl.	*as a last resort – als letzten Ausweg*
private practice	Privatpraxis		
nursing	Krankenpflege	VT	*to nurse*
intensive care	Intensivpflege		
waiting list	Warteliste		
non-urgent	nicht dringend	N	*urgency – Dringlichkeit*
equipment	Ausstattung	VT	*to equip*
recruitment	Einstellung	VT	*to recruit*
additional	zusätzlich	ADV	*in addition*
funding	Finanzierung	VT	*to fund*
medical insurance	Krankenversicherung	VT	*to insure*

http://www.io.com/%7Ewwwave/growing%2Dup/gu1.html

Adolescence and body image

Body image becomes a huge issue when puberty hits. Suddenly you're inundated with media images of gorgeous, impossibly thin women. Boys start taunting you if you don't meet these expectations, or if you do. You're suddenly gaining hips and breasts and the changes are unnerving. You're convinced you're nothing but a fat blob. This can lead you into an eating disorder. Eating disorders are distressingly common among adolescent girls, who use them as ways to deal with the problems that surface at this time.

There's anorexia, in which you diet yourself into starvation and malnutrition. You do this so that there is something in your life you have absolute control over. Maybe you exercise a lot, but over time you're more and more tired and can't do as much exercise as you did before. You're convinced that you're fat and flabby no matter how many people tell you how thin (and great) you look. Anorexia is a serious illness. You will reach a point at which you're tired all the time because you have no reserves of energy left. You've stopped your periods. You're dying.

Bulimia is more like an addiction. You submit to the urge to eat everything in front of you and then, in an attack of guilt, you make yourself vomit. The problem is, bingeing feels good, so you do it again. After a while, you don't like to eat with other people because you're afraid you'll lose control. Food has become an addiction that is difficult to break.

Compulsive eating is a third way young women use food to deal with their anxieties. Eating food feels good ... you often associate certain foods with good times, for example. Grandma's cookies, or mom's fresh baked pies bring back good memories. And gaining weight can become a shield to keep the boys away from you when you don't want to have to deal with your sexuality.

In all of these cases, you must truly want to change in order to get out of this pattern of self-destructive behavior. You must talk with someone who can give you more help than this web page.

adolescence	Adoleszenz	vgl. *youth – Jugend*
body image	Körperimage	vgl. *self image*
to become an issue	zu einem Problem werden	vgl. *to make an issue out of s.th.*
puberty ['pju:bətɪ]	Pubertät	ADJ *pubescent*
to hit	einsetzen	≈ *to strike*
to inundate ['ɪnʌnˌdeɪt]	überfluten	≈ *to flood*
gorgeous	hinreißend	≈ *lovely, beautiful*
to taunt	verspotten	≈ *to mock*
to meet an expectation	einer Erwartung entsprechen	VT *to expect s.th. of s.o.*
unnerving	beunruhigend	≈ *disconcerting*
eating disorder	Essstörung	
distressingly	erschreckend	
common	verbreitet	≈ *widespread*
adolescent	jugendlich, pubertär	
to deal with a problem	mit einem Problem fertig werden	
to surface	auftauchen	≈ *to emerge*
anorexia [ˌænə'reksiə]	Anorexie, Magersucht	ADJ *anorexic*
to diet	eine Schlankheitskur machen	N *diet*
starvation	Verhungern	VTI *to starve*
malnutrition	Unterernährung	VT *to malnourish*
to have control over	Kontrolle haben über	VT *to control*
flabby	schwabbelig	N UGS *flab*
reserves of energy	Energiereserven	vgl. *to have in reserve – in Reserve haben*
period	Periode	≈ *menstruation*
bulimia [bju:'lɪmiə]	Bulimie	ADJ *bulimic*
addiction	Sucht	VI *to be addicted (to)*
to submit to	nachgeben	≈ *to give in to*
urge	Drang	≈ *desire, craving*
attack of guilt	Anfall von Schuld	ADJ *guilty*
to vomit	sich erbrechen	≈ UGS *to throw up*
to binge	im Übermaß essen	N *binge*
to lose control	die Kontrolle verlieren	
to break an addiction	eine Sucht aufgeben	
compulsive	zwanghaft	N *compulsion*
anxiety [æŋ'zaɪəti]	Sorge	
to associate with	assoziieren mit	N *association*
to gain weight	zunehmen	≈ *to put on weight*
shield	Schutzschild	≈ *barrier*
sexuality	Sexualität	ADJ *sexual*
pattern of behavior	Verhaltensmuster	UK *behaviour*
self-destructive	selbstzerstörerisch	

Radio interview: Advice to parents

Interviewer Dr Walsh, what general advice would you give to parents of teenagers?

Walsh It's very important to strike the right balance between the parental instinct to nurture on the one hand, and allowing your child to grow into an independent, mature adult on the other. Try not to be overprotective or patronizing, but make sure they understand that you are there to give emotional support and practical advice if they need it.

Interviewer Would you say that parents often overestimate their children's problems?

Walsh Definitely. It's natural for adolescents to be rebellious: behaving differently from the rest of the family and not "joining in" is usually a response to the need to establish a separate identity. But watch out for signs of real isolation and alienation, because adolescence can be a time of insecurity and emotions which are difficult to articulate.

Interviewer What about sex education? Should parents leave this to teachers and other professionals?

Walsh Absolutely not! Sex education has a poor record in this country: young people grow up with an understanding of the mechanics of sexual reproduction, but very little idea of how to relate this to a loving relationship. Hence the huge number of unplanned teenage pregnancies. Many adolescents are coerced into becoming sexually active by peer group pressure. There is no excuse for parents who are prudish in this area – it's pure selfishness. Talk to your kids frankly about sex and relationships, make sure that they can make informed decisions. Studies have shown that, far from encouraging promiscuity, detailed sexual knowledge tends to delay first sexual experiences.

Interviewer And what about parents' other great fear: drugs?

Walsh There's always a problem about adults warning young people not to take drugs. Hysterical overreactions destroy adults' credibility, because adolescents know that occasional use of soft drugs mostly doesn't lead to heroin addiction. That's why the 'Just Say No' campaign didn't work. Inform yourself fully about the real dangers, because 'white lies' and scare stories will be met with youthful cynicism.

Interviewer Dr Walsh, that's all we have time for. Thank you.

to strike the right balance	das richtige Verhältnis finden	≈	*to find the right balance*
parental instinct	elterlicher Instinkt	ADJ	*instinctive*
to nurture	umhegen		
mature	reif	N	*maturity*
overprotective	überängstlich	<>	*negligent*
patronizing	herablassend	≈	*condescending*
emotional support	emotionale Unterstützung	ADJ	*supportive*
to overestimate	überbewerten	<>	*to underestimate*
rebellious [rɪ'beljəs]	rebellisch	VI	*to rebel*
to join in	teilnehmen	≈	*to participate*
response to	Reaktion auf	VI	*to respond (to)*
to establish a separate identity	eine eigene Identität aufbauen		
alienation	Entfremdung	VT	*to alienate*
insecurity	Unsicherheit	ADJ	*insecure*
to articulate	artikulieren		
sex education	Sexualerziehung		
to have a poor record	*hier:* nicht gut bestellt sein um		
mechanics	Technik		
sexual reproduction	sexuelle Fortpflanzung	VI	*to reproduce*
to relate to	in Zusammenhang bringen mit		
pregnancy	Schwangerschaft	ADJ	*pregnant*
to coerce into [kəʊ'ɜ:s]	nötigen zu	N	*coercion*
peer group pressure	Peergroup-Zwänge		
prudish	prüde	N	*prude* – prüde
selfishness	Egoismus	<>	*selflessness*
frankly	offen	N	*frankness*
to encourage	fördern	N	*encouragement*
promiscuity	Promiskuität (häufiger Partnerwechsel)	ADJ	*promiscuous*
to tend to	die Tendenz haben	N	*tendency*
to delay	aufschieben	N	*delay*
hysterical	hysterisch	N	*hysteria*
overreaction	Überreaktion	VI	*to overreact*
to destroy s.o.'s credibility	jds Glaubwürdigkeit untergraben	ADJ	*credible*
soft drug	weiche Droge	<>	*hard drug*
campaign	Kampagne	VI	*to campaign*
white lie	Notlüge		
scare story	Schauergeschichte	≈	*horror story*
cynicism ['sɪnɪsɪzəm]	Zynismus	ADJ	*cynical*

Recognizing addiction

Are you worried that a friend or relative may be addicted to drugs? If he or she suddenly starts to display some of these characteristics, this *may* be a sign of drug addiction:

- sudden mood swings
- sudden withdrawal from his or her usual group of friends
- erratic performance at school or at work
- hyperactivity and inability to concentrate
- obsession with parties and going out
- inexplicable lack of money
- trembling, sweating, agitation

Here are some of the common illegal drugs and their associated effects and side effects:

Cannabis, marijuana, hashish

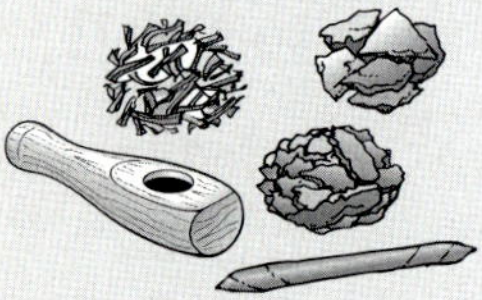

Smoking a 'joint' has a similar effect to drinking alcohol, breaking down inhibitions. Unlike alcohol, it does not tend to cause depression or aggression as negative side effects.

Side effects: Long-term use may lead to apathy and loss of concentration. Some users may eventually develop a psychological dependency. May be linked to some cancers.

Ecstasy

Ecstasy has an energizing effect and can induce trance-like states.

Side effects: Short-term effects include an increase in heart rate and blood pressure, accompanied by profuse sweating. There is a danger of heart, liver and kidney failure. Long-term effects are as yet unknown. Users may develop a psychological dependency.

>> FORTSETZUNG SEITE 12

addiction [ə'dɪkʃən]	Sucht	VGL	*addict* [*'ædɪkt*] – *Süchtige/r*
to be addicted to drugs	drogensüchtig sein	ADJ	*addictive*
to display a characteristic	ein Merkmal zeigen	ADJ	*characteristic* – *typisch*
mood swing	Stimmungswechsel	≈	*mood change*
withdrawal from	Zurückziehen aus	VTI	*to withdraw from*
erratic	stark schwankend	<>	*steady*
performance	Leistung	VI	*to perform*
hyperactivity	Hyperaktivität	ADJ	*hyperactive*
inability	Unfähigkeit	ADJ	*unable*
to concentrate	sich konzentrieren		
obsession with	besessenes Verlangen nach	VI	*to be obsessed (with)*
inexplicable	unerklärlich		
trembling	Zittern	≈	*shaking*
sweating ['swetɪŋ]	Schwitzen	N	*sweat* – *Schweiß*
agitation	Erregung	ADJ <>	*agitated* *calmness*
associated	*hier:* damit in Zusammenhang stehend		
side effect	Nebenwirkung		
to break down inhibitions	Hemmungen abbauen	vgl.	*uninhibited* – *ohne Hemmungen*
long-term	langfristig	ADV	*in the long term*
apathy ['æpəθi]	Apathie	ADJ	*apathetic* [*ˌæpə'θetɪk*]
concentration	Konzentration		
eventually	schließlich		
psychological dependency [dɪ'pendənsi]	psychische Abhängigkeit	vgl.	*dependent on* – *abhängig von*
cancer	Krebs	ADJ	*carcinogenic* – *krebserregend*
to energize	aufputschen		
to induce	herbeiführen	≈	*to bring about*
state	Zustand	≈	*condition*
short-term	kurzfristig	ADV	*in the short term*
heart rate	Herzschlagfrequenz	vgl.	*pulse* – *Puls*
blood pressure	Blutdruck	vgl.	*high blood pressure* – *Bluthochdruck*
accompanied by	begleitet von		
profuse [prə'fjuːs]	stark		
liver	Leber		
kidney	Niere		

>> Fortsetzung Seite 13

LSD

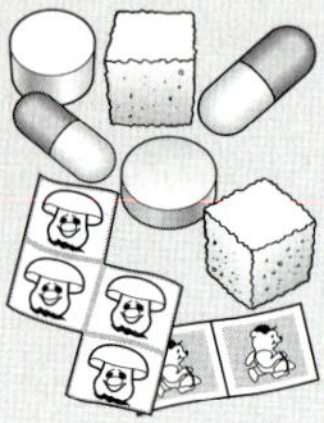

LSD is a powerful hallucinogen, inducing visions and euphoria.

Side effects: LSD is unpredictable in its effects, which may include nightmarish 'bad trips' and a dangerous inability to distinguish hallucinations from the physical world. In the longer term, use can lead to isolation, apathy and liver damage. Psychological dependency may begin with the user's first trip.

Cocaine

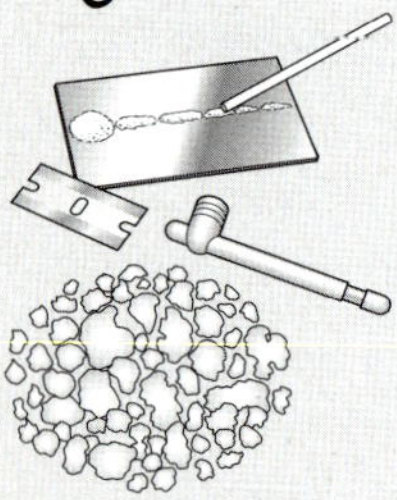

The use of cocaine induces euphoria, increased self-confidence and sexual excitement.

Side effects: 'Snorting' cocaine damages the nasal membranes; other physical effects include skin complaints, impotence and heart and circulatory problems. Psychological effects include paranoia and insomnia. Users may quickly form a strong psychological dependency on the drug.

Heroin and opiates

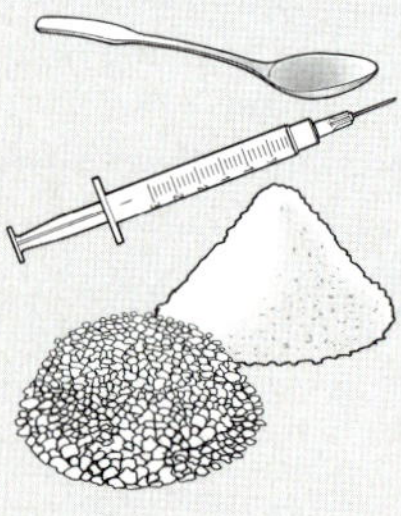

Heroin induces euphoric 'highs', reduces pain and anxiety.

Side effects: Long-term physical effects include severe damage to the immune system. Partly because of the variable purity of the heroin available from dealers, there is a high risk of taking an overdose. Sharing of syringes brings a danger of infection with AIDS and hepatitis. Psychological effects include delusions and isolation. A strong psychological and physical dependency develops almost immediately.

hallucinogen [ˌhæluːˈsɪnədʒən]	Halluzinogen	ADJ	*hallucinogenic [həˌluːsɪnəˈdʒenik]*
euphoria [juːˈfɔriə]	Euphorie		
unpredictable	unberechenbar		
nightmarish	alptraumartig	N	*nightmare*
bad trip	Horrortrip		
to distinguish from	unterscheiden von	N	*distinction*
hallucination	Halluzination	VI	*to hallucinate*
sexual excitement	sexuelle Erregung	ADJ	*sexually excited*
		≈	*sexual arousal*
to snort cocaine	Kokain schnupfen		
to damage	schädigen	N	*damage*
nasal membrane	Nasenschleimhaut		
skin complaint	Hautproblem		
impotence	Impotenz	ADJ	*impotent*
circulatory [ˌsɜːkjəˈleɪtəri]	Kreislauf-	N	*circulation*
paranoia	Paranoia, Verfolgungswahn	ADJ	*paranoid*
		≈	*persecution complex*
insomnia	Schlaflosigkeit	≈	*sleeplessness*
opiate	Opiat		
euphoric [juːˈfɒrɪk]	euphorisch		
anxiety	Angst		
severe	schwer, schlimm	N	*severity*
immune system	Immunsystem		
variable	unbeständig	<>	*consistent*
purity	Reinheit	ADJ	*pure*
		<>	*impurity*
overdose	Überdosis	VI	*to overdose (on)*
syringe	Spritze	vgl.	*to inject VTI – spritzen*
infection	Infektion	VT	*to infect (with)*
delusion	Wahnvorstellung		
physical dependency	physische Abhängigkeit	ADJ	*physically dependent*

Schools in the United Kingdom

The UK school system is highly centralized. Basic requirements such as course content and examination syllabuses are decided by government agencies and apply to all schools in England, Wales and Northern Ireland. Scotland has its own school system, but its examinations are compatible with the system in the rest of the United Kingdom.

The United Kingdom has state nursery schools, but compulsory education begins at the age of five with primary school, which all children attend until the age of 11, followed by secondary school from the age of 11 to 16. Over 90% of children of secondary school age attend comprehensive schools, which accept pupils of all levels of ability. There is also a small number of grammar schools, which select pupils by ability, and around 9 per cent of students attend independent schools.

Most pupils take the General Certificate of Secondary Education (GCSE) exams at the age of 16. These public examinations are based on the requirements of the National Curriculum, which defines three core subjects (English, maths and science) and seven foundation subjects (history, geography, music, art, technology, a modern language and physical education). Pupils are examined in all core subjects and a choice of foundation subjects.

After the age of 16, education is optional. However, most students choose to continue past this minimum school-leaving age, enrolling for a variety of academic and vocational courses in a variety of institutions. Some schools offer a sixth form, i.e. two years of full-time education from 16 to 18; otherwise, students go to a specialized sixth-form college or to a college of further education. Students who wish to go on to higher education must pass two or three A Levels ('A' for 'Advanced'). Recently, in an effort to broaden sixth-form education, AS Levels ('AS' for 'Advanced Subsidiary') were introduced – one-year courses with half the content of an A Level. There is also a system of GNVQs (General National Vocational Qualifications), which can be taken at four levels; the highest level is equivalent to A Level.

highly centralized	stark zentralisiert		
basic requirement	grundlegende Voraussetzung		
course content	Unterrichtsinhalt		
examination syllabus	Prüfungsinhalte		
government agency	Regierungsbehörde		
to apply to	gelten für	ADJ	*applicable*
to be compatible with	kompatibel sein mit		
state	staatlich	US	*public*
		<>	*private*
nursery school	Kindergarten	US	*kindergarten*
compulsory education	allgemeine Schulpflicht		
primary school	Grundschule	US	*elementary school*
to attend	besuchen	N	*attendance*
secondary school	weiterführende Schule	US	*high school*
comprehensive school	Gesamtschule		
level of ability	Leistungsniveau	ADJ	*able* – *fähig*
grammar school	Gymnasium		
to select	auswählen	N	*selection*
independent school	Privatschule	≈	*public school, private school*
secondary education	höhere Schulbildung	vgl.	*primary education* – *Grundschulbildung*
public examination	staatliche Prüfung		
to be based on	basieren auf	N	*basis*
to define	festlegen		
core subject	Pflichtfach		
foundation subject	Grundfach		
to examine	prüfen		
optional	freiwillig	<>	*compulsory*
school-leaving age	Schulabgangsalter		
to enrol for	sich einschreiben für	N	*enrolment*
academic	akademisch		
vocational	berufsbildend		
sixth form	Oberstufe	US	≈ *senior high school*
sixth-form college	Oberstufenkolleg	US	*college* – *Universität*
college of further education	Fachhochschule		
higher education	Hochschulbildung		
advanced	fortgeschritten		
to broaden	erweitern	ADJ	*broad*
subsidiary [səb'sɪdiəri]	Neben-	<>	*main*
to introduce	einführen	N	*introduction*
to be equivalent to	entsprechen	N	*equivalent*

education forum

Subject: Gender bias in education 10/25/2001 19:35 EST
From: Madeleine Hopper <mhopper@newnet.com>

Research shows that girls attain higher academic performance and develop higher career aspirations in a single-sex environment than they do in a coeducational environment. Women at all-female colleges are more likely to major in science, or to become doctors. So why aren't public schools offering single-sex classes? And why have so many private schools become coeducational?

Subject: Re: Gender bias in education 10/25/2001 22:16 EST
From: Marc Davis <marcdavis5@all.org>

You're quite right about the results, Madeleine, but you've got to look at the underlying causes. Girls receive less intensive teaching in coed schools and colleges. Why? Because boys demand attention, while too many girls become well-behaved spectators. Teachers are trained to respond to active students – who tend to be male. The result: boys get more attention, more help and more praise. The solution: we don't need single-sex education, just better teacher training. Educators need to analyse their own classroom behaviour and see how it discriminates against their female students.

Subject: Re: Gender bias in education 10/25/2001 22:41 EST
From: Gina Schultz <gischultz@io.com>

Another problem: the lack of strong female role models in coed schools, where men tend to monopolize positions of power. Nine out of ten high school principals are men! Girls need to take pride in their sex and its past and present achievements if they are to have aspirations for the future. This also means that women need to be more fairly and fully represented in the curriculum. How many female painters or scientists feature in school textbooks?

Subject: Re: Gender bias in education 10/25/2001 22:41 EST
From: Ant Babajee <ababajee@mass.ac.us>

Bear in mind that men are the victims of sexism just as much as women. Boys are forced into gender-defined roles even earlier than girls, also suffer widely from sexual harassment (e.g. challenges to their masculinity) and often grow up into alienated and lonely adults. Social pressures dissuade them from entering professions which are not considered "masculine", such as elementary teaching. Single-sex schools may actually exacerbate the problem of gender stereotyping.

to attain	erreichen	N	*attainment*
academic performance	intellektuelle Leistung		
career aspirations	Karrierestreben	VT	*to aspire to*
single-sex	gleichgeschlechtlich		
environment	Umgebung	≈	*surroundings*
coeducational	koedukativ		
all-female	Frauen-, Mädchen-		
college	Universität, College		
to major in	als Hauptfach belegen	UK	*to take as a main subject*
public school	staatliche Schule	UK	*state school*
		!	UK *public school – Privatschule*
underlying cause	tieferer Grund	<>	*apparent cause*
to demand	fordern	ADJ	*demanding*
spectator	Zuschauer/in	≈	*onlooker*
to train	ausbilden	N	*training*
to respond to	reagieren auf	N	*response*
praise	Lob	VT	*to praise*
educator	Erzieher/in	VT	*to educate*
analyse	analysieren	N	*analysis*
to discriminate against	diskriminieren	N	*discrimination*
role model	Rollenbild		
to monopolize	in Beschlag nehmen	N	*monopoly*
position of power	Machtposition		
high school	weiterführende Schule	UK	*secondary school*
principal	Direktor/in	UK	*head(teacher)*
to take pride in	stolz sein auf	≈	*to be proud of*
achievement	Leistung	VT	*to achieve*
to feature	vorkommen		
to bear in mind	nicht vergessen		
victim	Opfer		
to force into	zwingen in		
gender-defined	geschlechtsspezifisch		
sexual harassment	sexuelle Belästigung	VT	*to harass*
challenge to	Herausforderung an	VT	*to challenge*
masculinity	Männlichkeit	<>	*femininity*
alienated	entfremdet	N	*alienation*
social pressure	gesellschaftlicher Druck		
to dissuade from	abbringen von	N	*dissuasion*
elementary teaching	Grundschullehrberuf	UK	*primary teaching*
exacerbate	verschärfen	≈	*to worsen*
gender stereotyping	stereotype Geschlechterbeurteilung		

German Department
UNIVERSITY OF CAMFORD

We are based on the main campus in the Faculty of Languages. The Department has seven permanent academic staff (one professor and six lecturers) and three foreign language assistants. At present 390 undergraduate students are enrolled for honours degree courses provided by the Department, together with six postgraduate students.

Our aims:

- *to provide high-quality language tuition*
- *to encourage students to take responsibility for their own learning and to set their own personal goals*
- *to provide flexible courses of study through which students may develop their knowledge of the language, literature, culture and society of the German-speaking countries*

Your course is modular: after a foundation year, you concentrate on the aspects which interest you most. Tuition takes the following forms:

lectures	*Lecturers give talks on a variety of general topics to a large audience.*
seminars	*Six to ten students take turns to give presentations on specialized topics under the guidance of a lecturer.*
tutorials	*One or two students receive feedback on written work from their tutor.*

Developing a high level of proficiency in spoken and written German is a core skill for all our students. Language workshops are led by our native speaker assistants.

Your course lasts four years, of which you will spend the third year in a German-speaking country. Many students apply for a teaching assistantship in a school or spend two semesters as an exchange student at a university. A work placement is a popular third option.

We place emphasis on preparing our graduates for the world of work. You will finish your degree course not only with linguistic skills and academic knowledge, but also with transferable skills – including analytical, collaborative and IT skills. Our graduates are in demand amongst employers, and you will benefit from the advice and support of the University's careers service when applying for jobs.

department	Fachbereich, Seminar		
faculty	Fakultät		
academic staff	akademische Mitarbeiter/innen		
lecturer	Dozent/in	VTI	*to lecture*
foreign language assistant	Fremdsprachen-assistent/in		
undergraduate student	(nicht graduierte/r) Student/in		
honours degree course	*Studiengang zur Erlangung eines akademischen Grades im Spezialfach*		
postgraduate student	Postgraduierte/r	UGS	*postgrad*
tuition [tjuː'ɪʃən]	Unterricht	≈	*teaching*
to take responsibility for	die Verantwortung übernehmen für	≈	*to assume responsibility for*
to set goals	Ziele setzen		
course of study	Studiengang		
modular	*hier:* nach dem Kurs-system aufgebaut	N	*module*
foundation year	Basisjahr		
lecture	Vorlesung	vgl.	*talk* – Vortrag
specialized	Fach-	<>	*general*
under the guidance of	unter Anleitung + *Gen.*	VT	*to guide*
tutorial [tjuːtɔːriəl]	Kolloquium		
level of proficiency	Leistungsstand	ADJ	*proficient*
core skill	wesentliche Fertigkeit		
language workshop	Sprachkurs		
native speaker	Muttersprachler/in	<>	*non-native speaker*
to apply for	sich bewerben für	N	*application*
teaching assistantship	Stelle als Fremdsprachen-assistent/in		
exchange student	Austauschstudent/in		
work placement	Praktikum		
option	Möglichkeit		
to place emphasis on	Wert legen auf	≈	*to emphasize*
to prepare for	vorbereiten auf	N	*preparation*
graduate ['grædjuːət]	Absolvent/in	VI	*to graduate* ['grædjuːeɪt]
linguistic skills	sprachliche Fertigkeiten		
transferable [træns'fɜːrəbl]	übertragbar	<>	*non-transferable*
analytical	analytisch	VT	*to analyse*
collaborative [kə'læbərətɪv]	Kooperations-	N	*collaboration*
to be in demand	gefragt sein	≈	*to be sought after*
to benefit from	profitieren von	N	*benefit*
support	Unterstützung	VT	*to support*
careers service	Berufsberatung		

BOOK REVIEW – Stan Potapov

A Colorblind Society?

As F. Scott Fitzgerald says in *The Great Gatsby* "The past is a foreign country; they do things differently there". Nowhere is this more true than in the field of race relations. As recently as 1967, interracial marriage was illegal in many US states.

Three decades later, a *USA Today*/Gallup poll of teenagers across America found that 57 per cent had dated someone of another ethnic group. An even greater proportion (64 per cent) said that their parents would not object to their forming interracial relationships. Other polls confirm that the overall trend is towards interracial tolerance.

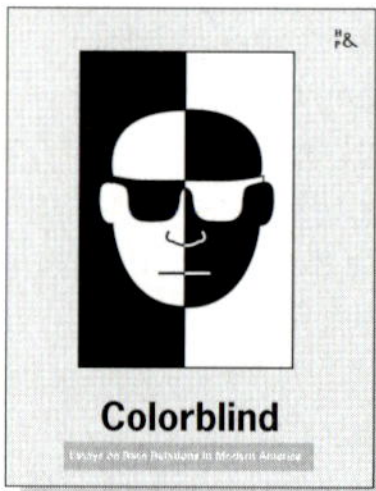

Does this suggest that we are heading for a future of interracial harmony – or even a future without cultural differences? Three writers explore this question in ***Colorblind:*** *Essays on Race Relations in Modern America* (Hawker & Paul, 129 pp., $ 14.95).

Isabelle Martinez warns against polarizing the issue into black and white: the ethnic makeup of the US comprises not just Afro-Americans and Caucasians – but also Asians, Hispanics and Native Americans, "and within each of these groups we must differentiate between many diverse and distinct cultures – each with its own prejudices and anxieties."

Ayelee Lanclos writes about her personal experience of romance outside her race (Filipino), in spite of her family's opposition. "One thing I have realized: Filipino parents will always interfere in their children's love lives."

Mark Chan claims that integration and intermarriage actually increase racial tension, as "traditionalists" within each culture complain of "betrayal" by members of their community who look for partners outside it, and competition from outsiders for "their" men or women. Chan describes an imbalance in the trend towards intermarriage which disadvantages Asian men and Afro-American women – hence the bitter opposition of many young Asian men and Afro-American women to interracial relationships. "This is a painful topic to explore honestly," writes Chan, "yet addressing resentments is a first step towards healing the rift."

colorblind	farbenblind	N	*colorblindness*
		UK	*colourblind*
race relations	Beziehungen zwischen den Rassen		
interracial	gemischtrassig		
poll	Umfrage	≈	*survey*
to date	ausgehen mit	UK	*to go out with*
ethnic	ethnisch	N	*ethnicity*
proportion	Anteil	≈	*share*
to object to	Einwände erheben gegen	N	*objection*
to form a relationship	eine Beziehung eingehen		
to confirm	bestätigen	N	*confirmation*
tolerance	Toleranz	VT	*to tolerate*
		ADJ	*tolerant*
to head for	auf dem Weg sein in		
cultural	kulturell		
to polarize	polarisieren		
makeup	Zusammensetzung	≈	*composition*
to comprise	umfassen	≈	*to consist of*
Afro-American	Afroamerikaner/in		
Caucasian	Kaukasier/in		
Asian	Asiate/Asiatin		
Hispanic	Hispanoamerikaner/in		
Native American	Indianer/in		
to differentiate between	unterscheiden zwischen	N	*differentiation*
diverse	unterschiedlich	N	*diversity*
distinct	eigen, individuell	N	*distinction*
prejudice	Vorurteil	ADJ	*prejudiced*
anxiety	Angst	ADJ	*anxious*
romance	Romanze	ADJ	*romantic*
opposition	Widerstand	VT	*to oppose*
to interfere in	sich einmischen in	N	*interference*
intermarriage	Mischehen	VI	*to intermarry*
racial tension	Rassenspannung		
betrayal	Verrat	VT	*to betray*
community	*hier:* Bevölkerungsgruppe		
competition	Konkurrenz	VI	*to compete*
outsider	Außenstehende/r		
imbalance	Ungleichgewicht	ADJ	*unbalanced*
to disadvantage	benachteiligen	N	*disadvantage*
bitter	erbittert		
to address	zur Sprache bringen		
resentment	Ressentiment	VT	*to resent*
to heal the rift	*hier:* den Graben überwinden		

OPERATION ATHENA

a step in the right direction

LONDON is one of the world's most culturally and ethnically diverse cities. Approximately 25 per cent of its 7 million citizens come from 'visible ethnic minorities', i.e. ethnic minorities easily identified by their physical appearance.

Relations between these minority communities and London's police, the Metropolitan Police Force ('the Met') have always been uneasy, and on occasions have been strained to breaking point (e.g. the Brixton riots of the 1980s and 1990s). This is reflected in recruitment figures: in the 1990s, the Met only recruited 3 per cent of its officers from ethnic minorities.

Many black and Asian Londoners in particular felt that the Met was treating them as second-class citizens. There were allegations of police harassment of blacks and Asians, of racist insults and occasionally of physical brutality. A number of notorious cases in the 1990s indicated that a less overt form of racism was widespread in the Met: officers were not taking racially motivated crimes seriously.

A senior judge, Sir William Macpherson, headed an enquiry into one such case: the Met's failure to catch the white racists who killed the black teenager Stephen Lawrence in April 1993. The 'Macpherson Report' was published in 1998, and confirmed what the minority communities had always claimed: the Metropolitan Police Force was an 'institutionally racist' organization, i.e. it was permeated with unconscious racial prejudice and racist stereotyping. The report made 70 recommendations for dealing more effectively with racist crime, combatting racism in the force itself, and winning the trust of the minority communities.

One result of the report has been Operation Athena, a racial and violent crime task force headed by Deputy Assistant Commissioner John Grieve. In the first year of Operation Athena, there was a 158 per cent rise in prosecutions for racist crime, and the credibility of the Met among London's ethnic minorities seems to be improving. However, progress is slow and fragile. It remains to be seen whether Grieve's well-intentioned and determined efforts will have any long-term effect on entrenched attitudes. ***N. Sargent***

ethnically	ethnisch	ADJ	*ethnic*
diverse	vielfältig	<>	*homogenous*
visible	erkennbar		
ethnic minority	ethnische Minderheit		
physical appearance	äußerliche Erscheinung		
relations	Beziehungen		
uneasy	prekär	<>	*comfortable, relaxed*
to strain to breaking point	bis zum Zerreißen belasten		
riot	Aufstand	VI	*to riot*
to reflect in	widerspiegeln	N	*reflection*
recruitment figures	Einstellungszahlen		
to recruit	einstellen	N	*recruit – neue/r Mitarbeiter/in*
allegation	Behauptung	VT	*to allege*
harassment	Schikanierung	VT	*to harass*
racist	rassistisch		
physical brutality	körperliche Gewalt	ADJ	*brutal*
notorious	berüchtigt	N	*notoriety*
overt	unverhohlen	<>	*covert, hidden*
racism	Rassismus	vgl.	*bigotry – eifernde Borniertheit*
widespread	weit verbreitet	≈	*common*
racially motivated	rassistisch motiviert	N	*motivation*
senior	hoch	<>	*junior*
to head	vorsitzen	≈	*to lead*
enquiry into	Untersuchung + *Gen.*		
failure	Misserfolg	<>	*success*
racist	Rassist/in	vgl.	*bigot – Eiferer*
to permeate ['pɜːmieɪt]	durchdringen		
unconscious	unbewusst	vgl.	*subconscious – unterbewusst*
racial prejudice	Rassenvorurteil		
racist stereotyping	stereotype Rassenbeurteilung	vgl.	*stereotype – Klischee(vorstellung)*
recommendation	Empfehlung	VT	*to recommend*
to combat	bekämpfen	≈	*to fight (against)*
trust	Vertrauen	VT	*to trust*
task force	Sondereinheit		
prosecution	Anklage	VT	*to prosecute*
credibility	Glaubwürdigkeit	ADJ	*credible*
progress ['prəʊgres]	Fortschritt	VI	*to progress [prə'gres]*
fragile ['frædʒaɪl]	anfällig	N	*fragility [fræ'dʒɪlɪti]*
well-intentioned	wohlmeinend	≈	*well-meaning*
long-term	langfristig	<>	*short-term*
entrenched attitude	verwurzelte Haltung	≈	*set idea*

LETTERS TO THE EDITOR

"Cults" in the USA

Zora Stokes' article "Faith in the USA" (*Modern Revue* Nov. 17) was a convenient summary of popular ignorance, misconception and prejudice about alternative religions in America today.

Ms Stokes refers several times to "cults", which she defines as "a small, recently formed religious group led by a charismatic leader". Yet some of the religions she discusses – such as Voodoo – have no central leaders, and others – e.g. Druidism and Zoroastrianism – have existed for thousands of years.

By her use of the word "cult" Ms Stokes implies that these are not "real" religions; thus she uses the word "religion" only of the mainstream faiths, e.g. Judaism, Islam and the main denominations of Christianity. However, the *American Heritage Dictionary* states: "Religion: a set of beliefs, values and practices based on the teachings of a spiritual leader". There is no mention here of which beliefs, teachings or leader! Moreover, all world religions started off as "cults" with a handful of adherents – often suffering persecution from orthodox bigots who feared and despised them as heretics or subversives.

Equally misleading is Ms Stokes' use of the term "New Age". Only some of the religions she discusses fall into the New Age mindset, which we might define as "seeking truth and unity beyond the constraints of organized religious thought and worship".

Another myth perpetuated by the article is that alternative religions use brainwashing to recruit members. With few exceptions, these allegations are unfounded: most new members enter alternative religious groups (including NRMs) of their own volition, and leave when the group no longer satisfies their need for emotional support, religious certainty and moral guidelines. On average, they stay for less than two years.

The actions of movements such as Heaven's Gate and Aum Shinrikyo have led the media to portray all alternative religions as proponents of suicide or homicide. In reality, most teach values such as charity and honor which are wholly compatible with the laws of the USA and the teachings of Christ.

Dr. William C. Tucker

cult	Kult		
faith	Glaube		
ignorance	Ignoranz	ADJ	*ignorant*
misconception	Verkennung	≈	*misunderstanding*
prejudice [ˈpredʒudɪs]	Vorurteil	ADJ	*prejudiced*
charismatic	charismatisch		
mainstream	Haupt-	<>	*minor, alternative*
denomination	Konfession		
Christianity [ˌkrɪstiˈænɪti]	Christentum	vgl.	*Christian* – *Christ/in; christlich*
belief	Glaube, Überzeugung	VTI	*to believe*
practice	Praktik	VT	*to practice,* UK *to practise*
teachings	Lehren		
spiritual	geistig, geistlich	N	*spirituality*
adherent	Anhänger/in	≈	*follower, disciple*
to suffer	erleiden	N	*suffering*
persecution	Verfolgung	VT	*to persecute*
bigot [ˈbɪɡət]	Frömmler/in, religiöse/r Eiferer/in	vgl.	*bigotry* – *Bigotterie, Frömmelei*
to despise	verachten	ADJ	*despicable*
heretic	Ketzer/in, Häretiker/in	vgl.	*heresy* – *Ketzerei*
mindset	Geisteshaltung		
unity	Einheit	ADJ	*unified, united*
constraint	Zwang, Beschränkung	≈	*limit*
worship	Verehrung, Anbetung	VT	*to worship*
myth	Mythos	ADJ	*mythical*
to perpetuate [ˌpɜːˈpetjuːeɪt]	aufrechterhalten		
brainwashing	Gehirnwäsche	VT	*to brainwash*
to recruit	werben	N	*recruitment*
allegation	Behauptung	VT	*to allege*
unfounded	aus der Luft gegriffen	<>	*well-founded*
NRM	Neue Religiöse Bewegung	–	*New Religious Movement*
of one's own volition	aus freiem Willen	≈	*of one's own free will*
emotional support	emotionale Unterstützung	VT	*to support*
certainty	Gewissheit	<>	*uncertainty*
moral guideline	moralische Leitlinie	vgl.	*to guide* – *leiten*
proponent of	Befürworter/in von		
suicide	Selbstmord	vgl.	*to commit suicide* – *Selbstmord begehen*
homicide	Totschlag, Mord	≈	*murder*
charity	Nächstenliebe		
honor	Ehre	UK	*honour*
compatible with	vereinbar mit	<>	*incompatible with*

talkback.com/lawandorder

talkback

Is it time to amend the Second Amendment?

"A well regulated Militia being necessary to the security of a free State, the right of the people to keep and bear Arms, shall not be infringed." Second Amendment to the United States Constitution

All human beings have a right to self-defense. In the United States, this is also a constitutional right. Criminals will always be able to obtain weapons – so how can a law-abiding citizen defend him- or herself against an armed attacker? By carrying a handgun, and undergoing appropriate training in using it. If handguns are outlawed, only outlaws will carry them! **Pawel, New Jersey**

In the 1770s, the Second Amendment was necessary. In the 2000s, we have the National Guard, so militias are obsolete, and there is no longer any reason for civilians to bear arms. This part of the Constitution is clearly out of date, yet Congress – watched by the powerful pro-gun lobby – continues to avoid the issue. There are around 20,000 state and local weapons laws, but no effective federal firearms legislation. **Louise, Illinois**

The self-defense argument just doesn't stand up. Research suggests that keeping a gun in the home places the residents in great jeopardy. Suicides are five times more likely in homes where guns are kept; homicides are three times more likely. According to the FBI, more than 12,000 people were shot dead in the USA last year – but amongst this carnage there were only 180 justifiable homicides. The rational conclusion: gun ownership does little to promote self-defense, much to increase the risk of accidental or deliberate killing of innocent people. **Joseph, Michigan**

Occasional massacres by a few deranged individuals shouldn't make us forget that the majority of guns are used for legitimate purposes. There are 20 million hunters in our country, and none of us want to see our sport stopped as a result of strict gun legislation. In farming communities, shotguns and rifles are necessary for pest control. Automatic weapons are another matter. It's a disgrace that civilians should have access to this kind of military equipment. **Christina, Arkansas**

to amend [ə'mend]	ändern	≈	*to alter*
amendment	Zusatz zu Gesetzen		
security	Sicherheit	ADJ	*secure*
to bear arms	Waffen tragen		
to infringe	antasten	N	*infringement*
constitution	Verfassung	ADJ	*constitutional*
self-defense	Selbstverteidigung	UK	*self-defence*
constitutional right	verfassungsmäßiges Recht		
weapon	Waffe		
law-abiding	gesetzestreu	<>	*criminal*
to defend o.s.	sich verteidigen	<>	*to attack s.o.*
armed	bewaffnet	<>	*unarmed*
handgun	Handfeuerwaffe	vgl.	*firearm – Schusswaffe*
to undergo training	sich einer Ausbildung unterziehen		
to outlaw	ächten, gesetzlich verbieten		
outlaw	Geächtete/r, Verbrecher	≈	*criminal*
obsolete ['ɒbsəliːt]	überholt, veraltet		
civilian	Zivilist/in	ADJ	*civilian*
out of date	unzeitgemäß	<>	*up-to-date, modern*
federal	Bundes-		
firearms legislation	Waffengesetze		
to stand up	überzeugen	≈	*to be convincing*
to place in jeopardy ['dʒepədɪ]	einer Gefahr aussetzen	≈	*to jeopardize, to endanger*
suicide	Selbstmord	vgl.	*to commit suicide*
homicide	Totschlag, Mord	≈	*murder*
to shoot dead	erschießen	vgl.	*to wound – verletzen*
carnage	Gemetzel		
justifiable homicide	begründete Tötung		
to promote	fördern	<>	*to hinder*
accidental	versehentlich	N	*accident*
deliberate	absichtlich		
innocent	unschuldig	<>	*guilty*
massacre	Massaker	VT	*to massacre*
deranged	gestört		
legitimate [lə'dʒɪtɪmət]	rechtmäßig	<>	*illegitimate*
hunter	Jäger/in	VTI	*to hunt*
shotgun	Schrotflinte		
rifle	Gewehr		
pest control	Schädlingsbekämpfung		
automatic weapon	Automatikwaffe		
disgrace	Schande	VT	*to disgrace*
military equipment	militärisches Gerät		

READERS' FORUM

In last week's Readers' Forum we invited your views on the following issue:

The latest figures released by the Home Office show that there are now nearly 69,000 people in prison in England and Wales. As a proportion of the total population, more people are jailed here than in any other western European country apart from Portugal. Does this mean that our criminal justice system is failing? And if so, what can be done about it?

Here are extracts from some of your replies:

"Tackling crime means addressing problems which are deeply rooted in our society – problems such as truancy, drug abuse and long-term unemployment. The punitive approach – locking people up for longer and longer – just doesn't work." ***J. Palmer***

"Judges and magistrates should be more flexible in sentencing offenders, rather than just imposing custodial sentences. Take probation orders, for example. These curtail the offender's freedom without putting him or her in prison. Offenders can be made to take part in programmes which address particular problems linked to their offence, e.g. addiction or violence." ***N. Singh***

"Who says prison isn't working? England and Wales have one of the lowest murder rates in western Europe, and car thefts have fallen by over 120,000 cases a year since 1995. The reason? A tough sentencing policy really is a deterrent. If the cost of a safer society is more prisons, this is a price worth paying." ***Mike McCullen***

"What about community service? More use should be made of this alternative to prison. Up to 240 hours of unpaid work is not a soft option! As well as being a punishment, this type of sentence allows the offender to make reparation to the community for his or her offence. Offenders who have done community service are 20% less likely to reoffend than people who have served a custodial sentence. Where necessary, electronic tagging and curfews can be used to give additional protection to the public." ***Paula Davies***

"There's too much emphasis on punishment, and not enough on the rehabilitation of prisoners. Most people come out of prison worse, not better, which means that prison is failing to protect the public. There should be more programmes to help prisoners to integrate into society after their release." ***Terri O'Donnell***

Home Office	Innenministerium	vgl.	*Home Secretary – Innenminister/in*
to jail	ins Gefängnis sperren	N	*jail – Gefängnis*
criminal justice system	Strafjustizsystem		
to tackle	anpacken	≈	*to deal with*
to address	ansprechen		
deeply rooted	tief verwurzelt		
truancy	Schuleschwänzen	vgl.	*to play truant – die Schule schwänzen*
drug abuse	Drogenmissbrauch	vgl.	*alcohol abuse*
long-term unemployment	Langzeitarbeitslosigkeit		
punitive	Straf-	VT	*to punish*
approach	Methode		
judge	Richter/in	VT	*to judge*
magistrate	Amtsrichter/in		
to sentence	verurteilen	N	*sentence – Strafe*
offender	(Straf)Täter/in	VI	*to offend*
to impose	verhängen		
custodial sentence	Gefängnisstrafe		
probation order	Bewährungsurteil	vgl.	*probation officer – Bewährungshelfer/in*
to curtail	beschränken	≈	*to restrict*
offence	Straftat	≈	*crime*
addiction [ə'dɪkʃn]	Sucht	vgl.	*addict – Süchtige/r*
violence	Gewalt	ADJ	*violent*
murder	Mord	VT	*to murder*
		vgl.	*murderer – Mörder/in*
theft	Diebstahl	vgl.	*robbery*
tough	hart, streng	<>	*lenient*
sentencing policy	Verurteilungspraktiken		
deterrent [dɪ'terənt]	Abschreckungsmittel	VT	*to deter [dɪ'tɜː]*
community service	Sozialdienst		
soft option	milde Alternative		
to make reparation	Wiedergutmachung leisten		
to reoffend	rückfällig werden		
to serve a sentence	eine Strafe verbüßen		
electronic tagging	elektronische Markierung		
curfew	Ausgangssperre		
emphasis	Betonung	VT	*to emphasize*
punishment	Bestrafung	vgl.	*retribution – Vergeltung*
rehabilitation [riːəˌbɪlɪ'teɪʃn]	Resozialisierung	VT	*to rehabilitate*
to integrate into	sich integrieren in	N	*integration*
release	Entlassung	VT	*to release*

B The Environment

1 The Living World

2 Environmental Problems – First World

3 Environmental Problems – Third World

4 Sustainable Development

http://www.foe.co.uk/

How our countryside has changed

The British Isles support an amazing diversity of wildlife. Rich in wetlands, peatlands, grasslands, heaths, ancient woodlands, we have one of the most dramatic coastlines in the world. The UK is home to thousands of wild species.

As humans colonized the British Isles they changed the landscape by hunting the large grazing animals and transforming the UK's wild woodlands and wetlands into farmland. This has profoundly changed the distribution and diversity of species and habitat types throughout these islands. Many species that were once common in the UK have now been lost because they did not exist comfortably alongside humans; bear, wolf, beaver, lynx, wild cattle, wild horses, storks and bustards are among the casualties.

Some human impacts, however, have not been disastrous. Grazing with cattle or sheep can be similar to grazing by bison, and cutting back woodlands acts like the wind blowing down trees and browsing by deer. Thus we have inherited a 'semi-natural' landscape where natural communities of species can exist within habitats that are managed in one way or another by humans.

This inheritance of semi-natural landscapes shows how harmonious our relationship with the natural world can be. Wildlife thrives in this environment and we can still appreciate how rich in wildlife our countryside must have been just a few generations ago by looking at our Sites of Special Scientific Interest (SSSIs), our best remaining wild places.

The Industrial Revolution and agricultural 'improvement', however, have consigned this sustainable landscape to just a few per cent of the UK. Changes to agriculture have led to draining and ploughing of grasslands and wetlands, the conversion of colourful meadows rich in flowers to drab monocultures of wheat and oil seed rape and the removal of woodlands and hedgerows to make way for prairie fields sprayed with pesticides and chemical fertilizers.

to support	Lebensraum bieten für		
diversity	Vielfalt	ADJ	*diverse*
wildlife	Tierwelt	≈	*fauna*
wetland	Feuchtgebiet	vgl.	*bogland – Sumpf*
peatland	Moor(landschaft)	≈	*moorland*
grassland	Grasland(schaft)		
heath	Heideland(schaft)		
ancient woodland ['eɪnʃənt]	Urwald, altes Waldland	vgl.	*plantation – Plantage*
coastline	Küste	ADJ	*coastal*
species ['spiʃiz]	Art, Spezies		
to colonize	besiedeln	≈	*to settle*
to hunt	jagen		
grazing animal	grasendes Tier		
to transform	umwandeln	N	*transformation*
farmland	Ackerland	≈	*agricultural land*
profoundly	tiefgreifend	<>	*superficially*
distribution	Verteilung	VT	*to distribute*
habitat	Lebensraum		
common	verbreitet	<>	*rare*
beaver	Biber		
lynx	Luchs		
casualty ['kæʒuəlti]	Opfer	≈	*victim*
impact ['ɪmpækt]	Einwirkung	VT	*to impact on [ɪm'pækt]*
disastrous	katastrophal	≈	*catastrophic*
to graze	abweiden		
to browse	äsen		
deer	Reh		
to inherit	erben, übernehmen	vgl.	*heir – Erbe/Erbin*
community	Gemeinschaft		
to manage	bewirtschaften		
inheritance	Erbe		
harmonious [hɑː'məʊniəs]	harmonisch	N	*harmony ['hɑːməni]*
to thrive	gedeihen	≈	*to flourish*
site	Gebiet, Ort		
sustainable	zu erhaltend		
to drain	entwässern	N	*drainage*
to plough [plaʊ]	(um)pflügen	N	*plough – Pflug*
meadow ['medəʊ]	Wiese		
drab	trist	<>	*colourful, vibrant*
wheat	Weizen	vgl.	*rye – Roggen*
oil seed rape	Raps		
hedgerow	Hecke		
pesticide	Pestizid	vgl.	*pest – Schädling*
chemical fertilizer	Kunstdünger	VT	*to fertilize*

North America – Natural Vegetation

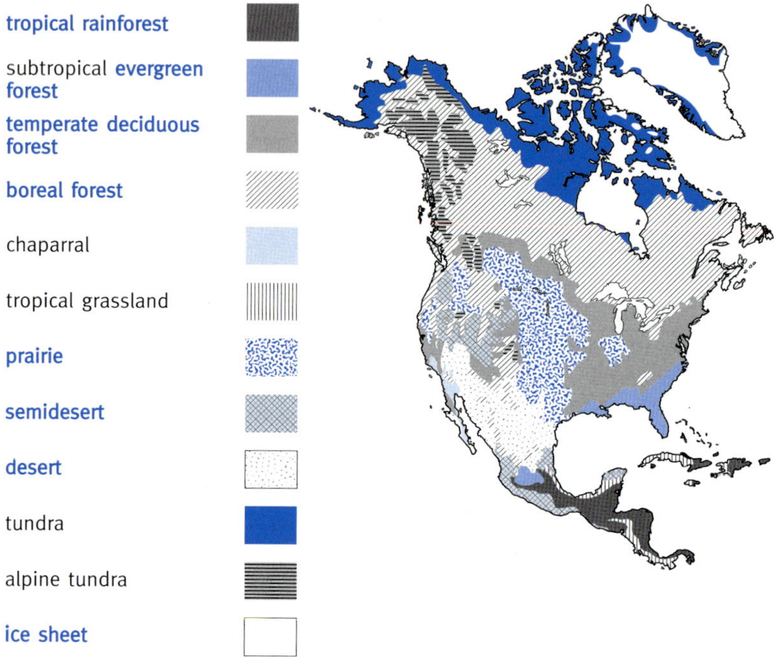

ICE SHEET covers most of Greenland; on the North American continent it is confined largely to glaciers. This is one of the most barren and inhospitable climates on Earth.

TUNDRA stretches across the far north of Canada and Alaska, a vast marshy region of low-growing, extremely hardy vegetation. During the brief arctic summer, the tundra is visited by many millions of migratory birds, for whom it is a vital feeding and breeding ground. Mammals which have adapted to this harsh climate include polar bears, herds of caribou and packs of timber wolves. Similar vegetation (ALPINE TUNDRA) occurs at high altitudes to the south of the arctic tundra.

BOREAL FOREST extends across northern Canada from Newfoundland to Alaska, one of the world's largest areas of forest. In the west of the continent, the forest extends southwards: coniferous forest along the Pacific coast from Alaska to California contains immense redwoods and firs. The forest supports large and impressive animal species such as moose, beaver, lynx, black and grizzly bears.

>> Fortsetzung Seite 36

tropical	tropisch		
rainforest	Regenwald		
evergreen forest	immergrüner Wald		
temperate	gemäßigt		
deciduous forest [dɪ'sɪdjuəs]	Laubwald		
boreal forest	borealer Nadelwald, Taiga		
prairie	Prärie		
semidesert	Halbwüste		
desert ['dezət]	Wüste		
ice sheet	Eisschicht	≈	*ice cap*
confined to	begrenzt auf	≈	*limited to*
glacier ['glæsiə]	Gletscher	ADJ	*glacial*
barren	karg, unfruchtbar	<>	*fertile*
inhospitable [ˌɪnhɒ'spɪtəbl]	unwirtlich	≈	*bleak*
climate	Klima		
marshy	sumpfig	N	*marsh – Sumpf*
low-growing	kleinwüchsig	<>	*tall*
hardy	widerstandsfähig	N	*hardiness*
migratory bird [maɪ'greɪtəri]	Zugvogel	VI	*to migrate*
vital	lebenswichtig	≈	*essential*
feeding ground	Nahrungsgebiet		
breeding ground	Brutstätte		
mammal	Säugetier		
to adapt to	sich anpassen an	N	*adaptation*
harsh	rau	<>	*gentle*
polar bear	Eisbär		
herd	Herde		
pack	Rudel		
wolf	Wolf	PL	*wolves*
altitude	Höhe	<>	*depth*
to extend	sich ausdehnen	N	*extent*
coniferous forest	Nadelwald		
fir	Tanne	vgl.	*pine – Kiefer;* *oak – Eiche;* *birch – Birke;* *beech – Buche;* *ash – Esche;* *elm – Ulme*
moose	Elch		
black bear	Schwarzbär		
grizzly bear	Grislibär		

>> FORTSETZUNG SEITE 37

TEMPERATE DECIDUOUS FOREST has been cleared in most low-lying areas in the densely populated east of the continent, but persists in mountainous areas, merging into mixed forest in the north. Indigenous species include white-tailed deer, squirrels, mink and skunks.

PRAIRIE is a type of temperate grassland, dominated by tall grasses. It was the natural vegetation of the great plains of central North America. It has been virtually eradicated by human cultivation.

CHAPARRAL is composed of shrubs that form dense thickets. It occurs from Oregon southward through the coast ranges of California and the foothills of the Sierra Nevada. The chaparral environment is harsh, with low annual rainfall mainly occurring between November and April, yet it has many resident animal species, such as deer, coyotes, rattlesnakes, tortoises and many rodents.

DESERTS are arid areas where more water is lost through evaporation than is gained from precipitation. Less than one per cent of the North American desert consists of sand dunes. Desert wildlife is surprisingly rich, including wild sheep, coyotes, hares, rattlesnakes and numerous lizards.

SEMIDESERT is a region of transition between arid and humid climates, and is subject to great climatic variability. It is agriculturally very productive, but is vulnerable to desertification. It is dominated by scrub and shorter grasses, with cacti in the more arid areas.

SUBTROPICAL EVERGREEN FOREST grows in the southeastern United States, where Florida's Everglades and the Louisiana swamps are rich in reptile species such as alligators and snakes. Birdlife is plentiful and varied, including herons, ibis and vultures.

TROPICAL RAINFOREST in Central America supports a great diversity of plant and animal species, including mammals such as the jaguar and several species of monkey, parrots and other exotic bird species and many amphibians. Despite their appearance of fertility, rainforests are fragile ecosystems.

TROPICAL GRASSLAND or savanna exists around the rainforests of Central America, and is expanding as a result of forest clearance by humans.

to clear	roden	N	*clearance*
low-lying	tief gelegen		
to persist	sich halten	ADJ	*persistent*
mountainous	gebirgig		
to merge into	übergehen in		
indigenous [ɪn'dɪdʒənəs]	einheimisch	≈	*native*
squirrel	Eichhörnchen		
mink	Nerz		
to dominate	beherrschen		
plain	Ebene	vgl.	*plateau* – Hochebene
to eradicate [ɪ'rædɪkeɪt]	vernichten	≈	*to wipe out*
cultivation	Kultivierung	VT	*to cultivate*
to be composed of	sich zusammensetzen aus	N	*composition*
shrub	Strauch, Busch		
dense	dicht	<>	*sparse*
thicket	Dickicht		
foothill	Ausläufer		
rainfall	Niederschlag	≈	*precipitation* (auch Schnee usw.)
resident	heimisch		
rattlesnake	Klapperschlange		
rodent	Nagetier		
arid	trocken, dürr	N	*aridity*
evaporation	Verdunstung	VTI	*to evaporate*
hare	Hase		
lizard	Eidechse		
transition	Übergang		
humid	feucht	N	*humidity*
to be subject to	unterworfen sein + *Dat.*		
climatic variability	Klimaschwankung		
agriculturally	landwirtschaftlich	N	*agriculture*
vulnerable to	anfällig für	N	*vulnerability*
desertification	Wüstenvormarsch		
scrub	Gestrüpp		
plentiful	reichhaltig	<>	*scarce*
heron	Reiher		
vulture	Geier	vgl.	*eagle* – Adler
amphibian	Amphibie		
fertility [fə'tɪlɪti]	Fruchtbarkeit	ADJ	*fertile*
fragile ['frædʒaɪl]	empfindlich	N	*fragility*
ecosystem	Ökosystem		
to expand	sich ausdehnen	N	*expansion*
forest clearance	Waldrodung	≈	*deforestation*

Climate Change

Earth's climate is subject to natural change. Some change is gradual, e.g. the long-term fluctuations which produce ice ages; some is sudden and catastrophic, e.g. temperature changes caused by major volcanic eruptions or meteorite strikes. Geological evidence shows that gradual changes give ecosystems time to evolve and adapt to new conditions, whereas rapid changes cause mass extinctions and the collapse of ecosystems.

However, over the last few centuries a new factor has begun to affect the climate of our planet in a major way. We are that factor.

Many human activities affect the climate. Most important are those that lead to the emission of carbon dioxide (CO_2). In particular, the burning of fossil fuels releases large quantities of CO_2 into the atmosphere. CO_2 is a greenhouse gas, i.e. it traps solar heat in the atmosphere. Over the last 200 years, the level of CO_2 in the atmosphere has risen by nearly 30%.

There are still many uncertainties in scientific understanding of global warming, but it seems likely that human activities will result in an average global temperature rise of around 1.4°C by the year 2050. (Other estimates range from almost no change to around 3.5°C.) This should not result in the melting of the polar ice caps, but a slight rise in sea level is expected. This will probably be too little to cause widespread flooding of coastal regions; however, it will make hurricanes and other storms more destructive, and the higher temperatures may also make these storms more intense and frequent.

There will also be consequences for life away from the coasts. A small but rapid climate change could result in migration or extinction of natural plant species and changes in insect pests. The distribution of rainfall may change, causing local drought and desertification. If nothing is done to halt the process – or the estimates prove to have been too conservative – the consequences will be more severe.

We know that there is a problem. Let's act now before it becomes a crisis.

climate change	Klimaveränderung		
to be subject to	unterworfen sein + *Dat.*		
gradual	allmählich	<>	*sudden*
fluctuation	Schwankung	VI	*to fluctuate*
ice age	Eiszeit		
catastrophic [ˌkætə'strɒfɪk]	verheerend	N	*catastrophe [kə'tɑːstrəfi]*
major	groß	<>	*minor*
volcanic eruption	Vulkanausbruch	VI	*to erupt*
meteorite strike	Meteoriteneinschlag	VTI	*to strike*
ecosystem	Ökosystem		
to evolve	sich entwickeln	N	*evolution*
to adapt to	sich anpassen an	vgl.	*adaptable – anpassungsfähig*
rapid	schnell	N	*rapidity*
mass	Massen-		
extinction	Aussterben	ADJ	*extinct*
collapse	Zusammenbruch	VI	*to collapse*
carbon dioxide	Kohlendioxid		
fossil fuel	fossiler Brennstoff		
to release	freisetzen	N	*release*
greenhouse gas	Treibhausgas		
to trap	stauen		
level	Anteil		
uncertainty	Ungewissheit		
global warming	globale Erwärmung		
estimate ['estɪmət]	Schätzung	VTI	*to estimate ['estɪˌmeɪt]*
polar ice cap	Polkappe	vgl.	*pole – Pol*
sea level	Meeresspiegel		
widespread	weit verbreitet	<>	*localized*
flooding ['flʌdɪŋ]	Überschwemmung		
coastal region	Küstenregion	vgl.	*coast – Küste*
hurricane	Hurrikan		
destructive	zerstörerisch	N	*destructiveness*
intense	heftig	N	*intensity*
consequence	Folge	≈	*result*
insect pest	Insektenschädling		
distribution	Verteilung		
drought [draʊt]	Dürre		
desertification	Wüstenvormarsch	vgl.	*desert – Wüste*
to halt	zum Stillstand bringen		
conservative	vorsichtig		
severe [sɪ'vɪə]	schlimm	N	*severity [sɪ'verəti]*
crisis	Krise	≈	*emergency*

http://www.greenpeace.org/~toxics/

Greenpeace Toxics Campaign

The production, trade, use, and release of many synthetic chemicals is now widely recognised as a global threat to human health and the environment. Yet the world's chemical industries continue to produce and release thousands of chemical compounds every year, in most cases with no or very little testing or understanding of their impacts on people and the environment. Of these chemical compounds, Greenpeace has prioritized the Persistent Organic Pollutants or POPs. The Greenpeace International Toxics Campaign seeks an end to the manufacture, use and disposal of hazardous synthetic substances.

POPs These substances are generally extremely toxic in small amounts, and because they travel long distances via air currents, they endanger people and wildlife all over the world. We now also know that POPs are carried by the atmosphere towards polar environments where they are deposited. This is believed to account for the high concentrations of POPs in arctic environments, and in the indigenous peoples that live there.

POPs cannot easily be broken down by natural processes – in other words they are persistent. In some cases, when breakdown does occur, it creates chemicals that are even more hazardous than the original substances.

PVC is one of the most widely used types of plastics. During its production, dioxins, some of the most toxic chemicals known, are created and released. Over their lifetime, PVC products can leak harmful additives. Furthermore, at the end of their lifetime, PVC products must be either burned or buried. Burning creates and releases more dioxins and other compounds that contaminate our land and waterways. Attempts to recycle PVC have proven difficult, so much of it ends up in landfills.

TOXIC TRADE: Greenpeace has documented hundreds of cases where industrialized countries have either traded or transferred toxic waste problems to newly industrializing countries. Not only is this type of trade immoral and environmentally destructive to countries and their peoples, but it also prevents developed countries from investing in proper solutions to pollution and developing new markets in more appropriate technologies or products.

toxics	Giftstoffe	≈	*toxic substances*
campaign [kæm'peɪn]	Kampagne	VI	*to campaign*
trade	Handel	VTI	*to trade*
release	Freisetzung	VT	*to release*
synthetic chemical [sɪn'θetɪk]	synthetische Chemikalie	VT	*to synthesize*
threat to	Bedrohung für	VT	*to threaten*
chemical compound	chemische Verbindung		
impact on	Auswirkung auf	≈	*effect on*
to prioritize [praɪ'ɒrətaɪz]	Priorität einräumen	N	*priority – Priorität*
persistent	beständig	VI	*to persist*
pollutant	Schadstoff	VT	*to pollute*
manufacture	Herstellung	VT	*to manufacture*
disposal	Entsorgung	VT	*to dispose of*
hazardous	gefährlich	N	*hazard*
toxic	giftig	≈	*poisonous*
air current	Luftstrom		
to endanger	gefährden	N	*danger*
wildlife	Tierwelt	≈	*fauna*
to deposit	ablagern	N	*deposit*
to account for	der Grund sein für		
indigenous [ɪn'dɪdʒənəs]	eingeboren	≈	*native*
to break down	zersetzen	VI	*to decompose*
breakdown	Zersetzung	≈	*decomposition*
plastic	Kunststoff	ADJ	*plastic*
to leak	freisetzen	N	*leakage*
harmful	schädlich	VT	*to harm*
additive	Additiv, Zusatz	VT	*to add*
to contaminate	vergiften	N	*contamination*
waterway	Wasserweg	vgl.	*river – Fluss, Strom; stream, brook – Bach*
to end up	enden, landen		
landfill	Deponie		
to document	dokumentieren	N	*documentation*
industrialized country	Industriestaat		
immoral	unmoralisch	vgl.	*unethical – unethisch*
environmentally destructive	umweltzerstörend	N	*environmental destruction*
to prevent from	hindern an	N	*prevention*
to invest in	investieren in	N	*investment*
solution	Lösung	VT	*to solve*
pollution	Umweltverschmutzung		
appropriate [ə'prəʊpriət]	geeignet	<>	*inappropriate*

Marine pollution in the North Sea

The North Sea is one of the world's most intensively used bodies of water. It serves as a route for shipping, its reserves of fossil fuels are exploited by numerous oil and gas installations, its fisheries are trawled by the fishing fleets of most European nations.

In addition to the environmental impacts of all these human activities, the North Sea has to absorb the waste products generated by all the industrialized countries which border upon it. Pressure on its marine and shoreline ecosystems is intense.

The dumping of industrial and radioactive wastes into the North Sea, and the incineration of toxic waste at sea, are now prohibited by international conventions, although illegal and accidental discharges still occur. However, discharges and emissions *on land* are the source of around 90% of all marine pollution.

Oil pollution Supertanker accidents can devastate marine and shore life, but far more oil spillage results from other human activities. The major culprit is run-off from our roads: oil from motor vehicles is washed into our streams and rivers, and eventually finds its way into the sea. The roads of one major city provide as much oil pollution per annum as one major oil spill. In addition, oily exhaust fumes mostly find their way out to sea.

Radioactive waste Radioactive waste is still routinely discharged into the sea from the nuclear reprocessing plants at Sellafield (England's Irish Sea coast), Dounreay (northern Scotland) and La Hague (French Atlantic coast). Although supporters of reprocessing claim that the environmental impact is negligible, neighbouring countries are alarmed by the levels of radioactivity to be found in the foodchain.

Toxic waste It is now recognized that a number of toxic substances are liable to 'bioaccumulate', i.e. to be absorbed by and build up in living organisms, leading eventually to levels which are hazardous to the environment and to human health. The North Sea countries have agreed to reduce discharges, emissions and losses of such substances, with the ultimate aim of eliminating them totally by 2020.

marine	Meeres-		
body of water	Wassermasse		
shipping	Schifffahrt		
to exploit	ausbeuten	N	*exploitation*
oil installation	Bohrinsel	≈	*oil rig*
fishery	Fischereizone	VI	*to fish*
to trawl	mit dem Schleppnetz durchziehen	N	*trawler*
fishing fleet	Fischereiflotte		
environmental	Umwelt-	N	*environment*
to absorb	aufnehmen	N	*absorption*
to generate	erzeugen	≈	*to produce*
to border upon	grenzen an	N	*border*
pressure	Belastung		
intense	massiv	N	*intensity*
dumping	Verklappung	VT	*to dump*
waste	Abfall, Müll		
incineration	Verbrennung	VT	*to incinerate*
to prohibit	verbieten, untersagen	≈	*to forbid*
convention	Abkommen	≈	*agreement, treaty*
discharge	Einleitung	VTI	*to discharge*
source	Quelle		
to devastate ['devəsteɪt]	vernichten	N	*devastation*
oil spillage	Ölverschmutzung	VTI	*to spill*
culprit	Schuldige/r	vgl.	*guilty* – schuldig
run-off	Ablauf	VI	*to run off*
motor vehicle ['vi:əkl]	Kraftfahrzeug		
oil spill	Ölpest		
exhaust fumes	Auspuffgase		
routinely	routinemäßig		
nuclear reprocessing plant	atomare Wiederaufbereitungsanlage	VT	*to reprocess*
supporter	Befürworter/in	VT	*to support*
negligible ['neglɪdʒəbl]	unbedeutend	≈	*insignificant*
to alarm	beunruhigen		
radioactivity	Radioaktivität	ADJ	*radioactive*
foodchain	Nahrungskette		
to bioaccumulate [ˌbaɪəʊə'kju:mjəleɪt]	sich biologisch akkumulieren		
to build up	sich anreichern	≈	*to accumulate*
ultimate	End-		
to eliminate	beseitigen	≈	*to get rid of*

http://www.foe.co.uk/

Wild Britain is under threat

Sadly, much of the wildlife in the UK is under threat. Important habitats are constantly being destroyed by developers, mineral extractors and industrialists, all for the sake of short-term profit. Factory-style farming, which results from perverse agricultural subsidies, also takes its toll.

Our wild places are disappearing fast – ploughed up, polluted, drained or covered in concrete. With the loss of habitat there has been a drastic decline in species. Over 300 of our most important wildlife sites (called 'Sites of Special Scientific Interest' or SSSIs) are damaged every year, threatening many rare and endangered species with extinction. Also, many of the species that live outside these recognized wildlife havens are also under threat, in the wider countryside and in the marine environment. Time and again the pressures of agriculture and development ride roughshod over nature conservation.

Threatened marine wildlife

As a set of islands, the UK's relationship with the oceans that surround it is intimate. The UK has a highly significant population of marine mammals including bottlenose dolphins, harbour porpoises and grey seals. They are under threat from a range of activities:

* Fishing 'bycatch' – the catching of non-commercial species during fishing operations – wipes out some 2,200 harbour porpoises a year in the Celtic Sea alone. That is about six per cent of the local population.
* Overfishing further depletes their prey of marine wildlife.
* Disturbance: noise from shipping and industry can drive away marine mammals, as can insensitive dolphin watching.
* Pollution from land-based sources or at sea poisons marine mammals and their prey.
* Coastal change: changes to the immediate coast such as development or dredging have an impact on the sea bed and fish spawning grounds.
* Global climate change: changes in the temperature of the sea influence reproduction and species distribution.

to be under threat	bedroht sein	≈	*to be threatened*
developer	Bauplaner und -entwickler	VT	*to develop*
mineral extractor	Bergbauunternehmer/in	VT	*to extract*
industrialist	Industrielle/r		
for the sake of	um … willen		
short-term	kurzfristig	<>	*long-term*
perverse	widersinnig		
subsidy	Subvention	VT	*to subsidize*
to take its toll	*hier:* das Seine dazu beitragen		
to plough up [plaʊ]	umpflügen	N	*plough – Pflug*
to pollute	verschmutzen	N	*pollutant – Schadstoff*
to drain	entwässern	N	*drainage*
decline	Abnahme	VI	*to decline*
to threaten	bedrohen	≈	*to endanger*
rare	selten	<>	*common*
endangered	gefährdet	VT	*to endanger*
haven	Zufluchtstätte		
development	Bebauung		
to ride roughshod over ['rʌfʃɒd]	rücksichtslos hinweggehen über		
conservation	Schutz	VT	*to conserve*
intimate	eng	≈	*very close*
marine mammal	Meeressäugetier		
dolphin	Delphin		
porpoise	Tümmler		
seal	Seehund		
bycatch	Beifang		
non-commercial	nicht kommerziell		
to wipe out	vernichten	≈	*to eradicate*
overfishing	Überfischung		
to deplete	vermindern	N	*depletion*
prey	Beute	VT	*to prey on*
disturbance	Störung	VT	*to disturb*
to drive away	vertreiben	<>	*to attract*
to poison	vergiften	N	*poison*
dredging	Ausbaggern	VTI	*to dredge*
sea bed	Meeresboden		
spawning ground	Laichplatz, -grund	VI	*to spawn*
		vgl.	*to breed – Junge haben, brüten*
to influence	beeinflussen	N	*influence*
reproduction	Fortpflanzung	VTI	*to reproduce*

Earthfacts.com : desertification

Desertification

Desertification is the term used to describe the degradation of land in arid and semi-arid regions (drylands). It does not refer to the expansion of natural deserts. Degradation is taking place in the biological productivity and biodiversity of the drylands. That is to say, less vegetation is able to grow on the land, supporting smaller populations of animals, and fewer plant and animal species are able to survive there.

Drylands cover one third of the Earth's land area. They are naturally resilient: dryland plants and animals respond quickly to fluctuations in the availability of fresh water, and recover easily from periods of drought. The human populations of dryland regions traditionally protected their natural resources by evolving suitable methods of land management, such as nomadic herding. These practices were sustainable: they did not exhaust the land, and they allowed people to respond flexibly to fluctuations in climate.

Today, dryland ecosystems are being destroyed by new and unsustainable practices. Over 70 per cent of the world's drylands have been degraded by overexploitation, by deforestation and by the use of irrigation. This change in land use is largely a result of new economic and political pressures, e.g. the cultivation of cash crops for sale to the developed world. However, the causes of desertification are complex.

Degraded drylands lose their ability to cope with naturally occurring periods of drought. Stripped of its vegetation by overgrazing, fertile soil is eroded by the wind; plants are buried by wind-blown dust and nutrients are washed out of the cracked earth when the rains finally come. Unsuitable irrigation practices can raise the water table, allowing salts to build up on the waterlogged land.

The results of desertification include huge social and economic problems – including famine, poverty and mass migration – and long-term environmental damage.

LINKS:

- **Desertification Information Network**
- **United Nations Convention to Combat Desertification**
- **United Nations Commission for Sustainable Development**

desertification	Wüstenvormarsch	vgl.	*desert – Wüste*
arid	trocken, dürr	N	*aridity, aridness*
productivity	Produktivität	ADJ	*productive*
biodiversity	Artenvielfalt	vgl.	*diverse – vielfältig*
to support	*hier:* ernähren		
species ['spiːʃiːz]	Spezies, Art		
resilient [rɪ'zɪliənt]	unverwüstlich	N	*resilience*
fluctuation	Schwankung	VI	*to fluctuate*
availability	Verfügbarkeit	ADJ	*available*
fresh water	Süßwasser		
to recover from	sich erholen von	N	*recovery*
drought [draʊt]	Dürre	<>	*flooding*
to evolve	entwickeln	N	*evolution*
		VI	*to evolve – sich entwickeln*
suitable	geeignet	N	*suitability*
land management	Landbewirtschaftung	VT	*to manage*
nomadic herding	nomadische Hirtenkultur	VT	*to herd – hüten*
practice	Praktik		
sustainable	nachhaltig	N	*sustainability*
to exhaust [ɪgzɔːst]	auslaugen	N	*exhaustion*
to degrade	auslaugen	N	*degradation*
overexploitation	Übernutzung	VT	*to overexploit*
deforestation	Entwaldung	VT	*to deforest*
irrigation	Bewässerung	VT	*to irrigate*
pressure	Druck		
cultivation	Anbau	VT	*to cultivate*
cash crop	zum Verkauf bestimmte Feldfrucht		
to cope with	bewältigen		
to strip of	berauben + *Gen.*	≈	*to deprive of*
overgrazing	Überweidung	VTI	*to graze*
fertile ['fɜːtaɪl]	fruchtbar	<>	*barren*
soil	Boden	≈	*earth*
to erode	erodieren	N	*erosion*
nutrient	Nährstoff	VT	*to nourish*
water table	Grundwasserspiegel		
to build up	sich anlagern	≈	*to accumulate*
waterlogged	wasserdurchtränkt	<>	*parched – verdorrt*
famine ['fæmɪn]	Hungersnot		
poverty	Armut	adj	*poor*
mass migration	Massenabwanderung	VI	*to migrate*
		vgl.	*refugee – Flüchtling*
to combat	bekämpfen	≈	*to fight against*

Tropical Deforestation

THE SCALE OF THE PROBLEM

There are 1700 million hectares of tropical forest – half of the Earth's total forest area. We destroy 16 million hectares of this unique natural resource each year, and the rate of destruction is accelerating.

CAUSES OF DEFORESTATION

Slash-and-burn cultivation. Around 60% of tropical deforestation is caused when peasant farmers clear forest for subsistence farming. However, the farmers are not to blame. Often they have been displaced from more fertile areas by large landowners creating vast monoculture plantations of cash crops for export. The problem is not overpopulation as such, but the unfair distribution of land, together with the economic interests of the developed world.

Livestock grazing. Clearing of forest to create pasture is another major cause of deforestation. However, cattle ranching is often a pretext to claim title to the land for mining. Some of the largest ranches in Amazonia have never sent cattle to market.

Firewood collection. Worldwide, nearly 3 billion people use firewood as their main energy source: half of the wood cut in the world is burned as fuel. Poverty is the underlying cause.

Commercial logging. In most tropical countries, logging is largely unregulated, with poor natural regeneration and little reforestation. Logging also opens up the forests to colonization.

ENVIRONMENTAL EFFECTS OF DEFORESTATION

Land degradation. The soil of forested areas is mostly unsuitable for cultivation or grazing, so farming is not sustainable in the long term.

Loss of biodiversity. Tropical forests, whether rainforest, dry forest or coastal mangrove swamps, are among the world's richest habitats. Of the 30 million species believed to exist, around 12 million are indigenous to tropical forests.

Water management problems. Forests absorb excess rain and release it gradually, producing a steady supply of fresh water. When they are cleared, there may be catastrophic flooding downstream. Disruption of the water supply leads to shortages of water for drinking and irrigation. Silt washed downstream destroys coastal fisheries and coral reefs.

scale	Ausmaß		
unique	einzigartig	N	*uniqueness*
rate	Tempo	≈	*speed*
destruction	Zerstörung	VT	*to destroy*
to accelerate [ək'seləreɪt]	sich beschleunigen	<>	*to slow down*
slash-and-burn cultivation	Wanderackerbau mit Brandrodung		
peasant farmer	(armer) Bauer		
to clear	roden	N	*clearance*
to displace	verdrängen	N	*displacement*
vast	riesig	≈	*huge, enormous*
plantation	Plantage		
overpopulation	Überbevölkerung	ADJ	*overpopulated*
livestock grazing	Viehweidewirtschaft	VTI	*to graze*
pasture	Weideland		
cattle ranching	Viehwirtschaft		
pretext	Vorwand		
to claim title to	Besitzrechte beanspruchen auf		
mining	Bergbau	VTI	*to mine*
energy source	Energiequelle		
fuel	Brennstoff	vgl.	*firewood* – Brennholz
underlying cause	eigentlicher Grund		
logging	Holzfällen	VT	*to log*
unregulated	unkontrolliert	N	*regulation* – Kontrolle
reforestation	Aufforstung	VT	*to reforest*
colonization	Besiedlung	VT	*to colonize*
in the long term	langfristig	ADJ	*long-term*
rainforest	Regenwald		
mangrove swamp	Mangrovensumpf		
habitat	Lebensraum		
indigenous to [ɪn'dɪdʒənəs]	beheimatet in	≈	*native to*
water management	Wasserwirtschaft	VT	*to manage*
to absorb	aufnehmen	N	*absorption*
excess	überschüssig	vgl.	*excessive* – übermäßig
steady	beständig	<>	*variable, unreliable*
supply	Versorgung	VT	*to supply*
downstream	stromabwärts	<>	*upstream*
disruption	Störung	VT	*to disrupt*
shortage	Mangel	<>	*excess*
silt	Schlick		
fishery	Fischereigebiet		
coral reef	Korallenriff		

RADIO INTERVIEW: SUSTAINABLE DEVELOPMENT

INTERVIEWER: Dr McNamara: 'sustainable development' seems to be in vogue at the moment, but what does it actually mean?

McNAMARA: The Brundtland Commission defined it as 'development that meets the needs of the present without compromising the ability of future generations to meet their own needs'.

INTERVIEWER: So we just need to convert to more ecologically friendly means of production? Recycled paper and suchlike?

McNAMARA: No, the challenge is far greater than that. First let's consider 'the needs of the present': 1,3 billion people lack access to clean water, and 300 million people suffer from malnutrition, while the developed countries enjoy excessive levels of consumption. This imbalance must be rectified, and the essential needs of the world's poor must be given priority. Secondly, we are still behaving as if our natural resources – like soil, water, forests and minerals – are inexhaustible, despite all the evidence to the contrary. Achieving sustainable development requires a massive shift in attitudes and lifestyles.

INTERVIEWER: But people are mainly concerned with their own needs, and politicians are only interested in quick fixes. Sustainable development is just a utopian dream.

McNAMARA: On the contrary: 'business as usual' is no longer an option. Complacency and inertia are still rife, it's true, but change will come. We can do this the easy way – prompt action before more irreversible damage is done – or the hard way – postponing action until it is more expensive, more painful, more disruptive.

INTERVIEWER: So, tell us about 'the easy way'.

McNAMARA: We are treating our natural resources as if they were free. They are not: they have a value. Prices of goods and services must reflect the true cost to society of the use of these resources. To put it another way: environmental costs must become an integral part of business calculations. When resources are priced realistically, resource-intensive goods will become more expensive – and less attractive to consumers. There will be an incentive for companies to reduce their environmental impacts. We don't need authoritarian, interventionist policies: the competition inherent in free market economies will be the driving force towards sustainability.

INTERVIEWER: Dr McNamara, thank you.

sustainable development	nachhaltige Entwicklung		
to be in vogue	in Mode sein	≈	*fashionable*
to compromise	gefährden	VI	*to compromise – einen Kompromiss schließen*
to convert to	sich umstellen auf	≈	*to switch over to*
ecologically friendly	umweltfreundlich	≈	*environmentally friendly*
means of production	Produktionsmittel	VT	*to produce*
challenge	Herausforderung	VT	*to challenge*
access to ['ækses]	Zugang zu		
to suffer from	leiden an	<>	*to enjoy*
malnutrition	Unterernährung	ADJ	*malnourished*
excessive	übermäßig	<>	*insufficient*
consumption	Konsum	VT	*to consume*
imbalance	Ungleichgewicht	ADJ	*unbalanced*
to rectify	korrigieren	≈	*to correct*
to give priority to	Priorität geben + *Dat.*		
natural resources	natürliche Ressourcen		
inexhaustible [ɪnɪgzɔːstəbl]	unerschöpflich	VT	*to exhaust – erschöpfen*
evidence to the contrary	gegenteilige Beweise		
shift	Wandel	VTI	*to shift*
quick fix	schnelle Lösung	<>	*long-term solution*
utopian	utopisch	N	*utopia*
complacency	Selbstzufriedenheit	ADJ	*complacent*
inertia [ɪ'nɜːʃə]	Trägheit		
rife	weit verbreitet	≈	*common, widespread*
prompt	unverzüglich	≈	*timely*
irreversible [ɪrə'vɜːsəbl]	nicht rückgängig zu machen	<>	*reversible*
to postpone	verschieben	≈	*to delay*
disruptive	störend	VT	*to disrupt*
to reflect	widerspiegeln	N	*reflection*
consumer	Verbraucher/in		
incentive [ɪn'sentɪv]	Anreiz		
environmental impact	Umweltbelastung		
authoritarian	autoritär		
interventionist	interventionistisch	VI	*to intervene*
competition	Wettbewerb	VI	*to compete*
inherent in [ɪn'hɪərənt]	eigen, innewohnend + *Dat.*		
free market economy	freie Marktwirtschaft		
driving force	treibende Kraft		

• GROW ORGANIC, BUY ORGANIC, GROW ORGANIC, BUY ORGANIC •

Modern intensive agriculture uses synthetic fertilizers, pesticides, fungicides and herbicides to compensate for unsustainable farming methods. In the short term, synthetic chemicals increase yields, but they pollute the environment and leave toxic residues in our food. As soil quality deteriorates and pests develop resistance, more and more chemicals are needed. In the long term, this kind of agriculture just isn't viable.

Organic farming is about working with nature, not fighting against it. We don't use synthetic chemicals. So how do we nourish the soil and control pests, weeds and diseases?

Soil nutrition

Every time a crop is harvested, nutrients are removed from the soil. To maintain fertility, farmers must replace these nutrients. Organic farmers use composted natural waste to do this. Healthy soils retain water and produce nutritious crops.

Weed control

We do all of our weeding by tractor or by hand, which is very labour intensive. So we try to stop weeds germinating in the first place – by not letting them produce seed. By watering with pipes at ground level instead of overhead sprinklers, we water the crop instead of the whole field – including the weeds.

Pest control

Conventional monoculture produces vast areas of one crop, allowing equally vast populations of insect pests to build up, which are then sprayed with highly toxic chemicals. The organic alternative is balanced cultivation using a variety of crops. We also plant flowering plants along field margins to attract beneficial insects which prey on pest species.

Disease control

Healthy soil is full of beneficial fungi and bacteria which keep harmful organisms in check. Synthetic chemicals destroy these beneficial organisms – forcing conventional farmers to use ever more chemicals. Using natural fertilizers (organic matter full of living organisms) helps the soil to fight back, and crop rotation stops diseases from building up year on year.

Buying organic produce is a commitment to the health of our families and our planet.

GROW ORGANIC, BUY ORGANIC, GROW ORGANIC, BUY ORGANIC

agriculture	Landwirtschaft	≈	*farming*
synthetic [sɪn'θetɪk]	Kunst-	<>	*natural*
fertilizer	Dünger	VT	*to fertilize*
pesticide	Pestizid		
fungicide	Fungizid		
herbicide	Herbizid		
to compensate for	ausgleichen	N	*compensation*
yield	Ertrag	VT	*to yield*
to pollute	verschmutzen	N	*pollution*
toxic	giftig	N	*toxin*
residue	Rückstand	ADJ	*residual*
soil	Boden		
to deteriorate [dɪ'tɪəriəreɪt]	sich verschlechtern	<>	*to improve*
pest	Schädling		
to develop resistance	Resistenzen entwickeln	ADJ	*resistant*
viable	rentabel	N	*viability*
to nourish ['nʌrɪʃ]	mit Nährstoffen anreichern		
weed	Unkraut	VTI	*to weed – jäten*
nutrition	Anreicherung mit Nährstoffen		
crop	Feldfrucht, Nutzpflanze		
to harvest	ernten	N	*harvest*
nutrient	Nährstoff		
to maintain	erhalten	N	*maintenance*
fertility	Fruchtbarkeit	ADJ	*fertile*
to compost	kompostieren	N	*compost*
nutritious	nahrhaft	≈	*nourishing*
labour intensive	arbeitsintensiv		
to germinate	keimen		
seed	Same	vgl.	*to set seed – sich aussäen*
to water	bewässern	≈	*to irrigate*
to spray	spritzen	N	*spray*
balanced	ausgewogen		
cultivation	Anbau	VT	*to cultivate*
beneficial [benɪ'fɪʃl]	nützlich		
to prey on	Beute machen auf	N	*prey – Beute*
fungus	Pilz	PL	*fungi*
bacteria	Bakterien	SG	*bacterium*
to keep in check	in Schach halten		
harmful	schädlich	<>	*beneficial*
crop rotation	Fruchtwechsel	VTI	*to rotate*

environment forum

Subject: Is recycling wasteful? **Date: 06/18/2001**
Author: fiz <fiz@the.vineyard>

Recycling is about people's emotional needs – it's not about ecology. Recyclers want to feel that they are making their contribution to saving the planet. Here are some reasons why recycling is wasteful – of city budgets and citizens' time:

1 Recycling is neither cost-effective nor ecologically effective.
Taking into account the cost of collection as well as the cost of cleaning, sorting and processing recyclable garbage, recycling costs more than traditional garbage collection and disposal. Every time a sanitation department truck picks up a load of recyclables from the curbside, it burns fuel and produces air pollution.

2 There is no real market for recycled materials.
The market price of most recycled materials is lower than the cost of producing them. Government regulations have produced an artificial demand for recycled materials (e.g. by requiring that newspapers be made from recycled paper), but the whole recycling industry is based on ideology, not economics. Only a few materials are worth recycling – e.g. aluminium.

3 Landfills are a safe, economical alternative to recycling.
Landfill capacity in the USA is abundant. Modern dumps for household waste are environmentally friendly and create employment in rural communities. If US citizens continue to produce garbage at the present rate, it will take us 1000 years to fill one landfill 100 yards deep and 35 miles square!

4 There is nothing wrong with making paper from trees.
Recycling paper doesn't save forests: trees for paper manufacturing are an agricultural product grown for that purpose. More trees are planted in the USA each year than are felled. Timber is a renewable resource, and conserving trees by recycling paper makes as much ecological sense as conserving wheat by reducing bread consumption.

5 There is nothing wrong with disposables.
It's true that plastic packaging doesn't break down in landfills. However, whilst paper and other organic materials are theoretically biodegradable, studies have shown that they don't actually tend to break down in the airless conditions of a landfill. Effective packaging prevents the spoilage of foodstuffs – and reduces garbage.

wasteful	verschwenderisch	VT	*to waste*
ecology	Ökologie	ADJ	*ecological*
to make a contribution	einen Beitrag leisten	≈	*to contribute*
cost-effective	kosteneffizient		
ecologically	ökologisch		
effective	wirkungsvoll	N	*effectiveness*
to take into account	berücksichtigen	<>	*to ignore*
collection	Abholung	VT	*to collect*
to sort	sortieren		
to process ['prəʊses]	verarbeiten		
recyclable	wiederverwertbar		
garbage ['gɑːbɪdʒ]	Müll	UK	*rubbish*
disposal [dɪ'spəʊzl]	Entsorgung	VT	*to dispose of*
sanitation department	Stadtreinigung		
fuel	Kraftstoff	vgl.	*petrol* – *Benzin*
pollution	Verschmutzung	VT	*to pollute*
regulation	Verordnung		
artificial	künstlich	<>	*natural*
demand for	Nachfrage für/nach	VT	*to demand*
to require	verlangen, erfordern	N	*requirement*
to be based on	basieren auf	N	*basis*
ideology	Ideologie	ADJ	*ideological*
economics	Ökonomie	ADJ	*economic*
landfill	Mülldeponie		
economical	wirtschaftlich		
capacity	Kapazität		
abundant	reichlich	N	*abundance*
dump	Müllkippe	VT	*to dump*
household waste	Haushaltsabfall		
environmentally friendly	umweltfreundlich		
rural community	ländliche Gemeinde		
manufacturing	Herstellung	VT	*to manufacture*
agricultural	landwirtschaftlich	N	*agriculture*
to fell	fällen		
timber	(Nutz)Holz		
renewable	erneuerbar	VT	*to renew*
to conserve	erhalten	N	*conservation*
consumption	Verbrauch	VT	*to consume*
disposable [dɪ'spəʊzəbl]	Einwegartikel		
packaging	Verpackung(en)	VT	*to package*
to break down	sich zersetzen	≈	*to disintegrate*
organic	organisch		
biodegradable	biologisch abbaubar		
to prevent	verhindern	N	*prevention*
spoilage	Verderben	VTI	*to spoil*
foodstuff	Nahrungsmittel		

environment forum

Subject: Re: Is recycling wasteful? Date: 06/18/2001
Author: Jude Kilpatrick <drjudek@aol.com>

Fiz, for someone who doesn't believe in recycling, you sure have recycled a whole lot of ill-informed garbage!

› 1 Recycling is neither cost-effective nor ecologically effective.

1 The economics: we don't require landfills or incinerators to pay for themselves, so neither should we require this of recycling schemes. The real issue is this: how much does recycling add to the cost of production over the long term, compared to traditional waste management? This depends on economies of scale – the more waste we recycle, the cheaper the process becomes. Also it depends on fluctuations in the market prices of recycled materials. On the whole, though, recycling compares favourably with disposal.

2 The environmental impact: modern recycling paper mills don't produce hazardous levels of air and water pollution or toxic byproducts, whereas the traditional paper industry is one of the world's largest generators of pollutants. That's just one example.

› 2 There is no real market for recycled materials.

Recycling garbage provides manufacturing industry with raw materials which are less expensive than virgin sources. This applies not just to aluminium cans, but also waste paper, scrap metal and a number of other materials.

› 3 Landfills are a safe, economical alternative to recycling.

Landfills are not innocuous. They produce methane – a greenhouse gas – and highly toxic chemicals which can contaminate the groundwater. Large, modern landfills have better environmental safeguards, it's true. However, they are mostly distant from population centers, so the cost of transporting garbage to them is high.

› 4 There is nothing wrong with making paper from trees.

Recycling paper reduces the pressure to turn natural forests into sterile plantations. It's true that we are planting more trees than we are felling, but we are seeing a steady erosion of our natural forests, resulting in a loss of biodiversity and animal habitats.

› 5 There is nothing wrong with disposables.

If by "disposables" you mean synthetic, non-biodegradable packaging, e.g. polystyrene food containers: the chemicals used in manufacturing these products are extremely harmful to the environment, and they use up non-renewable resources.

ill-informed	schlecht informiert	<>	*well-informed*
incinerator [ɪn'sɪnəreɪtə]	Müllverbrennungs-anlage	VT	*to incinerate*
recycling scheme	Recyclingprogramm		
over the long term	langfristig	<>	*in the short term*
waste management	Abfallentsorgung		
economy of scale	Einsparung durch erhöhte Produktion	VI	*to economize*
fluctuation	Fluktuation	VI	*to fluctuate*
to compare favourably with	günstig abschneiden im Vergleich mit		
environmental impact	Auswirkung auf die Umwelt	VT	*to impact upon*
paper mill	Papierfabrik		
hazardous ['hæzədəs]	gefährlich	≈	*dangerous*
toxic	giftig	≈	*poisonous*
byproduct	Nebenprodukt		
generator	Erzeuger	VT	*to generate*
pollutant	Schadstoff		
manufacturing industry	verarbeitende Industrie	VT	*to manufacture*
raw material	Rohstoff(e)		
virgin source	natürliche Quelle		
waste paper	Altpapier		
scrap metal	Schrott		
innocuous [ɪ'nɒkjuəs]	harmlos	≈	*harmless*
methane ['miːθeɪn]	Methan		
greenhouse gas	Treibhausgas	vgl.	*greenhouse effect*
chemical	Chemikalie		
to contaminate	verschmutzen	N	*contamination*
groundwater	Grundwasser		
environmental	Umwelt-	N	*environment*
safeguard ['seɪfgɑːd]	Schutz(vorrichtung)	VT	*to safeguard*
population center	Bevölkerungszentrum		
to transport	transportieren	N	*transportation*
pressure ['preʃə]	Druck		
sterile	steril	N	*sterility*
plantation	Plantage		
erosion	Aushöhlung	VT	*to erode*
biodiversity [ˌbaɪəʊdaɪvɜːsəti]	Artenvielfalt	ADJ	*diverse – vielfältig*
habitat	Lebensraum		
synthetic	synthetisch	≈	*artificial*
polystyrene [ˌpɒlɪ'staɪriːn]	Polystyrol		
harmful to	schädlich für	VT	*to harm*
non-renewable	nicht erneuerbar		

C The Economy

1 National and Global Economy

2 The World of Business

3 Employment

4 Money Matters

The Industrial Revolution

DURING THE PERIOD 1760–1840 Britain underwent a transformation from an agrarian economy to one dominated by industry and mass production. This process, termed the Industrial Revolution, was made possible by technological and socioeconomic developments, including the invention of new machines which increased workers' productivity, the development of new methods of transport and the reorganization of labour into the factory system, characterized by division of labour and functional specialization. These changes made it possible for Britain to exploit its natural resources far more efficiently and manufacture goods on an unprecedented scale

Non-industrial developments also played an important part: improvements in farming enabled the land to support a larger urban, non-farming population, which in turn provided a labour pool for the new industries, and a wider distribution of wealth and the growth of international trade provided a demand for the new manufactured goods.

The British were of course aware of their head start, and took measures to consolidate their industrial leadership by banning the export of machinery, manufacturing techniques and skilled workers. However, in the long term the monopoly could not be sustained: British industrialists and entrepreneurs were soon tempted by profitable opportunities abroad – and continental European countries were anxious to attract British expertise. In the early nineteenth century the Industrial Revolution spread to Belgium and then to France. Political fragmentation and the lack of a wealthy, powerful middle class delayed the Industrial Revolution in Germany, but once favourable conditions had been established in the later nineteenth century, Germany was quick to challenge and then surpass Britain in important areas of industrial production. On the other side of the Atlantic, the United States with its immense natural resources and labour pool far outpaced European industrialization in the late nineteenth and early twentieth century.

to undergo	erleben	≈	*to experience*
transformation	grundlegende Umwandlung	VT	*to transform*
agrarian economy	Agrarwirtschaft		
mass production	Massenproduktion	VT	*to mass-produce*
technological	technologisch	N	*technology*
socioeconomic	sozioökonomisch		
invention	Erfindung	VT	*to invent*
productivity	Produktivität	ADJ	*productive*
reorganization	Neuorganisation	VT	*to reorganize*
labour	Arbeit		
division of labour	Arbeitsteilung	VT	*to divide*
specialization	Spezialisierung	VI	*to specialize (in)*
to exploit	nutzen	N	*exploitation*
natural resources	natürliche Ressourcen		
efficiently	effizient	<>	*inefficiently*
to manufacture	herstellen		
on a ... scale	in einem ... Ausmaß		
unprecedented	beispiellos		
urban	städtisch	<>	*rural*
population	Bevölkerung		
labour pool	Arbeitskraftreserve		
distribution	Verteilung	VT	*to distribute*
wealth	Wohlstand	ADJ	*wealthy*
manufactured goods	Fertigwaren		
head start	Vorsprung	≈	*lead*
to take measures	Maßnahmen ergreifen	≈	*to take steps*
to consolidate	festigen	N	*consolidation*
leadership	Führung		
manufacturing technique	Herstellungsverfahren		
skilled worker	Facharbeiter/in	vgl.	*skill* – Fertigkeit
monopoly [mə'nɒpəli]	Monopol		
to sustain	aufrechterhalten		
industrialist	Industrielle/r		
entrepreneur [ˌɒntrəprə'nɜː]	Unternehmer/in	ADJ	*entrepreneurial*
profitable	Gewinn bringend	N	*profitability*
to attract	anlocken	N	*attraction*
expertise [ˌekspɜː'tiːz]	Sachkenntnis	≈	*know-how*
middle class	Mittelstand	vgl.	*upper class; working class*
favourable	günstig	VT	*to favour*
to challenge	herausfordern	N	*challenge*
to surpass [sɜːpɑːs]	übertreffen		
to outpace	überholen		
industrialization	Industrialisierung		

Fact File: USA

The United States of America

The US has the most powerful and diversified economy in the world and one of the highest levels of gross national product (GNP) per capita. Government makes minimal intervention in the economy, with fiscal and monetary policy its main means of regulation. Competition is fostered through enforcement of antitrust laws. US businesses enjoy considerable flexibility and freedom in laying off surplus labor, expanding capital plant, and developing new products. US companies are at the forefront of information technology, medicine, the aerospace and arms industries.

However, the rapid advance of technology has increased inequalities between economic groups, as those lacking technical and professional training have been excluded from the economy's success. Since 1975, most rises in household income have been gained by the top-earning 20% of households. The late 1990s saw steady growth, low inflation rates and a drop in unemployment to below 5%, but economic problems include a lack of investment in infrastructure and the rising cost of pensions and medical care for an ageing population.

Primary sector

Agricultural production, fishing and forestry together generate only 2% of GNP, but production exceeds domestic demand in most cash crops and in dairy products, making the US the world's leading food exporter. Mining (also 2% of GNP) is well developed. The US is rich in mineral resources, including around 20 per cent of the world's reserves of high-quality coal.

Secondary sector

Manufacturing generates around 20% of GNP. Large corporations dominate the major manufacturing industries, which include steel, industrial machinery, automobiles, aerospace, electronics, telecommunications, food processing, chemicals, textiles, and plastics.

Tertiary sector

As in the other "postindustrial" nations, the service sector employs most of the labor force (around 75%). It produces the largest percentage of GNP (also around 75%). Over 87 million people work in the service industries, including the following: government; communications, transportation and public utilities; finance, insurance, and real estate; wholesale and retail trade; health care; tourism.

diversified	vielfältig		
gross national product	Bruttosozialprodukt	vgl.	*gross domestic product – Bruttoinlandsprodukt*
per capita	pro Kopf		
intervention	Eingriff	VI	*to intervene*
fiscal policy	Finanzpolitik		
monetary policy	Währungs-, Geldpolitik		
regulation	Regulierung	VT	*to regulate*
competition	Wettbewerb	VI	*to compete*
to foster	fördern	≈	*to encourage*
enforcement	Durchsetzung	VT	*to enforce*
antitrust law	Kartellgesetz	UK	*anti-merger law*
to lay off	entlassen, abbauen	≈	*to make redundant*
surplus ['sɜ:pləs]	überschüssig	N	*surplus*
to expand	ausbauen	<>	*to contract [kən'trækt]*
capital plant	Investitionsgüter	≈	*capital goods*
to be at the forefront	an der Spitze sein		
aerospace industry	Raumfahrtindustrie		
arms industry	Rüstungsindustrie		
advance	Fortschritt	VI	*to advance*
inequality	Ungleichheit	ADJ	*unequal*
to exclude from	ausschließen von	N	*exclusion*
drop	Rückgang	<>	*rise, increase*
pension	Rente	!	*rent – Miete*
medical care	medizinische Versorgung		
to generate	erzeugen	≈	*to produce*
to exceed	übersteigen	<>	*to fall short of*
cash crop	zum Verkauf bestimmte Feldfrucht		
dairy product ['deəri]	Molkereiprodukt		
exporter	Exporteur/in	VTI	*to export*
mining	Bergbau	vgl.	*mine – Bergwerk*
mineral resources	Bodenschätze		
corporation	Unternehmen		
to dominate	dominieren	ADJ	*dominant*
food processing	Lebensmittelverarbeitung	VT	*to process*
percentage	Prozentsatz	vgl.	*proportion – Anteil*
public utilities	öffentliche Versorgung		
finance	Finanzwesen	ADJ	*financial*
insurance	Versicherungswesen	VT	*to insure*
real estate	Immobilien	UK	*property*
wholesale trade	Großhandel	vgl.	*wholesaler – Grossist/in*
retail trade	Einzelhandel	vgl.	*retailer – Einzelhändler/in*

RADIO DEBATE: GLOBALIZATION

Presenter: We have in the studio with us today two leading economists, Professor Belinda Stratton and Dr Trudi van Kleef, to discuss globalization. Professor Stratton, what exactly *is* globalization?

Stratton: The free flow of jobs, capital and trade across national borders. This may be seen as a consequence of economic and technical developments: firstly, the growth of multinational companies with bases in a number of countries; secondly, a general liberalization of markets, including privatization of industries and the reduction or removal of protectionist barriers against imports and foreign acquisition of domestic companies; thirdly, improvements in communications technology, making it possible for parts of a company to be geographically dispersed, and enabling e-commerce, which in turn has allowed companies of all sizes to offer their goods and services to a global market via the Internet, processing transactions quickly and securely.

Presenter: 'Globalization' sounds very egalitarian – are all countries and all sectors of society benefiting from it, Dr van Kleef?

van Kleef: No, I'm afraid my colleague is being a little optimistic. The increasing mobility of multinational corporations has disrupted the balance of power between employers and employees – instead of meeting their social obligations, companies can shift production overseas to countries where wages are lower, working conditions less regulated, workers less protected from exploitation. Multinationals can coerce countries – particularly poorer countries – into granting large subsidies and cutting corporation tax, in effect transferring the burden of taxation from corporations to individuals.

Stratton: Yes, these are serious problems, but on the whole globalization stimulates trade, benefiting both rich and poor nations enormously. In most countries, foreign firms tend to create jobs faster than their domestic competitors, spend more on research and development, pay their workforce above the national average, and export more.

van Kleef: I hope that your optimism is justified, Professor. As Kofi Annan said in a recent speech: 'The central challenge we face today is to ensure that globalization becomes a positive force for all the world's people, instead of leaving billions of them behind in squalor.'*

* *Kofi Annan, Secretary General of the UN, 3 April 2000*

globalization	Globalisierung	ADJ	*global*
economist	Ökonom/in		
flow	Fluss	VI	*to flow*
capital	Kapital		
consequence	Resultat, Folge	ADJ	*consequential*
liberalization	Liberalisierung	ADJ	*liberal*
privatization	Privatisierung	<>	*to nationalize*
reduction	Herabsetzung	VT	*to reduce*
protectionist	protektionistisch	<>	*liberal*
barrier against	Hindernis gegen		
acquisition	Erwerb, Ankauf	VT	*to acquire*
dispersed	verstreut	N	*dispersal*
e-commerce	elektronischer Handel		
to process	abwickeln		
egalitarian	egalitär	<>	*elitist*
to benefit from	profitieren von	N	*benefit*
mobility	Mobilität	ADJ	*mobile*
to disrupt	stören	N	*disruption*
balance of power	Gleichgewicht der Kräfte		
to meet o's obligations	seinen Verpflichtungen nachkommen		
wages	Löhne	≈	*pay* SG
regulated	geregelt	N	*regulation*
exploitation	Ausbeutung	VT	*to exploit*
to coerce [kəʊ'ɜːs] into	zwingen zu	≈	*to force to*
to grant	gewähren	≈	*award*
subsidy	Subvention, Zuschuss	VT	*to subsidize*
to cut	senken	N	*cut*
corporation tax	Körperschaftssteuer	vgl.	***income tax*** – *Einkommenssteuer;* ***value added tax*** – *Mehrwertsteuer*
to transfer	übertragen	N	*transfer*
burden of taxation	Steuerlast	VT	*to tax*
to stimulate	beleben	≈	*to foster*
to benefit	nützen	vgl.	*benefit (oben)*
competitor	Konkurrent/in	VI	*to compete (with)*
research and development	Forschung und Entwicklung	ABK	*R&D*
workforce	Arbeiterschaft	≈	*labour force*
average	Durchschnitt	ADJ	*average*
to export	exportieren	N	*export*
justified	gerechtfertigt	N	*justification*
challenge	Herausforderung	VT	*to challenge*
squalor ['skwɒlə]	elende Verhältnisse	ADJ	*squalid*

Voxpop.com: Economics Forum

VOXPOP
• DISCUSSION FORUM •

Poverty, First World lending and Third World debt – a vicious circle?

It's up to the Third World to use development aid and loans sensibly. In many Third World nations, undemocratic or incompetent government means that money is frequently diverted or misappropriated. Instead of being spent on useful programmes of economic development, the money is spent on useless prestige projects – or finds its way into the pockets of corrupt government officials and the already wealthy economic élite. However, the First World is also to blame: private and public lending needs depend much more on the democratic values, economic prospects and creditworthiness of recipient countries. **Jon, Oxford UK**

The terms First World and Third World are misleading generalizations: each country has its own particular needs and potential. However, in many of the poorest countries, rapid industrialization along free market lines is not an appropriate path to follow – at least, not yet. What's needed is the application of intermediate technologies: relatively simple agricultural and industrial equipment that does not rely on imported spare parts and foreign technicians, combined with a programme of vocational and technical training. This kind of programme is best implemented through small-scale self-help projects which are relatively cheap to finance.
Lisa, Washington D.C.

Jon and Lisa, you are both missing the point: First World 'aid' to developing countries is in effect a form of market colonialism. After the world recession of the 1980s and the oil crises left many developing countries unable to service their debts, the World Bank and the IMF started to impose Structural Adjustment Programmes as a precondition for further lending. SAPs amount to enforced liberalization of markets – regardless of whether this is appropriate for the country concerned. Governments are forced to reduce their intervention in the economy and to privatize industries, to cut public spending – especially in 'unprofitable' areas like social services, health, education and food subsidies – to produce for export rather than for the domestic market, to reduce import tariffs and to facilitate foreign investment. Developing countries are being treated as reserves of cheap labor and raw materials. **Rosa, Mexico City**

poverty	Armut	<>	*prosperity, wealth*
lending	Kreditvergabe	<>	*borrowing*
debt [det]	Verschuldung	vgl.	*to be in ~* – verschuldet sein
vicious circle ['vɪʃəs]	Teufelskreis	<>	*virtuous circle*
development aid	Entwicklungshilfe	VT	*to aid*
loan	Kredit		
incompetent	unfähig	N	*incompetence*
to divert	zweckentfremden	N	*diversion*
to misappropriate [ˌmɪsə'prəuprieɪt]	veruntreuen		
government official	Regierungsbeamte/r	vgl.	*civil servant* – Beamte/r
economic prospects	wirtschaftliche Aussichten		
creditworthiness	Kreditwürdigkeit	ADJ	*creditworthy*
recipient	Empfänger-	VT	*to receive*
free market	freie Marktwirtschaft		
application	Anwendung	VT	*to apply*
intermediate	Zwischen-		
equipment	Geräte		
spare part	Ersatzteil		
technician [tek'nɪʃn]	Techniker/in		
vocational training	Berufsausbildung	vgl.	*profession* – Beruf
technical training	technische Ausbildung		
to implement	umsetzen	≈	*to carry out*
small-scale	klein angelegt	ADV	*on a small scale*
self-help project	Selbsthilfeprojekt		
developing country	Entwicklungsland		
colonialism	Kolonialismus	vgl.	*colony* – Kolonie
recession	Rezession	<>	*boom*
oil crisis	Ölkrise	PL	*crises*
to service debts	Schulden bedienen		
to impose	auferlegen	N	*imposition*
structural adjustment	Strukturanpassung	VTI	*to adjust*
precondition	Bedingung	≈	*prerequisite*
to enforce	erzwingen		
regardless of	ohne Rücksicht auf		
to privatize	privatisieren	<>	*to nationalize*
public spending	Ausgaben der öffentlichen Hand		
unprofitable	wenig einträglich	<>	*profitable, lucrative*
social services	Sozialdienste		
import tariff	Einfuhrzoll	≈	*customs duty*
to facilitate [fə'sɪlɪteɪt]	erleichtern		
raw material	Rohstoff		

BUSINESS NEWS

NEW MAN AT THE TOP

Synthetica's new MD optimistic for the future

BOB HOLBY took over as managing director of Synthetica following its restructuring in May last year, and has embarked upon his new role with enthusiasm. He points to a new £2 billion investment programme, joint ventures in eastern Europe and the opening of Synthetica's new plant in Inverness as achievements he is proud of.

Holby refuses to accept criticism of the way the company's restructuring was implemented, especially the sale of its unprofitable subsidiary PlasChem, which resulted in mass redundancy in the Tyneside plant. "That was very unfortunate, but necessary. PlasChem's buyers were able to keep 60% of the workforce, which wouldn't have happened if we had delayed the inevitable. Job losses elsewhere in the group were absorbed by voluntary redundancy."

Holby rejects rumours of a merger between Synthetica and its competitor GN Plastics. "I don't believe that the interests of the company, workforce or shareholders would be served by that." However, he does not rule out acquisitions: "We would consider acquisitions which offer economies of scale, increases in efficiency and cuts in overheads. It's a question of finding businesses which complement our main activities."

Holby sees potential for expanding Synthetica's existing businesses. "But it's not a question of size for size's sake – there's no point in increasing our turnover and market share unless we increase our profit margins also."

A key issue for Holby is the plastics industry's image. "We need to make people aware of the high standards we operate by, the employment we create, the revenue we generate for the country and the benefits our products bring to people's daily lives. We have to get the message across."

Another of Holby's key concerns is to recruit and develop the right personnel: "I believe very strongly in the people factor. If you look at businesses which have really boosted their performance in the long term, it's rarely been just the result of a market upturn or a technological breakthrough. It's *people* who've made the difference."

managing director (MD)	geschäftsführende/r Direktor/in	US	*chief executive officer (CEO)*
restructuring	Neustrukturierung		
to embark upon	beginnen		
investment	Investition	VTI	*to invest*
plant	Produktionsanlage		
achievement	Leistung	VT	*to achieve*
criticism	Kritik	VTI	*to criticize*
unprofitable	unrentabel	vgl.	*profitability – Rentabilität*
subsidiary [səb'sɪdiəri]	Tochtergesellschaft	<>	*parent company*
mass redundancy	Massenentlassung	vgl.	*to make redundant – entlassen*
workforce	Belegschaft	≈	*labour force*
inevitable	unvermeidbar	<>	*avoidable*
voluntary redundancy	freiwillige Aufgabe des Arbeitsplatzes		
to reject	zurückweisen	N	*rejection*
rumour	Gerücht		
merger	Fusion	VTI	*to merge*
competitor [kəm'petɪtə]	Konkurrent/in	≈	*rival*
shareholder	Aktionär/in	vgl.	*share – Aktie*
to rule out	ausschließen		
acquisition [ˌækwɪ'zɪʃn]	Erwerb, Ankauf	VT	*to acquire*
economy of scale	Größenvorteil		
efficiency	Effizienz	<>	*inefficiency*
overheads	allgemeine Kosten		
to complement	ergänzen	ADJ	*complementary*
to expand	erweitern	N	*expansion*
turnover	Umsatz		
market share	Marktanteil		
profit margins	Gewinnspannen		
key issue	Schlüsselfrage	≈	*vital issue*
employment	Arbeitsplätze	VT	*to employ*
revenue	Einnahmen		
to generate	*hier:* erwirtschaften		
to get the message across	die Botschaft rüberbringen		
concern	Anliegen		
to recruit	einstellen	N	*recruitment*
personnel	Personal		
to boost	enorm steigern	N	*boost*
performance	Leistung	VI	*to perform*
in the long term	langfristig	ADJ	*long-term*
market upturn	Marktaufschwung	<>	*market downturn*
breakthrough	Durchbruch		

EMPLOYMENT – Ella Martens

The glass ceiling

Job segregation in the US persists

By 2005, women will make up 48% of the US labor force, yet job segregation of women persists: 98% of secretaries are female, as are 80% of administrative support staff in general; 91% of nurses are female. This translates into lower income for women: average weekly earnings for full-time workers in 1998 were $456 for women and $598 for men. The average full-time male worker with a high-school education has a higher income than the average full-time female worker with a college degree.

Even amongst female high-achievers, sexual inequality has not been removed by 40 years of anti-discrimination legislation. Although women occupy around 40% of all executive, management and administrative positions, and comprise more than a third of business school graduates, senior management remains a largely male preserve. In America's biggest 500 companies, only 3% of senior executives and fewer than 6% of corporate directors are female.

In her book *Breaking the Glass Ceiling* Ann Morrison describes the problem as a barrier which is "so subtle that it is transparent, yet so strong that it prevents women from moving up the corporate hierarchy". Here are three factors which contribute to the "glass ceiling":

Firstly, female executives tend to be employed in personnel, PR and marketing, rather than as line managers. These areas provide little opportunity for promotion to the top levels of corporations, and few opportunities for female executives to show leadership qualities and prove themselves as policy makers.

Secondly, male senior managers tend to be complacent. There is a tendency to assume that now that women are well-represented in middle management, it is only a matter of time before they achieve parity at senior level. Failure of promising female executives to achieve their full potential is often attributed to the difficulty of combining family and career.

Thirdly, there is active discrimination. Male bosses tend to promote people like themselves (the "old boy network"), so the gender bias is perpetuated. Sexual harassment is still tolerated by large corporations, intimidating women.

job segregation	berufliche Ausgrenzung	VT	*to segregate*
to persist	anhalten	<>	*to cease*
administrative support staff	Verwaltungshilfskräfte	vgl.	*administration – Verwaltung*
income	Einkommen	<>	*expenditure*
average	durchschnittlich	N	*average*
high school	weiterführende Schule	UK	*secondary school*
college degree	Universitätsabschluss	UK	*university degree*
female high-achievers	leistungsstarke Frauen	vgl.	*achievement – Leistung*
anti-discrimination legislation	Gleichstellungsgesetz	VT	*to discriminate against*
executive	leitend		
administrative	Verwaltungs-		
business school graduate ['grædjuət]	Wirtschaftsschul-absolvent/in	VI	*to graduate ['grædjueɪt]*
male preserve	männliche Domäne		
senior executive	leitende/r Angestellte/r		
corporate director	Unternehmensleiter/in		
barrier	Barriere	vgl.	*obstacle – Hindernis*
to prevent from	hindern an	<>	*to enable to*
corporate hierarchy ['haɪərɑːki]	Unternehmens-hierarchie		
personnel	Personalabteilung	≈	*human resources*
line manager	leitende/r Angestellte/r		
opportunity	Möglichkeit		
promotion	Beförderung		
corporation	Unternehmen	≈	*company*
leadership	Führung	VTI	*to lead*
policy maker	Gestalter/in von Geschäftspolitik		
complacent	selbstzufrieden	N	*complacency*
to assume	ausgehen von	N	*assumption*
parity	Gleichstellung		
promising	viel versprechend		
to attribute to	zurückführen auf	≈	*to ascribe to*
to promote	befördern		
old boy network	Alte-Kameraden-Prinzip		
gender bias	geschlechtsspezifische Voreingenommenheit		
to perpetuate [pə'petʃueɪt]	aufrechterhalten	<>	*to put an end to*
sexual harassment	sexuelle Belästigung	VT	*to harass*
to tolerate	tolerieren	≈	*to condone*
to intimidate	einschüchtern	N	*intimidation*

Getting it right ...

... RECRUITMENT *and* SELECTION

"What are the legal requirements?"

Job applicants who consider they have been discriminated against on the grounds of their race, sex or disability or refused employment on the grounds of membership or non-membership of a trade union may make a claim to an industrial tribunal. If the tribunal finds in the applicant's favour, it may award compensation. It is a criminal offence to employ a person with no immigration authorization to work in the UK.

"Why is good recruitment and selection important?"

A more effective, better motivated workforce can result. Absenteeism, low morale, ineffective management and supervision, disciplinary problems, dismissals and possible unfair dismissal complaints can be avoided.

"How do I get it right?"

- ✔ Prepare a person specification. This should briefly describe the ideal person to fill the job. It is a profile of the personal skills and characteristics to look for in recruitment and selection. By writing a person specification you can help avoid inadvertent discrimination.
- ✔ An effective equal opportunities policy can help you ensure that no job applicant is treated less favourably on grounds of sex, race, colour, nationality, ethnic or national origin or on the grounds of disability.
- ✔ Attract applicants by using the best recruitment method(s), e.g.:
  - — *internal recruitment*
  - — *local schools, colleges, universities*
  - — *Jobcentres of the Employment Service*
  - — *commercial employment agencies*
  - — *newspapers and magazines.*
- ✔ An application form can help you to sift out unsuitable candidates.
- ✔ Consider a variety of selection methods, such as:
  - — *an interview*
  - — *selection tests*
  - — *taking up references.*
- ✔ When carrying out interviews you should make sure that you:
  - — *put the candidate at ease*
  - — *inform the candidate about your organization and the job*
  - — *tell the candidate when to expect the result of the interview*
  - — *do not ask questions which may be considered discriminatory*
  - — *list beforehand the points you wish to raise.*

recruitment [rɪ'kruːtmənt]	Personalbeschaffung	VT	*to recruit*
selection	Auswahl	VT	*to select*
legal requirement	rechtliche Voraussetzung	VT	*to require*
job applicant	Stellenbewerber/in	VI	*to apply (for)*
to discriminate against	diskriminieren	N	*discrimination*
on the grounds of	aufgrund + *Gen.*	≈	*on the basis of*
race	Rasse	ADJ	*racial*
disability	Behinderung	ADJ	*disabled*
trade union	Gewerkschaft		
to make a claim to	anrufen		
industrial tribunal	Arbeitsgericht		
to find in s.o.'s favour	für jdn befinden	<>	*to find against s.o.*
to award compensation	eine Entschädigung zuerkennen	VT	*to compensate*
criminal offence	strafbare Handlung	≈	*crime*
authorization	Genehmigung	VT	*to authorize*
motivated	motiviert	N	*motivation*
workforce	Arbeiterschaft	≈	*staff, employees, personnel*
absenteeism [ˌæbsən'tiːɪzm]	Nichterscheinen am Arbeitsplatz		
morale [mə'rɑːl]	Moral	!	*moral* ['mɒrəl] – *moralisch*
supervision	Aufsicht	VT	*to supervise*
disciplinary	Disziplin-	N	*discipline*
dismissal	Entlassung	VT	*to dismiss*
person specification	Personenbeschreibung		
skill	Fähigkeit, Fertigkeit		
inadvertent	unbeabsichtigt	<>	*intentional, deliberate*
equal opportunities policy	Chancengleichheits-politik		
favourably	wohlwollend	VT	*to favour* – *begünstigen*
ethnic origin	ethnische Herkunft		
internal recruitment	firmeninterne Stellen-besetzung	<>	*external recruitment*
employment agency	Stellenvermittlung		
application form	Bewerbungsformular		
to sift out	aussieben		
unsuitable	ungeeignet	vgl.	*suitability* – Eignung
to take up references	Referenzen einholen		
to put at ease	die Befangenheit nehmen	<>	*to make uneasy*
discriminatory [dɪs'krɪmɪnətəri]	diskriminierend	vgl.	*biased* – *voreingenommen*
to raise	ansprechen	≈	*to address*

Netpost: Mail in

REPLY FORWARD FILE IT DELETE

From: Maggie Gregan **To:** Alice Hanson

Subject: Going freelance **Date:** 05/05/2001

Hi Alice,

I was interested to hear that you're planning to go freelance, now that your position with YTech has been made redundant.

As you know, I've been freelance for some years. It does seem to be an increasingly popular choice. Some economists see "free agents", as they call us, as a new socioeconomic phenomenon, a sign of a transformation in society's relationship to work. In the 20th century, employment was viewed as a social contract: the individual gave the organization loyalty, and the organization gave the individual security – even self-esteem and a sense of identity. However, after decades of downsizing and outsourcing, that social contract seems to be disintegrating. In today's volatile business climate, companies tend to be short-lived – and how can you have long-term security with a company that only exists for a few years? In such a climate, having six clients is arguably more secure and stable than having one boss!

Personally, I find the freelance lifestyle very rewarding: I can better utilize and develop my skills and interests, and I can be selective about the projects I take on. Nor is freelance work always solitary – I often collaborate with other freelances on specific projects, where we pool our complementary skills before moving on to the next contract and the next challenge. If you have the sort of personality which is suited to this way of earning a living, it can be very liberating – no one else dictates when, where or how you work.

At the same time, you'll miss a lot of the things you take for granted now: not just fringe benefits like your company car, 30 days' paid annual leave and a company pension plan, but also chats with colleagues, planned training and development, a clear career structure ... But don't let me put you off!

Good luck!
Maggie &:-)

to go freelance	freiberuflich tätig werden		
to make redundant	streichen	N	*redundancy*
free agent	frei Agierende/r		
socioeconomic	sozioökonomisch		
phenomenon	Phänomen	PL	*phenomena*
transformation	Verwandlung	VT	*to transform*
social contract	Gesellschaftsvertrag		
loyalty	Loyalität	ADJ	*loyal*
security	Sicherheit	<>	*insecurity*
self-esteem	Selbstachtung	≈	*self-respect*
sense of identity	Identitätsgefühl		
to downsize	rationalisieren und Stellen abbauen		
to outsource	extern beschaffen/ vergeben	vgl.	*source – Quelle*
to disintegrate	sich auflösen	N	*disintegration*
volatile	unbeständig	<>	*stable*
business climate	Wirtschaftsklima		
short-lived	kurzlebig		
secure	sicher	<>	*insecure*
stable	stabil	N	*stability*
lifestyle	Lebensstil	≈	*way of life*
rewarding	vorteilhaft		
to utilize	einsetzen	≈	*to use*
selective	wählerisch	UGS	*choosy*
solitary	einsam		
to collaborate [kə'læbəreɪt]	zusammenarbeiten	N	*collaboration*
freelance	Freiberufler/in	ADJ	*freelance*
to pool	zusammenfassen		
complementary [ˌkɒmplɪ'mentri]	sich ergänzend	!	*complimentary – schmeichelhaft*
contract	Auftrag	≈	*commission*
challenge	Herausforderung	VT	*to challenge*
to earn a living	sich seinen Lebensunterhalt verdienen		
liberating	befreiend	<>	*restrictive, restricting*
to dictate	diktieren		
to take for granted	als selbstverständlich hinnehmen		
fringe benefit	zusätzliche Leistung		
annual leave	Jahresurlaub		
pension plan	betriebliche Altersversorgung	vgl.	*to retire – in den Ruhestand gehen*
colleague ['kɒliːg]	Kollege, Kollegin		
career structure	beruflicher Werdegang		

What is Economic and Monetary Union?

Economic and Monetary Union (EMU) is a single currency area within the European Union single market in which people, goods, services and capital move without restrictions. It creates the framework for economic growth and stability and is underpinned by an independent central bank and legal obligations on the participating Member States to pursue sound economic policies and to coordinate these policies very closely. The rules, institutions and objectives of EMU are set down in the Maastricht Treaty.

Why a European Economic and Monetary Union?

European Economic and Monetary Union is an economic necessity as the natural complement to the European single market. The euro removes high transaction costs brought about by currency conversions and the uncertainties linked to exchange rate instability. A more efficient single market helps to boost growth and employment, while the euro strengthens international monetary stability. Easy comparison of prices in euro makes companies more competitive and will deliver stable, and in some cases lower prices to consumers. In general, the single currency strengthens European unity and fosters stability, peace and prosperity.

How does Economic and Monetary Union work?

Economic and Monetary Union is based on two concepts: the coordination of economic policies and an independent monetary institution, the European System of Central Banks (ESCB). The Council of Finance Ministers (which brings together the Ministers for Economic Affairs and Finance of the Member States) is responsible for defining the major orientations of economic policy. It can put pressure on the participating states for them to respect their budgetary commitments. The ESCB consists of the central banks of the Member States and the European Central Bank (ECB). The ESCB is independent and therefore cannot receive instructions either from the Member States or from the European institutions. The ECB was formally constituted on 1 June 1998 and fully operational from 1 January 1999. Its main objective is to ensure price stability.

economic and monetary union	Wirtschafts- und Währungsunion		
single currency area	Gebiet mit einheitlicher Währung		
single market	Binnenmarkt		
service	Dienstleistung		
capital	Kapital		
restriction	Beschränkung	VT	*to restrict*
framework for	Rahmen für		
stability	Stabilität	<>	*instability*
to underpin	stützen		
legal obligation	gesetzliche Verpflichtung		
to pursue [pə'sjuː]	verfolgen	N	*pursuit*
sound	solide	N	*soundness*
to coordinate	koordinieren	N	*coordination*
objective	Ziel	≈	*aim, goal*
to set down	schriftlich niederlegen		
treaty	Vertrag	vgl.	*agreement – Abkommen*
necessity [nə'sesəti]	Notwendigkeit	ADJ	*necessary*
complement to	Ergänzung + *Gen.*	ADJ	*complementary*
to bring about	verursachen	≈	*to cause*
currency conversion	Währungsumtausch	VT	*to convert*
uncertainty	Unsicherheit		
exchange rate	Wechselkurs		
to boost	ankurbeln	<>	*to depress*
employment	Beschäftigung	VT	*to employ*
to strengthen	stärken	<>	*to weaken*
competitive [kəm'petətɪv]	konkurrenzfähig	N	*competitiveness*
stable	stabil		
consumer	Verbraucher/in	VT	*to consume*
unity	Einheit	<>	*disunity*
prosperity	Wohlstand	ADJ	*prosperous*
council	Rat		
finance minister	Finanzminister/in		
economic affairs	Wirtschaft		
orientation	Kurs, Ausrichtung	VT	*to orientate*
to put pressure on	Druck ausüben auf	≈	*to pressurize*
to respect a commitment	einer Verpflichtung nachkommen		
budgetary	Finanz-		
instruction	Anweisung	VT	*to instruct*
to constitute	einrichten		
operational	im Einsatz		
to ensure	sicherstellen		

D Literature

1 General

2 Prose

3 Poetry

4 Drama

Figurative language

EVEN WHEN they express extremes, such as 'beautiful' and 'ugly', everyday words rarely appeal to the imagination. Thus authors seek new ways to convey thoughts, perceptions and feelings – ways which are more striking and effective, which attract the reader's attention, excite his or her imagination and maybe arouse strong feelings.

One such method is figurative language, i.e. a use of language which departs from the literal meaning of the words. Classical rhetoric identified several hundred such 'figures of speech', but here are some of the more common:

Simile occurs when one thing is expressly compared to another which, taken literally, is fundamentally dissimilar to it, e.g. 'My blood, it is like light'.[1] Logic tells us that blood cannot possibly be like light, but we understand that the writer is alluding to certain attributes or characteristics of light – it is bright, swift and weightless. Applying these characteristics to 'blood' creates a forceful expression of joy and energy.

If the writer does not state that a comparison is being made – i.e. does not use a word such as 'like' or 'as' – simile becomes **metaphor**, e.g. 'Once my heart was a summer rose'.[2] Sometimes the object of comparison is implied rather than stated, e.g. 'Faith in their hands shall snap in two'[3] – where the implied image is that of breaking a stick.

Figurative language often makes an impact by comparing an abstract concept – such as faith in the last example – to something concrete, i.e. something which can be perceived by the senses. This has the effect of making the concept much more immediate. When figurative language is used to evoke pictures in the reader's mind, it is also called 'imagery'.

The **literary symbol** may be defined as something which means itself *and something more as well*, i.e. it is to be understood in both a literal and a metaphorical sense. Thus when 'man and shadow meet'[4], the shadow is both the man's literal shadow, meeting him as he falls to the ground, and a symbol of death. Often, a symbol is not clear-cut, but is open to various interpretations, which can make it very subtle and complex.

1 Thom Gunn, 'Rites of passage' **2** Edith Sitwell, 'Song' **3** Dylan Thomas, 'And death shall have no dominion' **4** Keith Douglas, 'How to kill'

figurative ['fɪgərətɪv]	bildlich	<>	*literal*
to express	ausdrücken	ADJ	*expressive*
extreme	Extrem	ADJ	*extreme*
everyday	alltäglich	≈	*commonplace*
to appeal to	ansprechen	N	*appeal*
imagination	Vorstellungskraft, Phantasie	ADJ	*imaginative*
to convey	vermitteln		
perception	Wahrnehmung	VT	*to perceive*
striking	eindrucksvoll		
effective	wirkungsvoll	N	*effect*
to attract s.o.'s attention	jds Aufmerksamkeit erregen		
to excite	anregen		
to arouse	erwecken	≈	*to evoke*
to depart from	abweichen von	N	*departure*
literal	wörtlich	<>	*figurative*
figure of speech	Redewendung		
simile ['sɪməli]	Gleichnis	vgl.	*metaphor* SIEHE UNTEN
expressly	ausdrücklich	≈	*explicitly*
fundamentally	grundlegend	<>	*superficially*
to allude to	anspielen auf	N	*allusion*
attribute	Merkmal		
characteristic	Eigenschaft	≈	*property*
to apply to	verwenden für	ADJ	*applicable*
forceful	kraftvoll, eindringlich	N	*force, forcefulness*
metaphor	Metapher	vgl.	*simile* SIEHE OBEN
to imply	implizieren, andeuten	ADJ	*implied, implicit*
image	Bild		
to make an impact	eine Wirkung erzielen		
abstract	abstrakt		
concept	Vorstellung	≈	*idea*
concrete	konkret		
to perceive	wahrnehmen	vgl.	*perceptive – scharfsinnig*
immediate	unmittelbar, direkt	<>	*remote*
to evoke	hervorrufen	ADJ	*evocative*
imagery	Metaphorik		
literary	literarisch		
metaphorical [ˌmetə'fɒrɪkl]	metaphorisch, bildlich	<>	*literal*
clear-cut	klar, eindeutig	<>	*vague ['veɪg]*
subtle ['sʌtl]	subtil, hintergründig	<>	*crude*
		N	*subtlety*
complex	komplex	N	*complexity*

Discussion: Reading Preferences

Megan: ... I mostly read long historical novels – pure escapism. I can get really immersed in a long novel with a well thought-out plot and believable characterization. Characters become as familiar as old friends.

Paula: Hmm ... I prefer non-fiction, in the form of biographies and travel accounts – they're so much more informative than invented accounts of fictional characters and events, and the truth is often so much more interesting and surprising than fiction.

Chris: How can you read that dry, factual stuff? I prefer something more imaginative. Short stories and novellas are my favourites, ones with clever twists in the plot. Because they're so much more concise than novels, the writer needs to be much more skilful in depicting characters. I tend to find novels rather predictable.

Dirk: Well, I love poetry because it's so much more intense and expressive than prose. The vivid imagery you find in poetry appeals so strongly to your imagination. Also, poetry is concerned with the sounds of words and their emotional and imaginative associations, not just with their literal meaning. And a poem can often be understood on different levels. You can suddenly find new meanings in a poem you have known all your life.

Paula: Personally, I find a lot of modern poetry rather obscure and self-indulgent. Its interpretation is too subjective. I prefer to *know* what the author is trying to say. 'Poetic' language is often just an excuse for a lack of clarity.

Chris: Drama, of course, can be written in poetry or prose – I think it's the most versatile form of literature. It also has an added dimension, in that it is written to be performed. But I can quite happily sit and read a play, and at the same time visualize actors performing it on a stage.

1 General

reading preferences	Lektürevorlieben	VT	*to prefer*
novel	Roman	vgl.	*novelist* – *Romanschriftsteller/in*
escapism	Wirklichkeitsflucht	ADJ	*escapist*
to get immersed in	sich vertiefen in		
well thought-out	gut durchdacht		
plot	Handlung	≈	*storyline*
believable	glaubhaft	≈	*credible*
characterization	Charakterisierung	VT	*to characterize*
familiar	vertraut	N	*familiarity*
non-fiction	Sachbücher		
travel account	Reisebericht		
informative	informativ	VT	*to inform*
fictional	erfunden	<>	*factual, real*
character	(Roman)Gestalt		
event	Ereignis		
fiction [fɪkʃən]	Fiktion		
factual	sachlich	N	*fact* – *Tatsache*
imaginative	phantasievoll	N	*imagination*
novella	Novelle		
twist	Wendung		
concise	kurz, bündig		
to depict	darstellen, beschreiben	N	*depiction*
predictable [prɪ'dɪktəbl]	vorhersehbar, absehbar	VT	*to predict*
poetry	Lyrik, Poesie	vgl.	*poet* – *Dichter/in*
intense	intensiv	N	*intensity*
expressive	ausdrucksvoll	VT	*to express* – *ausdrücken*
prose	Prosa		
vivid	anschaulich	N	*vividness*
to be concerned with	zu tun haben mit		
association	Assoziation	VT	*to associate*
poem	Gedicht		
level	Ebene		
obscure	schwer verständlich	<>	*clear*
self-indulgent [-ɪn'dʌldʒənt]	selbstverliebt	N	*self-indulgence*
subjective	subjektiv	<>	*objective*
poetic	poetisch, dichterisch		
clarity	Klarheit	ADJ	*clear*
versatile	vielseitig	N	*versatility*
to perform	aufführen	N	*performance*
play	(Theater)Stück, Drama		
to visualize ['vɪʒʊəlaɪz]	sich vorstellen	N	*visualization*
actor	Schauspieler/in	VTI	*to act*
stage	Bühne		

Radio interview: the role of the narrator

Interviewer: What problems do you face as an author?

Author: One of my main problems is finding a satisfactory narrative viewpoint. After all, where there's a story, there has to be a storyteller, a narrator. In my early novels, the narrator was of the conventional kind – unobtrusive and anonymous, not a character in his own right, and not distinct from me, the author. But that wasn't a good solution.

Interviewer: Why not?

Author: An omniscient narrator inevitably tells the reader what to think, how to react to the characters – no matter how impartial the author tries to be. Some authors – like Milan Kundera or maybe Salman Rushdie – deliberately exaggerate this, presenting the narrator as the reader's guide, even the controller or inventor of the action. That kind of narrator makes the characters into puppets, so that it's difficult for the reader to empathize with them and get involved in the plot. Also, it can seem pretentious and excessively intellectual. I don't think that my readers like being manipulated: they want to make up their own minds.

Interviewer: So, how do you let them do that?

Author: I've experimented with various storytelling techniques. In one novel I tried the epistolary form – constructing the novel entirely from letters written by the main characters. In effect, first-person narration by three narrators.

Interviewer: An unsuccessful experiment?

Author: Yes. It's a device that appears quite artificial, contrived – how did all these letters come to be in one place? Who selected them? Also, it can be very restrictive, because there are things that you want to express as author which you can't plausibly put into the mouth of one of your characters.

Interviewer: And your latest works?

Author: In the novel I'm writing now, there are two narrators, who both stand outside the action. Neither of them fully understands the story that she is telling – you could call them both 'unreliable observers'. This device has the advantage that the reader is invited to read between the lines.

role	Rolle		
narrator [nə'reɪtə]	Erzähler/in	VTI	*to narrate*
satisfactory [ˌsætis'fæktəri]	befriedigend	VT	*to satify*
narrative ['nærətɪv]	erzählerisch	N	*narrative – Erzählung*
viewpoint	Standpunkt, Perspektive	≈	*standpoint*
conventional	traditionell	N	*convention*
unobtrusive	unauffällig	<>	*conspicuous*
anonymous [ə'nɒnɪməs]	anonym	N	*anonymity [ˌænə'nɪmɪti]*
character	(Roman)Gestalt, (Roman)Figur	–	*sonst: Charakter, Persönlichkeit*
in o.'s own right	selber		
distinct from	abgegrenzt, unterschieden von	vgl.	*distinctive – unverkennbar, typisch*
omniscient [ɒm'nɪsɪənt]	allwissend	≈	*all-knowing*
react to	reagieren auf	N	*reaction*
impartial	unparteiisch	N	*impartiality*
to exaggerate [ɪg'zædʒəreɪt]	übertreiben	N <>	*exaggeration* *to understate*
guide	Führer/in	VT	*to guide*
controller	Lenker/in	VT	*to control*
action	Handlung		
puppet	Marionette		
to empathize with	sich hineinversetzen in	N	*empathy*
to get involved in	sich einlassen auf	N	*involvement*
pretentious [prɪ'tenʃəs]	anmaßend	N	*pretentiousness*
intellectual [ˌɪntə'lektʃʊəl]	intellektuell	N	*intellect ['ɪntəlekt]*
to manipulate [mə'nɪpjuleɪt]	manipulieren	N	*manipulation*
to make up o.'s own mind	sich eine eigene Meinung bilden		
to experiment with	experimentieren mit	≈	*to try out*
technique	Technik		
epistolary [ɪ'pɪstələri]	Brief-		
to construct	aufbauen	N	*construction*
first-person narration	Ich-Erzählung		
device	Kunstgriff, Mittel		
artificial	künstlich	<>	*natural*
contrived	gestellt		
to select	auswählen	ADJ	*selective*
restrictive	beschränkend	VT	*to restrict*
to express	ausdrücken	ADJ	*expressive*
plausibly [plɔ:zəbli]	überzeugend	<>	*implausibly*
put into s.o's mouth	jdm in den Mund legen		
unreliable	unzuverlässig	VT	*to rely on*
observer	Beobachter/in	VTI	*to observe*

The British novel post-1945

After World War II, a new generation of British novelists focused on humanity's more sinister qualities. In novels such as *Lord of the Flies* (1954), William Golding placed individuals or small groups in extreme situations: as the rules of civilized society become weaker, his characters quickly degenerate into violence and brutality. George Orwell presented a similiarly pessimistic view of humanity in his satirical fable *Animal Farm* (1945) and in his futuristic novel *1984* (1949). In *The Prime of Miss Jean Brodie* (1961) Muriel Spark portrayed a schoolteacher whose control of her pupils is really Fascism on a small scale. The small, enclosed world created in each of these works can be seen as an allegory of society in general, or a parable of human nature.

In contrast to these symbolic novels was a new type of social realism: novels about contemporary life in Britain, written in an accessible style and focusing on the lives of young working-class people whom a wide readership could recognize and identify with. Two famous works of this type were John Braine's *Room at the Top* (1957) and Alan Sillitoe's *Saturday Night and Sunday Morning* (1958). The anti-Establishment tone of this type of writing caused its authors to be known as the Angry Young Men. Iris Murdoch began in this realist tradition but she quickly found her own style in works such as *A Severed Head* (1961), in which character study is combined with complicated plots and supernatural incidents. Her novels have been described as psychological detective stories.

Britain found its ex-Empire a rich topic for narrative fiction. Paul Scott in his 'Raj Quartet' (1966–1975) portrayed Anglo-Indian relationships and the personal, political, racial and religious conflicts which arise from them, presenting events from various viewpoints which only gradually reveal the whole picture. Indian independence was given a far more lively treatment by Salman Rushdie in novels such as *Midnight's Children* (1981), written in the style known as Magic Realism, in which realistic characters and events mingle with the fantastic and the allegorical. The Anglo-Caribbean writer V.S. Naipaul explored problems of nationality and identity in novels such as *In a Free State* (1971) and short stories such as those in the collection *A Flag on the Island* (1967).

novelist	Romanschriftsteller/in	vgl.	*novel* – Roman
to focus on	sich konzentrieren auf	≈	*to concentrate on*
sinister ['sɪnɪstə]	düster	≈	*dark*
extreme	extrem	≈	*exceptional*
to degenerate into	entarten in	ADJ	*degenerate*
to present [prə'zent]	bieten		
pessimistic	pessimistisch	N	*pessimism*
view	Sicht		
satirical	satirisch	N	*satire*
fable	Fabel		
futuristic	futuristisch	<>	*historical*
to portray	darstellen	N	*portrayal*
allegory ['æləgəri]	Allegorie		
parable	Parabel		
symbolic	symbolisch	N	*symbolism*
social realism	sozialer Realismus		
contemporary [ˌkən'temprəri]	zeitgenössisch	N	*contemporary* – Zeitgenosse/genossin
accessible [ək'sesəbl]	zugänglich	<>	*obscure, difficult*
readership	Leserschaft		
to identify with	sich identifizieren mit		
tone	Ton		
character study	Charakterstudie	VT	*to characterize*
plot	Handlung	≈	*storyline*
supernatural	übernatürlich		
incident	Ereignis	≈	*event, happening*
psychological [ˌsaɪkə'lɒdʒɪkl]	psychologisch	N	*psychology*
detective story	Kriminalroman		
topic	Thema	≈	*subject*
narrative fiction	Erzählliteratur		
relationship	Beziehung		
racial	rassisch, Rassen-	N	*race* – Rasse
to arise from	entstehen aus	!	*arise–arose–arisen*
event	Ereignis	≈	*incident, happening*
to reveal	erkennen lassen	<>	*to conceal*
lively	lebendig	<>	*dull, staid*
treatment	Behandlung, Bearbeitung	VT	*to treat*
to mingle with	sich (ver)mischen mit		
fantastic	phantastisch		
allegorical [ˌælə'gɒrɪkl]	allegorisch		
identity	Identität		
short story	Kurzgeschichte		
collection	Sammlung		

BOOK REVIEW – Antony McMullen

The novels of Patrick O'Brian

Anglo-Irish author Patrick O'Brian's historical novels are popular with readers in all parts of the English-speaking world, and have been translated into languages as diverse as German and Japanese. They are set on the background of the Royal Navy during the Napoleonic Wars and concern the same two protagonists, ship's captain Jack Aubrey and doctor and intelligence agent Stephen Maturin – two very different characters who form a close and complex friendship.

Although the more technical descriptions of ships and sailing may be difficult to follow, O'Brian's novels are not generally a challenging read. The reader finds the same familiar pattern repeated in each; but skilful characterization, gentle humour and a vivid portrayal of warfare at sea grip the reader's attention even when the general sequence of events is quite predictable. O'Brian excels in straightforward, unpretentious storytelling.

The plot of each novel is linear, occasionally separating into two strands as Aubrey and Maturin go their own separate ways, but always converging again within a few chapters. Although the characters are fictional, the events are taken from the real political and military history of the period, with minor alterations in timescale.

However, O'Brian is not just interested in external action, but also in the internal development of his protagonists. Characterization takes place through the narrator's exposition and through witty, natural-sounding dialogue. One of O'Brian's particular strengths is the ability to use authentic 19th-century language without sounding stilted. His diction throughout the novels is slightly old-fashioned, and he delights in period detail in speech and manners. O'Brian's narrator is gently humorous, sympathetic towards the protagonists but dispassionate even in the description of shocking violence.

The pace of the narrative reflects the rhythms of life at sea: at times it is slow, and the characters have time for contemplation; then tension builds as an enemy ship is sighted, to be released in swift and bloody action as battle takes place. Many of the novels end on an exhilarating climax in which Jack Aubrey's ship defeats an opponent.

review	Rezension	VT	*to review*
to be set	spielen		
background	Hintergrund		
challenging	anspruchsvoll	VT	*to challenge*
skilful	kunstfertig	N	*skill*
characterization	Charakterisierung		
vivid	lebendig	N	*vividness*
portrayal	Darstellung	VT	*to portray*
to grip s.o.'s attention	jds Aufmerksamkeit fesseln		
sequence ['siːkwəns]	Abfolge		
predictable	vorhersehbar	VT	*to predict*
straightforward	einfach, klar	<>	*complex*
unpretentious	nicht anmaßend		
storytelling	Erzählen	≈	*narration*
linear	gradlinig	<>	*non-linear*
strand	Handlungsfaden		
to converge	zusammenlaufen	<>	*diverge*
fictional	erfunden	<>	*real, true-life*
alteration	Abänderung	VT	*to alter*
timescale	zeitlicher Rahmen	≈	*timeframe*
external action	äußere Handlung		
internal development	innere Entwicklung		
exposition	Erläuterung		
witty	geistreich	N	*wit*
authentic [ɔː'θentɪk]	authentisch	N	*authenticity*
stilted	gestelzt, gespreizt	≈	*artificial*
diction	Diktion, Ausdrucksweise		
period detail	zeitgenössische Details		
manners	Sitten (und Gebräuche)		
sympathetic towards	mitfühlend gegenüber	N	*sympathy*
dispassionate	objektiv	vgl.	*passionate* – *leidenschaftlich*
shocking	schockierend	≈	*appalling*
violence	Gewalt	ADJ	*violent*
pace	Tempo		
to reflect	widerspiegeln	≈	*to mirror*
rhythm ['rɪðəm]	Rhythmus	ADJ	*rhythmic*
contemplation	Besinnung	VTI	*to contemplate*
tension	Spannung	ADJ	*tense*
to build	sich aufbauen	≈	*to build up, to mount*
to release	lösen	N	*release*
exhilarating [ɪg'zɪləreɪtɪŋ]	aufregend	N	*exhilaration*
climax	Höhepunkt	ADJ	*climactic*
to defeat	besiegen	N	*defeat*
opponent [ə'pəʊnənt]	Gegner/in	VT	*to oppose*

Discussion: what is poetry?

Ben: How would you define poetry?

Lisa: How about: a piece of writing that rhymes?

Ben: But rhyme isn't an essential part of poetry – look at Shakespeare's blank verse, for example, or a lot of modern poetry.

Lisa: But a regular rhythm or metre *is* essential – a regular pattern of stressed and unstressed syllables, which you don't get in prose. There may also be other sound patterns, such as rhyme, alliteration or assonance.

Hazel: But political speeches and other kinds writing intended to be persuasive sometimes use these things as rhetorical devices. Does that make them poetry?

Lisa: I suppose not ... OK, how about this? Poetry is written in lines – the line breaks are important, and you can't just change them arbitrarily to fit the width of the page. Prose is organized into sentences according to rules of grammar, and into paragraphs according to its content. But poetry is organized into lines and stanzas – that is to say, it has a sound structure.

Ben: So poetry is meant to be read aloud.

Hazel: But so are political speeches. And so are plays, which may be in verse or in prose. So that doesn't get us far. Also, if you wrote out a poem as prose – without line breaks – would it then be prose or still poetry?

Lisa: Hmm, I'm not sure ... Another characteristic of poetry is that it need not follow the normal rules of syntax.

Hazel: These are all just formal criteria. Isn't the important thing the content? Poems are much more concise than prose and much more intense in their emotional appeal, expressing in a few lines what might take a whole essay or a whole novel to express in prose.

Lisa: That's a very subjective definition. Also, what about epic poetry, which can be as long as a novel? Or verse drama?

Ben: OK, OK. Maybe there's no single criterion. But if a text is organized into lines and contains regular patterns of sound, if it is emotionally intense, if it uses a lot of imagery, if it uses unusual syntax – then it's clearly poetry. If none of these things is true, then it's clearly prose.

Lisa: And if only some are true, then it may be poetic prose – or prosaic poetry!

poetry	Lyrik, Poesie	vgl.	*poet – Dichter/in*
to define	definieren	N	*definition*
to rhyme	(sich) reimen		
rhyme	Reim	ADJ	*rhyming*
essential	wesentlich	<>	*non-essential*
blank verse	Blankvers		
regular	regelmäßig	N	*regularity*
		<>	*irregular*
rhythm ['rɪðəm]	Rhythmus	ADJ	*rhythmic*
metre	Metrum	ADJ	*metrical*
pattern	Schema, Muster		
syllable	Silbe		
prose	Prosa		
alliteration	Alliteration, Stabreim	ADJ	*alliterative*
assonance	Assonanz		
to intend	vorhaben	N	*intent(ion)*
persuasive	überzeugend	N	*persuasion*
rhetorical device	rhetorisches Mittel	vgl.	*rhetoric – Rhetorik*
line break	Zeilenumbruch		
arbitrarily [ˌɑːbɪ'trerɪli]	willkürlich	ADJ	*arbitrary*
to organize into	einteilen in	N	*organization*
according to	entsprechend	≈	*in accordance with*
stanza	Strophe		
structure	Aufbau	ADJ	*structural*
play	Theaterstück, Drama		
in verse	in Versform		
characteristic	Merkmal	ADJ	*characteristic*
		≈	*quality*
criterion	Kriterium	!	PL *criteria*
concise	knapp	<>	*verbose*
intense	intensiv	N	*intensity*
emotional appeal	emotionale Anziehungskraft	VT	*to appeal to*
to express	ausdrücken	ADJ	*expressive*
subjective	subjektiv	N	*subjectivity*
		<>	*objective*
epic poetry	Epik		
imagery	Metaphorik		
poetic	poetisch		
prosaic [prə'zeɪɪk]	prosaisch		

Ted Hughes and the Poetry of Violence

THERE IS A STARK CONTRAST between the poetry of Ted Hughes (1930–) and that of older contemporaries such as Philip Larkin (1922–1985) and John Betjeman (1906–1984). They are witty and ironic – he is intensely serious; they depict the attitudes of middle-class society – he concerns himself with nature and myth; their tone is conversational, understated – he freely expresses his awe and horror.

Hughes' most accessible poems take as their subjects commonplace features of the English countryside: garden birds; thistles growing in a field; a pond. Written in free verse (without the artificial structure of rhyme and metre), his poetry appeals powerfully to our senses, is always dynamic, full of strong verbs and nouns with few adjectives. His 'nature poems' are never purely descriptive, and certainly never the gentle, idyllic images we traditionally associate with this subject matter. To Hughes, garden birds can be more terrifying than any monster:

> Terrifying are the attent sleek thrushes on the lawn
> More coiled steel than living … *

Where we are used to seeing a small brown bird, Hughes sees a ruthless killing machine. This vision could seem exaggerated, even ridiculous, and some have found Hughes' preoccupation with death and violence to be excessive and morbid. Yet Hughes is a convincing, accurate observer of animal behaviour. With his farming background, he knows that nature is a fight for survival – automatic, unquestioning, without our human doubts and excuses. As Hughes' hawk says:

> … the one path of my flight is direct
> Through the bones of the living.
> No arguments assert my right … *

This implicit contrast between nature's directness and its weak, self-doubting human observer is a central theme of Hughes' poetry. We sense that Hughes admires and even envies animals for their honesty, their inability to be self-conscious or hypocritical.

* 'Thrushes' and 'Hawk Roosting', both from *Lupercal*, 1960

stark contrast	krasser Gegensatz	VT	*to contrast*
contemporary	Zeitgenosse/genossin	ADJ	*zeitgenössisch*
witty	geistreich	N	*wit*
ironic	ironisch	N	*irony*
intensely	äußerst	N	*intensity*
attitude	Haltung		
to concern o.s. with	sich beschäftigen mit	N	*concern*
myth	Mythos	ADJ	*mythical*
conversational	leger, informell		
understated	subtil, unaufdringlich	<>	*overstated, exaggerated*
awe [ɔː]	Ehrfurcht	ADJ	*awesome – Ehrfurcht gebietend*
horror	Entsetzen	VT	*to horrify – entsetzen*
accessible [ək'sesəbl]	zugänglich	<>	*obscure*
commonplace	alltäglich, banal	≈	*banal*
free verse	freie Rhythmen		
artificial	künstlich	<>	*natural*
to appeal to	ansprechen	N	*appeal*
powerfully	stark	N	*power*
senses	Sinne	vgl.	*sensuous – sinnlich*
dynamic	dynamisch	<>	*static*
descriptive	beschreibend	vgl.	*narrative – erzählend*
idyllic	idyllisch	N	*idyll*
image	Bild, Vorstellung	vgl.	*imagery – Metaphorik*
to associate with	assoziieren mit	N	*association*
subject matter	Stoff, Thema		
terrifying	furchterregend	VT	*to terrify*
ruthless	unbarmherzig	N	*ruthlessness*
vision	Vorstellung		
exaggerated	übertrieben	N	*exaggeration*
ridiculous [rɪ'dɪkjələs]	lächerlich	≈	*laughable*
preoccupation	(ständige) Beschäftigung	≈	*obsession*
excessive	übertrieben	<>	*moderate*
morbid	krankhaft, morbid	<>	*healthy*
convincing	überzeugend	N	*conviction*
accurate	genau	<>	*inaccurate*
observer	Beobachter/in	vgl.	*observation – Beobachtung*
survival	Überleben	VTI	*to survive*
doubt	Zweifel	VT	*to doubt*
to admire	bewundern	N	*admiration*
to envy	beneiden	ADJ	*envious*
honesty	Ehrlichkeit	ADJ	*honest*
self-conscious	befangen	N	*self-consciousness*
hypocritical [ˌhɪpə'krɪtɪkl]	heuchlerisch	N	*hypocrisy [hɪ'pɒkrəsi]*

Literature Online: Genres: Comedy

Comedy

Throughout the history of the theatre there have been many attempts to define comedy. Many different types of play fall within this broad category.

In his *Poetics*, Aristotle claimed that comedy depicts human beings as worse than they are in reality, tragedy as better; comedy concerned the domestic lives of ordinary people, whereas tragedy concerned great events and noble characters. Some modern writers (such as Henri Bergson) have emphasized comedy's role in ridiculing and so correcting antisocial behaviour. Others emphasize the superiority which the audience feels when laughing at a comic character. A general definition might be that a comedy is a play which has a happy ending, in which the difficulties experienced by the protagonist(s) are resolved; such a play need not be humorous in the sense of trying to make the audience laugh.

Classical Greek and Roman comedy often used quite coarse language and dealt frankly with sexual themes. The plays of Aristophanes are satirical, mocking philosophers and parodying tragic drama. In the comedies of Terence and Plautius, young lovers have to outwit wicked or stupid characters who are obstacles to their happiness. Most classical comedy has stock characters who represent social types, with little individualization.

William Shakespeare's comedies (e.g. *As You Like It* and *A Midsummer Night's Dream*) often combine romantic plots with serious themes and exploration of the darker side of human nature; several of his plays do not fit conventional definitions of comedy or tragedy and so are called tragicomedies. In plays such *The Winter's Tale*, tragic errors are made and tragic suffering endured, but there is an unexpected (often artificial or improbable) resolution and a happy ending.

Modern comedy does not follow any particular pattern. The farces of numerous British writers feature slapstick, improbable situations and exaggerated characters. Oscar Wilde wrote lighthearted social satire of the type called comedy of manners. Samuel Beckett and Harold Pinter combined comedy and tragedy in plays which show the absurdity of life, portraying the breakdown of relationships and communication with black humour. In much modern drama, comedy is blended with realism in exploring the problems of daily life.

comedy	Komödie		
to depict	darstellen	≈	*to portray*
tragedy	Tragödie		
domestic life	häusliches Leben		
noble	edel; adlig	N	*nobility*
to ridicule	verspotten, verlachen	ADJ	*ridiculous* – *lächerlich*
antisocial	unsozial		
superiority [su:ˌpɪərɪ'ɒrəti]	Überlegenheit	<>	inferiority
comic	komisch		
to resolve	(auf)lösen		
humorous	lustig, komisch	N	*to have a sense of humour* US *humor*
coarse	derb	<>	*refined*
to deal with	behandeln		
frankly	offen	≈	*openly*
satirical	satirisch	N	*satire*
to mock	verspotten	N	*mockery*
to parody	parodieren	N	*parody*
to outwit	überlisten		
to be an obstacle to s.th.	einer Sache im Wege stehen	≈	*to stand in the way of*
stock character	Typ		
to represent	darstellen	N	*representation*
individualization	Individualisierung	vgl.	*individual* – *Individuum*
plot	Handlung	≈	*storyline*
exploration	Erforschung	VTI	*to explore*
human nature	menschliche Natur		
tragicomedy	Tragikomödie	ADJ	*tragicomic*
tragic	tragisch		
error	Fehler	≈	*mistake*
suffering	Leiden, Leid	VTI	*to suffer*
to endure	ertragen		
artificial	künstlich	≈	*contrived*
improbable	unwahrscheinlich	≈	*unlikely*
resolution	Auflösung		
slapstick	Klamauk		
exaggerated	übertrieben	N	*exaggeration*
lighthearted	leicht, vergnüglich	<>	*serious*
social satire	Gesellschaftssatire	vgl.	*satirist* – *Satiriker/in*
comedy of manners	Sittenkomödie		
absurdity	Absurdität		
breakdown	Zusammenbruch	VTI	*to break down*
relationship	Beziehung		
realism	Realismus	ADJ	*realistic*

Literature Online: Genres: Tragedy

Tragedy

A tragedy may be loosely defined as a play in which a sequence of events leads to a catastrophic conclusion.

The first definition of tragedy was given by Aristotle in his *Poetics*: a unified action which is serious and deals with events of importance, concerning the downfall of a person whose character is fundamentally good but not perfect: his or her downfall is caused by some flaw or error of judgement. The events arouse pity and fear in the audience.

Greek tragedy used familiar myths such as those found in Homer's works as its subject matter. As in Sophocles' *Oedipus the King*, their plots generally traced a development by which the hero or heroine becomes involved in a situation which is inescapable but intolerable, leading inevitably to disaster. In this suffering, the protagonist shows the most admirable aspects of his or her character, enduring his or her fate with courage and dignity.

In England around 1600, writers such as Christopher Marlowe and William Shakespeare made important developments in tragedy. In Shakespeare's great tragedies, the heroes are figures of high rank and great ability and virtue. They have many opportunities to choose paths which will not lead to disaster, but relentlessly make the wrong choices because of character flaws (e.g. Macbeth's ambition, Othello's jealousy) and the influence of evil, whether human or supernatural. The main plot is set in a context which involves many major and minor characters with their own viewpoints and motivations. There are subplots which mirror or contrast with the main plot.

French drama of the seventeenth century produced tragedies according to strict principles taken from Aristotle, adhering to the unities of time (the whole plot development to take no more than 24 hours), place (only one setting) and action (no subplots), and took their subject matter also from classical legend.

German tragic drama of the late eighteenth and early nineteenth century drew upon both the neoclassical and the English traditions. In northern and eastern Europe in the nineteenth century, Henrik Ibsen, August Strindberg and Anton Chekhov developed a new kind of tragedy which explored contemporary problems concerning how the individual relates to society.

sequence	Abfolge		
catastrophic	verhängnisvoll	N	*catastrophe* [kə'tæstrəfi]
conclusion	Schluss	VTI	*to conclude*
unified	einheitlich		
downfall	Niedergang	≈	*demise*
fundamentally	im Wesentlichen	<>	*superficially*
flaw	(Charakter)Schwäche	ADJ	*flawed*
error of judgement	Fehlurteil		
to arouse	erwecken	≈	*to evoke*
pity	Mitleid	VT	*to pity*
subject matter	Stoff		
to trace	verfolgen	≈	*to follow*
development	Entwicklung	VTI	*to develop*
hero/heroine [hɪərəʊ/'herəʊɪn]	Held/Heldin	ADJ	*heroic*
inescapable [ɪnɪ'skeɪpəbl]	unausweichlich		
intolerable	unerträglich	≈	*unbearable*
inevitably [ɪn'evɪtəbli]	zwangsläufig	N	*inevitability*
disaster	Katastrophe	ADJ	*disastrous*
admirable	bewundernswert	<>	*contemptible*
fate	Schicksal		
courage ['kʌrɪdʒ]	Mut	ADJ	*courageous* [kə'reɪdʒəs]
dignity	Würde	ADJ	*dignified*
rank	Stand	≈	*social position*
ability	Fähigkeit	≈	*capability*
virtue	Tugend	ADJ	*virtuous*
relentlessly [rɪ'lentləsli]	unaufhörlich		
ambition	Ehrgeiz	ADJ	*ambitious*
jealousy ['dʒeləsi]	Eifersucht	ADJ	*jealous*
influence	Einfluss	VT	*to influence*
evil	Böse(s)	<>	*good(ness)*
supernatural	übernatürlich		
major	Haupt-		
minor	Neben-		
viewpoint	Standpunkt	≈	*point of view*
subplot	Nebenhandlung		
to mirror	(wider)spiegeln	≈	*to reflect*
principle	Prinzip, Grundsatz		
to adhere to [əd'hɪə]	sich halten an	N	*adherence to*
unities of time, place and action	Einheit von Zeit, Ort und Handlung		
legend	Sage	ADJ	*legendary*
to explore	erforschen	N	*exploration*
contemporary	zeitgenössisch		

Discussion: Death of a Salesman

Teacher: Is *Death of a Salesman* a work of social criticism?

Student: Maybe "social and psychological observation" would be a more accurate description. I don't think Miller is delivering a moral message about society ... But he does demonstrate that the materialistic goals of his society *can* destroy those that aspire to them.

Teacher: Why doesn't Miller keep to the classical unity of time in this work?

Student: I think that's because he wants to reflect Willy's Loman's chaotic state of mind. The past and present, the real and imaginary are all equally real and present to Willy. He can't interact properly with the other "real" characters, who find his disconnected conversation and unpredictable moods strange and worrying. The play is a sequence of confrontations, with no transitional scenes.

Teacher: Why does Miller give such precise instructions about the stage set and lighting, do you think?

Student: The stage set intensifies the feeling of oppression: the tall buildings stand over Willy's fragile little house – just as reality threatens Willy's fragile illusion of success. The whole stage set has a dreamlike quality, matching Willy's fantasy world.

Teacher: Is Willy Loman a tragic hero?

Student: Well, he's a character with many good qualities who has a fatal flaw – his obsessive pursuit of success. His determination to go beyond his own capabilities leads him to self-delusion and ultimately to death. His refusal to accept defeat, to just be an ordinary man – an ageing man who can no longer compete with younger rivals – can be seen as heroic, or as pathetic. Miller isn't judgemental. There are no speeches which tell the audience how to interpret the play, and none of the characters clearly articulate the play's central theme – except maybe Biff, who finally achieves a clear understanding of his own and Willy's character.

Teacher: Doesn't that mean that the play itself is rather confused?

Student: Not at all: ambiguity and complex motives create a richer, more interesting play than certainty and a clear moral message.

social criticism	Gesellschaftskritik	!	*critic* – *Kritiker/in*
psychological	psychologisch	N	*psychology*
observation	Beobachtung	VTI	*to observe*
to deliver a moral message	eine moralische Botschaft vermitteln		
goal	Ziel		
to aspire to	streben nach	N	*aspiration*
to reflect	widerspiegeln	≈	*to mirror*
chaotic [keɪ'ɒtɪk]	chaotisch	N	*chaos*
state of mind	Geisteszustand	≈	*mental state*
to interact	interagieren	N	*interaction*
disconnected	zusammenhanglos		
unpredictable	unberechenbar	VT	*to predict* – *vorhersehen/-sagen*
mood	Stimmung	ADJ	*moody* – *launisch*
confrontation	Konfrontation	VT	*to confront*
transitional	Übergangs-	N	*transition*
scene	Szene		
precise	präzis(e)	<>	*imprecise, vague*
stage set	Bühnenbild	vgl.	*set designer* – *Bühnenbildner/in*
lighting	Beleuchtung	VT	*to light*
to intensify	verstärken	ADJ	*intense*
oppression	Bedrücktheit	ADJ	*oppressive*
fragile	zerbrechlich	N	*fragility*
to threaten	bedrohen	ADJ	*threatening*
quality	Eigenschaft		
to match	entsprechen	≈	*to correspond to*
obsessive	zwanghaft	N	*obsession*
pursuit [pə'sjuːt]	Jagd, Streben	VT	*to pursue*
determination	Entschlossenheit	ADJ	*determined*
capability	Fähigkeit	ADJ	*capable*
self-delusion	Selbsttäuschung	VT	*to delude*
ultimately	letztendlich	≈	*finally*
defeat	Niederlage	VT	*to defeat* – *besiegen*
to compete with	mithalten mit	N	*competition*
heroic	heroisch, heldenhaft	N	*heroism*
pathetic	erbärmlich		
judgemental [dʒʌdʒ'mentl]	wertend	N	*judgement* – *Urteil*
to interpret	interpretieren	vgl.	*to misinterpret*
to articulate [ɑː'tɪkjuleɪt]	darlegen		
confused	verworren	N	*confusion*
ambiguity [ˌæmbɪ'gjuːəti]	Mehr-, Vieldeutigkeit	ADJ	*ambiguous*
certainty	Gewissheit	ADJ	*certain*

E The Media

1 Broadcasting

2 The Press

3 Online

4 Censorship and Control

Question Time: THE FUTURE OF THE BBC

D.D.: ... A new question for the panel, from Norma Barry of Walthamstow: 'Is public-sector broadcasting obsolete in the age of cable television?' Lisa Hutchings?

L.H.: Definitely. It's absurd to fund the BBC through compulsory licence fees when most of us never watch BBC channels or listen to BBC radio stations. Viewers expect to see films on TV within a year of their cinema release, and to have access to live coverage of important sporting tournaments. In both respects, the BBC fails to deliver an adequate service: we get endless reruns of old films and only brief highlights of international games. So to get an acceptable standard of entertainment we pay for a package of cable channels – and have to pay the BBC licence fee as well!

D.D.: Mike O'Connell?

M.O'C: Well, it has been ten years since my family first subscribed to cable TV, along with the majority of UK households. In that time, there has been little improvement in the quality of programming. We can choose between 50 channels, but what's on offer? Cheap US imports – and repeats of popular BBC and ITV series. The only organizations to invest in making high-quality programmes are the BBC, the ITV franchises and Channel 4.

D.D.: Greta Wilson?

G.W.: Cable television has certainly increased the diversity of programmes available at any one time – there is now much more space in the schedule for minority interest programmes, and innovations like community TV channels, focusing on issues of local interest. Transmission via cable also improved the quality of reception – and now digital TV and radio are even better. ... However, the BBC still sets the standard which the commercial stations aim for. Also, it doesn't have intrusive commercial breaks.

D.D.: Madge Clarke?

M.C.: The best of the BBC programmes are very good indeed, but the average standard isn't high enough to justify the current licence fee. The BBC is too complacent about its special, protected status. There is still a place for the BBC, but it needs to try harder.

D.D.: And the audience? What do you think? ...

1 Broadcasting

public-sector	des öffentlichen Sektors	<>	*private-sector*
broadcasting	Rundfunk u. Fernsehen	VTI	*to broadcast*
obsolete ['ɒbsəli:t]	veraltet, überholt	N	*obsolescence*
cable television	Kabelfernsehen	vgl.	*satellite TV*
to fund	finanzieren	N	*funds* PL – *Gelder*
compulsory [kəm'pʌlsəri]	obligatorisch	≈	*obligatory*
licence fee	Fernsehgebühren	vgl.	*licence – Genehmigung*
channel	Kanal, Programm	!	*programme – Sendung*
radio station	Radiosender	vgl.	*pirate radio – Piratensender*
viewer	Zuschauer/in	VT	*to view*
cinema release	Kinodebüt	VT	*to release*
access to	Zugang zu	VT	*to access*
coverage	Berichterstattung	VT	*to cover*
sporting tournament	Sportturnier		
adequate	adäquat, ausreichend	<>	*inadequate*
rerun ['ri:rʌn]	Wiederholung	VT	*to rerun [ˌri:'rʌn]*
acceptable	akzeptabel	VT	*to accept*
entertainment	Unterhaltung	VT	*to entertain*
package	Paket		
to subscribe to	sich anmelden für	N	*subscription*
household	Haushalt		
programming	Programmgestaltung		
repeat	Wiederholung	VT	*to repeat*
series	Serie	!	PL. *series*
to invest in	investieren in	N	*investment*
franchise ['fræntʃaɪz]	Franchiseunternehmen		
diversity [ˌdaɪ'vɜ:səti]	Vielfalt	<>	*uniformity*
available	zur Verfügung stehend	N	*availability*
schedule ['ʃedju:l/'skedʒu:l]	Programmplan	VT	*to schedule*
minority interest programme	Sendung für eine spezielle Zuschauerschaft		
community	lokal, kommunal		
to focus on	sich konzentrieren auf	N	*focus*
transmission	Übertragung	VTI	*to transmit*
reception	Empfang	VT	*to receive*
commercial	kommerziell		
station	Sender		
intrusive	aufdringlich	N	*intrusion*
commercial break	Werbepause		
to justify	rechtfertigen	N	*justification*
complacent [kəm'pleɪsnt]	selbstzufrieden	N	*complacency*

The best and worst of TV

In our reader survey, we asked what were the best and worst aspects of television today. Here are some of your replies:

Jacqui Marks-Smythe

Best: Documentaries which find ways of making specialized subjects like archaeology and astrophysics intelligible to the general public without being patronizing.

Worst: Dull, high-brow arts programmes with conceited 'experts' who discuss awful paintings and horrible music.

Melissa Clayton

Best: Soap operas like *EastEnders* with superb acting and the courage to explore sensitive and difficult issues.

Worst: Popular science programmes with unnecessary special effects and 'artistic' camerawork.

Jarvis Barnes

Best: Current affairs programmes with intelligent interviewers like Jeremy Paxman. He asks searching questions, and insists on getting proper answers from his interviewees.

Worst: Boring Australian soap operas with poor acting, implausible storylines and cheap sets.

Nawaz Malik

Best: Stand-up comedians who have something original to say – who can be outrageous but get away with it because of their charm and wit.

Worst: Celebrity panel games populated by has-beens from sport and pop music. Most of the so-called 'spontaneous' humour is rehearsed before the show.

Will Davies

Best: Comedy dramas with strong casts, clever scripts and a subtle sense of humour.

Worst: Bland, contrived sitcoms with exaggerated studio laughter to signal even the weakest jokes. Apparently, the producers don't trust us to recognize a joke unless we hear a burst of hysterical laughter.

Kayleigh Howell

Best: Recent cinema releases and film classics on cable TV.

Worst: Home improvement and gardening shows. I can't stand the smug presenters!

documentary	Dokumentarfilm		
specialized	spezialisiert		
intelligible [ɪn'telɪdʒəbl]	verständlich	<>	*unintelligible*
patronizing	herablassend	VT	*to patronize*
high-brow	intellektuell	<>	*low-brow*
arts programme	Kultursendung		
conceited [kən'siːtɪd]	eingebildet	N	*conceit*
intellectual	intellektuell		
soap opera	Seifenoper	UGS	*soap*
acting	schauspielerische Leistung	N	*actor – Schauspieler/in*
courage	Mut	ADJ	*courageous*
sensitive	heikel	vgl.	*insensitive – taktlos*
issue	Thema	≈	*topic*
popular science programme	populärwissenschaft-liche Sendung		
artistic	künstlerisch	vgl.	*artist – Künstler/in*
camerawork	Kameraführung		
current affairs programme	Info-Magazin zu aktuellen Themen		
searching	bohrend	N	*search – Suche*
to insist on	bestehen auf		
interviewee	Interviewpartner/in	VT	*to interview*
implausible	unglaubhaft	<>	*plausible*
storyline	Handlung	≈	*plot*
set	Kulisse		
stand-up comedian	Alleinunterhalter/in		
outrageous [ˌaʊt'reɪdʒəs]	unverschämt	vgl.	*cheeky – frech*
to get away with	sich erlauben können		
wit	Witz	ADJ	*witty – geistreich*
celebrity [sə'lebrəti]	Prominente/r		
panel game	Ratespiel	vgl.	*panel – Rateteam*
has-been	vergessene Berühmtheit	<>	*wannabe* UGS *– Möchtegern*
spontaneous [spɒn'teɪniəs]	spontan	N	*spontaneity*
to rehearse [rɪ'hɜːs]	einstudieren	N	*rehearsal*
comedy drama	TV-Komödie		
cast	Besetzung		
subtle [sʌtl]	subtil, fein	N	*subtlety*
bland	fade	≈	*tame*
contrived	gekünstelt, gestellt	≈	*artificial*
sitcom	Situationskomödie		
classic	Klassiker		
home improvement	Heimverschönerungs-	≈	*DIY*
smug	selbstgefällig	N	*smugness*
presenter	Moderator/in	VT	*to present*

Netpost: Mail in

REPLY FORWARD FILE IT DELETE

From: Jo Edmundson **To:** Rudi Böttcher

Subject: The British press **Date:** 23/11/2003

Hi Rudi, here's the info you wanted for your assignment.

We divide our newspapers into broadsheets and tabloids. This distinction refers to their format (tabloids being half the size of broadsheets), but is also a quality judgement. 'Tabloid journalism' has come to mean a type of reporting which is populist, unreliable and sensationalist – although some tabloids really aren't too bad. The downmarket tabloids are sometimes given the derogatory label 'gutter press'. Although some of them pride themselves on their investigative journalism, they tend to distort the facts or exaggerate for the sake of a good story.

Of the tabloid dailies, *The Sun* has the highest circulation, with 3.5 million copies sold every day. *The News of the World* is the most popular tabloid weekly, with a readership of around 4 million. The tabloids are highly competitive, and try to come up with exclusives – interviews or reports which no other newspaper has. The ingredients of tabloid style include attention-grabbing headlines (involving very bad puns), short, moralizing articles written in a strange jargon (suspects are 'quizzed' by the police instead of being questioned; good-looking women are 'stunners'); gossip and supposition rather than fact; and soft-porn photos.

Broadsheets are often referred to as the 'quality' or 'serious' press and generally have a high standard of writing, including comprehensive coverage of the latest news, analysis of issues of long-term interest, and essays in which the writer expresses a point of view. They deal with serious issues in an authoritative way, but a dry, slightly facetious humour is valued as part of good journalistic style.

Broadsheet journalists often have greater freedom to express their opinions, even if these don't coincide with the editor's and the proprietor's political stance.

If you need more info on any of our papers, let me know. Alternatively, you can always take a look at their Websites. :-) Jo

broadsheet	großformatige Zeitung		
tabloid	kleinformatige Zeitung		
distinction	Unterscheidung	VT	*to distinguish*
quality judgement	Qualitätsbewertung	VT	*to judge*
journalism	Journalismus	vgl.	*journalist*
reporting	Berichterstattung	vgl.	*reporter*
populist	populistisch	N	*populism*
unreliable	unzuverlässig	≈	*untrustworthy*
sensationalist	reißerisch	N	*sensationalism*
downmarket	anspruchslos	<>	*upmarket*
derogatory	abfällig	≈	*pejorative*
gutter press	Boulevardpresse	vgl.	*gutter* – *Gosse*
investigative [ɪn'vestɪgətɪv]	Enthüllungs-	VTI	*to investigate*
to distort	verzerren	N	*distortion*
exaggerate	übertreiben	N	*exaggeration*
daily	Tageszeitung		
circulation	Auflage		
weekly	Wochenzeitung		
readership	Leserschaft		
competitive [kəm'petətɪv]	wettbewerbsorientiert	VI	*to compete*
exclusive	Exklusivbericht		
report	Bericht	VTI	*to report*
attention-grabbing	Aufmerksamkeit heischend	VT	*to grab* – *packen*
headline	Schlagzeile	vgl.	*to hit the ~s* – *Schlagzeilen machen*
pun	Wortspiel	≈	*play on words*
moralizing	moralisierend	≈	*moralistic*
article	Artikel	≈	*piece*
gossip	Klatsch	VI	*to gossip*
supposition	Mutmaßung	≈	*speculation*
comprehensive [ˌkɒmprɪ'hensɪv]	umfassend	<>	*partial* ['pɑːʃəl]
coverage	Berichterstattung	VT	*to cover*
analysis	Analyse	VT	*to analyse*
issue	Frage, Angelegenheit	≈	*topic*
long-term	langfristig	<>	*short-term*
authoritative [ɔː'θɒrɪtətɪv]	zuverlässig		
facetious [fə'siːʃəs]	spöttisch, witzelnd	N	*facetiousness*
to value	schätzen		
journalistic	journalistisch		
to coincide with	übereinstimmen mit	≈	*to match*
editor	Chefredakteur/in	VT vgl.	*to edit* – *redigieren* *editorial* – *Leitartikel*
proprietor [prə'praɪətə]	Besitzer/in	≈	*owner*
stance	Einstellung	≈	*attitude, standpoint*

THE NEWSPAPER

Here's what our readers say about us:

"*The Newspaper* keeps me up to date with current affairs. The news coverage is balanced and reliable. It's factual, not judgemental. The 'News in Brief' column is a useful synopsis of the very latest news."

L.G., Leicester

"*The Newspaper* employs some of the best columnists in the business. Their in-depth commentary and analysis is thought provoking and perceptive. *The Newspaper* is never afraid to challenge popular prejudices and stereotypes."

E.F., Barnsley

"On Thursdays I always turn to the Society section for Carolyn Barnes' provocative and witty pieces. She's controversial, opinionated but very clever – I rarely agree with a word she writes, but at least she's never predictable."

J.S., Gravesend

"What I like best are your special features. *The Newspaper* really explains the background to events, puts the news in context. You don't make assumptions about your readers' knowledge, but you're never patronizing."

L.M., Morecambe

"To be honest, we mainly buy *The Newspaper* for the television listings. Your critic Barry Skinner's reviews are great – a reliable guide to what's worth watching and what's not."

E.J. and N.J., Exeter

"*The Newspaper's* satirical cartoonist Steve Belling is brilliant. His wicked caricatures of public figures are a hilarious send-up of the pompous world of politics."

R.G., Harlech

"Your 'Leisure' supplement on Saturdays is one of the best – just the right balance between entertaining trivia and serious articles."

S.H., Hampstead

But don't take their word for it

THE NEWSPAPER

– because there are two sides to every story

up to date	auf dem Laufenden	<>	*out of touch*
current affairs	aktuelle Fragen		
balanced	ausgewogen	<>	*one-sided, biased*
factual	sachlich	N	*fact – Tatsache*
judgemental [dʒʌdʒ'mentl]	wertend	N	*judgement – Urteil*
in brief	Kurz-	ADJ	*brief – kurz*
column ['kɒləm]	Kolumne	vgl.	*columnist*
synopsis	Zusammenfassung	≈	*summary*
in-depth	umfassend, tiefgründig	<>	*superficial*
commentary	Kommentar		
thought-provoking	zum Nachdenken anregend		
perceptive	aufschlussreich	vgl.	*to perceive – erkennen*
to challenge	in Frage stellen	≈	*to question*
popular	weit verbreitet	N	*popularity*
prejudice	Vorurteil	ADJ	*prejudiced*
stereotype	Klischee(vorstellung)	ADJ	*stereotypical*
provocative [prə'vɒkətiv]	provokativ	N	*provocation*
witty	geistreich	N	*wit*
piece	Artikel	≈	*article*
controversial [ˌkɒntrə'vɜːʃl]	kontrovers	N	*controversy [kɒn'trɒvəsi]*
opinionated	selbstherrlich		
predictable	berechenbar	N	*predictability*
special feature	Sonderbeitrag		
background to	Hintergründe von		
context	Zusammenhang		
to make assumptions	Vermutungen anstellen	VT	*to assume – annehmen*
patronizing	herablassend		
television listings	Fernsehprogramm-übersicht		
critic	Kritiker/in	vgl.	*to criticize – kritisieren*
review	Rezension, Kritik	VT	*to review*
guide to	Führer für	VT	*to guide*
satirical	satirisch	N	*satire*
wicked	boshaft		
caricature	Karikatur	VT	*to caricature*
public figure	öffentliche Persönlichkeit		
hilarious [hɪ'leəriəs]	urkomisch		
send-up	Veralberung	VT	*to send up*
pompous	wichtigtuerisch	N	*pomposity*
supplement	Beilage		
entertaining	unterhaltend	N	*entertainment*
trivia	Trivialitäten	ADJ	*trivial*

Discussion: Websites

Dawn: Although I find e-mail essential for my work, and certain Websites invaluable for booking flights and hotels, most of this enthusiasm for the Web seems totally unjustified.

Jeremy: What makes you say that?

Dawn: For a start, most of it is just advertising. You have those annoying animated ads blinking – and sometimes playing silly tunes – at you and distracting your attention from the site. And then, most of the sites exist to promote the organization that created them – apart from e-commerce sites which actually sell merchandise or services. The purpose of most sites isn't to provide objective information – and that means that most of the information they *do* provide is superficial and unreliable.

Jeremy: Three things: firstly, does it matter why the information was put on the site, as long as it's useful? Secondly, not all sites are commercial – far from it. There are many sites produced by amateur enthusiasts, or academic institutions, which are not motivated by the desire to persuade anyone or promote anything. Thirdly, many of the sites which *are* produced by various organizations to raise public awareness of their activities are still very informative – take a look at the Greenpeace or Amnesty International Websites for example. Of course, these sites put forward a particular point of view, but that doesn't mean that they are necessarily unreliable or poorly researched – that would damage the organization's credibility.

Dawn: Sure, there are exceptions, but I still maintain that most Websites aren't terribly useful. Slick presentation – a few impressive graphics and an appearance of 'interactivity' – disguises a lack of original content and coherent structure.

Jeremy: You're right in a way: there are so many Websites out there that the quality is bound to be variable. For instance, there are some really dull sites that companies provide just because it has become fashionable to have a Web presence – and others put together by individuals with more enthusiasm than judgement. On the other hand, a large part of the skill of browsing lies in sifting search results for promising sites. Once you've found one good site, that usually leads you to others. But anyway, who says all Websites have to be informative? Some of my favourite sites are entertaining, creative or just completely wacky!

essential	(absolut) erforderlich	≈	*vital*
invaluable	von unschätzbarem Wert	vgl.	*valuable* – *wertvoll*
enthusiasm	Begeisterung	ADJ	*enthusiastic*
unjustified	ungerechtfertigt		
animated	animiert	N	*animation*
tune	Melodie		
to distract	ablenken	N	*distraction*
attention	Aufmerksamkeit		
to promote	Werbung machen für	N	*promotion*
merchandise ['mɜːtʃəndaɪz]	Ware(n)	≈	*goods*
purpose	Zweck	≈	*aim*
superficial	oberflächlich	N	*superficiality*
unreliable	unzuverlässig		
commercial	kommerziell		
academic institution	wissenschaftliche Institution		
to motivate	motivieren	N	*motivation*
desire	Wunsch		
to persuade [pə'sweɪd]	überzeugen	N	*persuasion*
public awareness	das öffentliche Bewusstsein		
activity	Aktivität		
to put forward	darstellen		
point of view	Standpunkt		
to research	recherchieren	N	*research*
to damage	schädigen	N	*damage*
credibility [ˌkredə'bɪləti]	Glaubwürdigkeit	ADJ	*credible*
slick	raffiniert, clever		
impressive	beeindruckend	VT	*to impress*
graphic	Grafik	ADJ	*graphic(al)*
appearance	Anschein	VI	*to appear*
interactivity	Interaktivität	ADJ	*interactive*
to disguise	verschleiern	≈	*to cover up*
coherent [kəʊ'hɪərənt]	schlüssig	<>	*incoherent*
variable	unterschiedlich	<>	*uniform*
fashionable	modisch	vgl.	*fashion* – *Mode*
judgement	Urteilsvermögen	VT	*to judge*
to sift	sieben	≈	*to filter*
search result	Suchergebnis	vgl.	*to search for* – *suchen*
promising	viel versprechend	N	*promise*
entertaining	unterhaltsam	N	*entertainment*
creative	kreativ	N	*creativity*
wacky	verrückt	N	*wackiness*

EDUCATION

An educ@tional experience

Instead of being suspicious of the Internet as a corrupting influence or a waste of time, educational psychologist STUART EVANS urges parents to start learning from their Internet-literate children.

TRADITIONAL subjects like maths and geography are still taught in schools, yet in many ways children today receive a different education from their parents, learning different skills and developing different aptitudes, even completely new approaches to learning.

These are some of the educational benefits being gained by the first "e-generation":

Flexibility: If you search online for a particular keyword or combination, the results you get are not usually (or not just) the ones you anticipated. Children are learning to adapt to the unexpected, to experiment and to learn by trial and error far more than we had the opportunity to.

Intuition: Lateral thinking is as important as logic in finding your way around the Internet – for example, in finding the most relevant search terms or the best place to look for information or an opinion. Interactive entertainment and learning materials are not structured in a linear way – they are not books which should be read from cover to cover, but adaptable learning resources.

Self-confidence: Children are growing up with a belief in their own ability to research topics and come to their own independent conclusions, forming opinions which are as valid as anyone else's. Now that their reading and research opportunities are not limited to the school library or the local bookshop, every student can come up with original combinations of ideas.

Curiosity: Every online document – whether the Website of a favourite pop group, an e-zine or an online encyclopaedia – has links to related material elsewhere on the Internet. Following up these links takes you to completely unexpected ideas and information. An enquiring mind is the best possible foundation for lifelong learning.

Critical thinking: The quality of information and clarity of presentation is very variable among Websites, so children need to become critical and selective. Their parents were brought up to believe that anything published is authoritative and reliable.

suspicious of	misstrauisch gegenüber	≈	*wary of*
corrupting	verderbend		
influence	Einfluss	VT	*to influence*
Internet-literate	Internet-bewandert	vgl.	*computer-literate*
skill	Fertigkeit	ADJ	*skilful*
aptitude	Begabung		
approach to	Ansatz + *Gen.*	VT	*to approach*
educational benefit	Bildungsvorteil	VT	*to benefit*
flexibility	Flexibilität	ADJ	*flexible*
keyword	Stichwort		
to anticipate [æn'tɪsɪpeɪt]	erwarten	≈	*to expect*
to adapt to	sich anpassen an	N	*adaptability*
to experiment	experimentieren	N	*experimentation*
trial and error	Ausprobieren	vgl.	*to try out –* ausprobieren
opportunity	Möglichkeit	≈	*chance*
lateral thinking	spielerisches Denken	VI	*to think laterally*
search term	Suchbegriff	VT	*to search s.th./for s.th*
learning materials	Lernmaterialien		
to structure	strukturieren	N	*structure*
adaptable	anpassungsfähig	VTI	*to adapt*
resources	Mittel		
self-confidence	Selbstvertrauen	ADJ	*self-confident*
belief in	Glaube an	VT	*to believe in*
to research	erforschen	N	*research*
topic	Thema	≈	*subject*
independent	unabhängig	N	*independence*
conclusion	Schlussfolgerung	VTI	*to conclude*
valid	gültig	N	*validity*
limited to	beschränkt auf	<>	*unlimited*
curiosity [ˌkjʊəri'ɒsəti]	Neugier	ADJ	*curious*
encyclopaedia [inˌsaɪklə'piːdiə]	Enzyklopädie	US	*encyclopedia*
related	verwandt		
to follow up	nachgehen	≈	*to pursue*
enquiring mind	forschender Geist	N	*enquiry*
foundation	Grundlage	≈	*basis*
lifelong	lebenslang		
critical	kritisch		
clarity	Klarheit	ADJ	*clear*
selective	wählerisch	N	*selectivity*
to publish	veröffentlichen	N	*publication*
authoritative [ɔː'θɒrɪtətɪv]	maßgebend		
reliable	zuverlässig	N	*reliability*

Interview: regulating the Internet

Interviewer: In the studio with me today is Dr Harriette Duncan, an expert on international law and the Internet. What measures can we use to combat Internet crime?

Duncan: There is a great deal of hysteria surrounding this subject, and little clarity. So, I would like to begin by defining the four main problem areas. Firstly, child pornography is being distributed via the Internet. By 'child pornography' I mean images of sexual acts involving minors. Secondly, minors are viewing Internet pornography – sexually explicit images and text which they would not be allowed to view in other forms, such as magazines. Thirdly, 'hard-core' pornography which is banned in the UK can be freely accessed by British Internet users. Fourthly, literature which incites racial hatred is accessible on the Internet.

Interviewer: What can the government and the international community do about these dangers?

Duncan: There are a number of possible approaches. Some of them are more acceptable to our ideas of democracy and free speech than others. None is perfect.

Interviewer: Please go on.

Duncan: OK. Most countries have laws to control the distribution of potentially harmful and corrupting material. We could simply work within the existing legal framework. After all, if it's illegal offline, it's illegal online too. Why make a distinction? Paedophiles who collect child pornography on their computers have been prosecuted in the UK and elsewhere under existing legislation.

Interviewer: And the problem with this approach?

Duncan: There are a number of problems. Firstly, it's technically difficult to detect that laws are being broken online. How do you know who is accessing what? And what if the material is on a Website in another country, where they have different laws about pornography? What about the Internet Service Providers – the organizations which provide access to the Internet and host their members' Websites on their servers – are they legally liable for the material uploaded by their users? And for preventing their users from *downloading* illegal material?

Interviewer: Are there any workable solutions?

Duncan: Technically, surveillance of Internet traffic by law enforcement agencies is feasible. In other words, if you

>> Fortsetzung Seite 116

to regulate	kontrollieren	N	*regulation*
measure ['meʒə]	Maßnahme	≈	*step*
to combat	bekämpfen	≈	*to fight*
hysteria [hɪ'stɪəriə]	Hysterie	ADJ	*hysterical*
clarity	Klarheit	<>	*confusion*
pornography	Pornografie	ADJ	*pornographic*
to distribute	verbreiten	≈	*to circulate*
image	Bild		
sexual act	sexuelle Handlung	vgl.	*sexual intercourse – Geschlechtsverkehr*
minor	Minderjährige/r	<>	*adult*
to view	betrachten	N	*viewer*
sexually explicit	unverhüllt sexuell		
to ban	verbieten	N	*ban*
to access	zugreifen auf		
to incite	aufhetzen zu	N	*incitement*
racial hatred	Rassenhass	VT	*to hate*
accessible [ək'sesəbl]	zugänglich		
community	Gemeinschaft		
approach	Ansatz	VTI	*to approach*
acceptable to	annehmbar für	N	*acceptability*
democracy [dɪ'mɒkrəsi]	Demokratie	ADJ	*democratic*
free speech	Redefreiheit	≈	*freedom of speech*
distribution	Verbreitung	≈	*circulation*
potentially [pə'tenʃəli]	potenziell	N	*potential*
harmful	schädlich	N	*harm – Schaden*
corrupting	verderbend		
legal framework	gesetzlicher Rahmen	vgl.	*law – Gesetz*
distinction	Unterschied	VT	*to distinguish*
paedophile ['pi:dəʊfaɪl]	Pädophile	US	*pedophile*
to prosecute	strafrechtlich verfolgen	N	*prosecution*
legislation	Gesetze, Gesetzgebung	VI	*to legislate*
technically	technisch		
to detect	entdecken	N	*detection*
to provide	zur Verfügung stellen	N	*provision*
access to	Zugang zu		
to host	bereitstellen		
liable for	haftbar für	N	*liability*
to prevent from	hindern an	N	*prevention*
workable	realisierbar	≈	*practicable*
surveillance [sɜ:'veɪləns]	Überwachung		
Internet traffic	Internetverkehr		
law enforcement agency	Organisation zur Durchsetzung von Gesetzen		
feasible	machbar	N	*feasibility*

>> Fortsetzung Seite 117

were viewing illegal material, someone might be monitoring you. It would only be possible to monitor a small proportion of Internet traffic, but the deterrent effect would be enormous. However, this Big Brother approach would be a severe infringement of civil liberties.

Interviewer: Yes, it certainly would. Tell us about other approaches.

Duncan: The government could put pressure on ISPs to regulate their own users, by making the ISPs legally responsible for the material they host on their servers. This might be an attractive solution for politicians, but it's unworkable due to the volume of material involved. Besides, this still doesn't solve the problem of material coming in from abroad.

Interviewer: Go on.

Duncan: Rather than adopting an authoritarian policy of enforcement, government could encourage voluntary self-regulation by the ISPs. On the face of it, this sounds a good solution. The problem is, ISPs are private organizations. They are not democratically accountable, and their decisions are not transparent. This means that they could actually be more severe than the law requires, so that you could end up with censorship of anything which could be considered sexually explicit – even a user's e-mail to her boyfriend.

Interviewer: I see.

Duncan: – Or you could rely on education and parental control. Sites can be – and are – vetted for their content, and provided with the equivalent of film certificates. Filters built into browser software can shield children from unsuitable material. It's not a perfect solution, but it is becoming more sophisticated. Of course, that doesn't tackle the other problems we talked about, such as paedophiles and racist material.

Interviewer: And what would be your ideal solution?

Duncan: I think that self-regulation is the most sensible and moderate path to go down, combined with better international collaboration to harmonize laws, probably involving a UN initiative. There will always be countries where distributors of extreme material will be safe from prosecution, but it will become more difficult for them to operate. We will never succeed in eradicating the problem, but we will protect users from harmful and offensive material, and that's probably the best we can hope for.

Interviewer: Dr Duncan, thank you.

to monitor	überwachen	vgl.	*monitor – Bildschirm*
deterrent effect	abschreckende Wirkung	VT	*to deter*
severe [sɪ'vɪə]	schwer	N	*severity*
infringement [ɪn'frɪndʒmənt]	Verletzung	VT	*to infringe*
civil liberties	Bürgerrechte		
to put pressure on	unter Druck setzen		
responsible for	verantwortlich für	N	*responsibility*
volume	Menge	≈	*amount*
to adopt a policy	eine Politik übernehmen		
authoritarian [ɔːˌθɒrɪ'teərɪən]	autoritär	N	*authoritarianism*
enforcement	Durchsetzung	VT	*to enforce*
voluntary	freiwillig	<>	*statutory*
self-regulation	Selbstkontrolle	VT	*to regulate*
democratically accountable	demokratisch verantwortlich	N	*accountability*
severe [sɪ'vɪə]	streng	<>	*lenient*
to require	erfordern	N	*requirement*
censorship	Zensur	VT	*to censor*
to rely on	sich verlassen auf	N	*reliance*
parental control	elterliche Aufsicht		
to vet	überprüfen		
film certificate	Filmfreigabe		
to shield from	abschirmen von	N	*shield*
sophisticated	ausgeklügelt, raffiniert	<>	*crude*
to tackle	bewältigen	≈	*to deal with*
moderate ['mɒdərət]	gemäßigt	<>	*excessive*
collaboration	Zusammenarbeit	VI	*to collaborate*
to harmonize	angleichen		
prosecution	strafrechtliche Verfolgung	VT	*to prosecute*
to operate	agieren, tätig sein		
to eradicate	ausrotten	N	*eradication*
offensive	anstößig	<>	*inoffensive, harmless*

Voxpop.com: Media Forum

VOXPOP
• DISCUSSION FORUM •

Is there too much violence on our screens?

Violent movies and computer games are an essential safety valve in our society. They offer a safe, harmless channel for aggression – rather like sport. **JD, Wisconsin**

A few deranged individuals imitate in real life the violence they see on the screen – but who can say whether they would have committed violent acts anyway? Did the movie make them homicidal, or did they become obsessed with that particular movie because they were already homicidal? **F Durand, Quebec**

When we watch an action movie, most of us understand that this genre has its own conventions. We are supposed to support the hero or heroine, whereas the villains deserve what they get. In the real world, of course, nobody is wholly good or bad, and nobody deserves to be beaten, humiliated or shot dead. But in action movies, we suspend our compassion – or we just choose not to watch. **P Kotecki, Florida**

The constant violence we see on TV or at the movies – or participate in when we play computer games – must have a corrupting, brutalizing influence on children. Young children are impressionable, and if they are given macho warriors as role models, they will grow up to believe that aggression and violence are acceptable. **Gil, UK**

Most children grow up able to distinguish right from wrong, despite a staple diet of violent movies and computer games. However, young children are easily traumatized by events which seem strange and frightening to them, and may suffer nightmares and phobias as a result of watching unsuitable material on television. **GWS, Utah**

There is a huge difference between action movies and realistic drama. An action movie is a fantasy in which moral issues are black-and-white. Violence is slick and gratuitous. In realistic drama as in real life, violence causes both physical and emotional harm to the victim and is deeply disturbing to those who witness it. Although this second kind of movie can be far more upsetting, I believe that it is less harmful to society than the casual violence of James Bond. **Raymond, Seattle**

violence	Gewalt	ADJ	*violent*
essential	notwendig	≈	*vital*
safety valve	Sicherheitsventil		
channel	Kanal	VT	*to channel*
deranged	geistesgestört	≈	*crazed*
to imitate	nachmachen	N	*imitation*
to commit a violent act	eine Gewalttat verüben		
homicidal [ˌhɒmɪ'saɪdl]	gemeingefährlich	N	*homicide* – *Mord*
obsessed with	besessen von	N	*obsession*
convention	Konvention	ADJ	*conventional*
to support	unterstützen		
hero/heroine	Held/in	ADJ	*heroic*
villain ['vɪlən]	Bösewicht, Schurke	ADJ	*villainous*
to deserve	verdienen	vgl.	*to get o.'s just deserts* – *bekommen, was man verdient hat*
to beat	schlagen	!	*beat–beat–beaten*
to humiliate [hjuː'mɪlieɪt]	demütigen	N	*humiliation*
to suspend	(vorübergehend) einstellen	N	*suspension*
compassion	Mitgefühl	ADJ	*compassionate*
to participate in	teilnehmen an	N	*participation*
to brutalize	brutalisieren	N	*brutality*
impressionable	leicht zu beeindrucken	N	*impression* – *Eindruck*
warrior ['wɒriə]	Krieger	≈	*fighter*
role model	Vorbild, Rollenbild		
to distinguish from	unterscheiden von	N	*distinction*
a staple diet of	Berieselung mit		
to traumatize ['trɔːmətaɪz/US traʊ-]	traumatisieren	N	*trauma*
nightmare	Alptraum		
phobia	Phobie		
unsuitable	ungeeignet	≈	*inappropriate*
fantasy	Fantasie	!	*imagination* – *Phantasie*
moral issues	moralische Fragen	N	*morality*
slick	glatt	N	*slickness*
gratuitous [grə'tjuːɪtəs/US -tuː-]	unnötig	≈ <>	*unnecessary* *necessary*
harm to	Schaden für	ADJ	*harmful*
to disturb	beunruhigend	≈	*unsettling*
to witness	(mit)erleben		
to upset	bestürzen, erschüttern	ADJ	*upset*
casual violence	beiläufige Gewalt		

LETTERS TO THE EDITOR

A gross intrusion

How dare your paper publish intimate photos of Laura Jarrod on holiday with her boyfriend? ('Saucy Laura reveals all', May 21) The photos were taken without her permission and knowledge after the official photo shoot. This is a gross intrusion into her privacy. Clearly, your paper is prepared to flout the voluntary code of practice in a most blatant and cynical way. There is no question of these photos being 'in the public interest', and there is no way the public has a 'right to know' about Ms Jarrod's taste in swimwear. It is high time that effective legislation is introduced to prevent unscrupulous so-called NEWSpapers from hounding people in this way, excusing their actions with the fact that their victims are in the public eye for one reason or another.

M. Merton, Warwick

The British press are not bound by any legislation to respect the privacy of individuals or their families. However, like other British newspapers, we abide by a voluntary code of practice drawn up by the Press Complaints Commission (PCC). This states that an individual's family life, home, health and correspondence should be respected, unless intrusions can be justified. The code also forbids the use of telephoto lenses to take pictures of individuals in places "where there is a reasonable expectation of privacy". In the case of Laura Jarrod, no laws or voluntary codes have been broken. – ***Editor***

Fair game

How hypocritical of Laura Jarrod to protest about the photos recently published in your paper. Far from being an innocent victim of press persecution, Laura Jarrod has systematically courted press attention to further her career and earn a great deal of money – far more than her talents as an actress deserve. This means that she is 'fair game' as far as media attention is concerned. The photos were not particularly revealing, and not in bad taste. Furthermore they were taken in a spot which is visible from a public beach. Ms Jarrod's libel action against your newspaper is one more example of her greed.

S. Singh, Leeds

gross [grəʊs]	grob, ungeheuerlich	≈	*outrageous*
intrusion	Verletzung	VI	*to intrude (on/upon)*
to publish	veröffentlichen	N	*publication*
intimate ['ɪntɪmət]	intim	N	*intimacy*
permission	Erlaubnis	VT	*to permit*
photo shoot	Fotosession	vgl.	*photographer – Fotograf/in*
privacy	Privatsphäre	ADJ	*private*
to flout	missachten	≈	*to ignore, to disregard*
code of practice	Verhaltenskodex		
blatant	unverfroren		
cynical ['sɪnɪkl]	zynisch	N	*cynicism*
in the public interest	von öffentlichem Interesse		
it is high time	es wird höchste Zeit		
effective	wirksam	N	*effectiveness*
unscrupulous	skrupellos		
to hound	jagen	≈	*to persecute*
to excuse [ɪk'skjuːz]	entschuldigen	N	*excuse [ɪk'skjuːs]*
victim	Opfer	VT	*to victimize*
in the public eye	im Blickpunkt der Öffentlichkeit		
to be bound by	verpflichtet sein durch		
to respect	respektieren	N	*respect*
to abide by	sich halten an	≈	*to adhere to*
to draw up	entwerfen, aufstellen		
correspondence	Korrespondenz	VI	*to correspond (with)*
to justify	rechtfertigen	N	*justification*
to forbid	verbieten	!	*forbid–forbade–forbidden*
telephoto lens	Teleobjektiv	≈	*zoom lens*
reasonable	berechtigt		
expectation	Erwartung	VT	*to expect*
fair game	Freiwild		
hypocritical [ˌhɪpə'krɪtɪkl]	heuchlerisch	N	*hypocrisy [hɪ'pɒkrəsi]*
to protest about	protestieren über	N	*protest*
innocent	unschuldig	<>	*guilty*
persecution	Verfolgung	VT	*to persecute*
systematically	systematisch	<>	*at random*
to court	buhlen um	≈	*to seek*
attention	Aufmerksamkeit	ADJ	*attentive*
to further	fördern		
revealing	enthüllend		
in bad taste	geschmacklos	≈	*in poor taste*
libel action ['laɪbl]	Verleumdungsklage	ADJ	*libellous*

Internet piracy is not a victimless crime

Piracy – the illegal duplication and distribution of software, videos, music or other creative works – is rife in the Internet community. It exists at all levels, from the individual who duplicates a piece of software for a friend or the music fan who swaps digital music tracks via an online chatroom, through to organized crime and the large-scale sale of pirated products. The pirating of music has become a particular problem in recent years with the widespread availability of digital tracks on the Internet. Since there is no reduction in quality with duplication, there is no technical barrier to illicit copying. The originators of the material can build in security measures to make duplication more difficult, but these are unlikely to deter the expert.

Some pirates try to justify their actions by claiming that they are making a political statement – challenging the monopoly of huge corporations like Microsoft – or acting as modern Robin Hoods – robbing the rich to give to the poor. Since the prices charged for music and software are artificially inflated, so their argument goes, there is nothing wrong in making them available at a reduced price – or for free.

These arguments are fallacious. Let's be clear about this: illegal copying and distribution is theft. If an artist has composed and recorded a song, then the result is his or her intellectual property. It is the artist's right to do with it as he or she wishes. That includes granting distribution rights to a record company in exchange for a royalty. In making illegal copies, the pirate is depriving the artist of his or her rightful income. There is no ethical distinction between this and picking someone's pocket in the street.

Not only is piracy (and knowingly receiving pirate copies) unethical and illegal, it is also self-defeating: ultimately, it undermines the industry it exploits. In the case of music, piracy makes recording less profitable for the artists and the record companies, decreasing the viability of new projects, and pushes up the prices of legitimate copies, making it more difficult for honest music lovers to acquire them.

If you have information about illegal duplication of software, film or music, phone our confidential hotline:

0700 1540154

Artists Against Copyright Crime

piracy ['paɪrəsi]	illegales Kopieren	–	WÖRTL *Seeräuberei*
victimless	ohne Opfer	N	*victim*
duplication	Vervielfältigung	≈	*copying*
rife	weit verbeitet	!	NICHT ATTRIBUTIV
to duplicate	vervielfältigen	≈	*to copy*
to swap	tauschen		
track	Stück		
large-scale	in großem Rahmen	ADV	*on a large scale*
to pirate ['paɪrət]	illegal kopieren		
barrier to	Hindernis gegen	vgl.	*to prevent – hindern*
illicit	verboten, illegal	<>	*legitimate, legal*
originator	Urheber/in	VTI	*to originate*
security measure	Sicherheitsmaßnahme	ADJ	*secure – sicher*
to deter [dɪ'tɜː]	abschrecken	<>	*to encourage*
statement	Aussage		
to challenge	anfechten	N	*challenge*
monopoly [mə'nɒpəli]	Monopol	VT	*to monopolize*
corporation	Unternehmen	≈	*(large) company/firm*
artificially [ˌɑːtɪ'fɪʃəli]	künstlich	<>	*naturally*
inflated	hoch getrieben		
fallacious [fə'leɪʃəs]	trugschlüssig	N	*fallacy ['fæləsi]*
theft	Diebstahl	vgl.	*thief – Dieb/in*
to compose	komponieren	N	*composer – Komponist/in*
to record	aufnehmen	N	*recording – Aufnahme*
intellectual property	geistiges Eigentum		
to grant	übertragen	N	*grant*
record company	Plattenfirma	≈	*record label*
in exchange for	im Austausch gegen	VT	*to exchange*
royalty	Tantieme	vgl.	*fee – Honorar*
to deprive s.o. of s.th.	jdm etw vorenthalten		
rightful	rechtmäßig	≈	*legitimate*
income	Einnahmen	≈	*earnings*
ethical	moralisch, ethisch	N	*ethics* PL
distinction	Unterschied	VTI	*to distinguish*
self-defeating	unsinnig		
to undermine	untergraben	<>	*to support*
to exploit	ausbeuten	N	*exploitation*
profitable	profitabel	N	*profitability*
viability [ˌvaɪə'bɪləti]	Rentabilität	ADJ	*viable*
legitimate [lɪ'dʒɪtɪmət]	legitim, rechtmäßig	<>	*illegitimate*
confidential	vertraulich	N	*confidentiality*

F Politics

1 Systems and Institutions

2 Policies and Issues

3 Campaigning and Protest

4 Conflict and Oppression

DIALOGUE: ELECTIONS IN THE UNITED STATES

A: I don't really understand the electoral system here in the US. For example, what exactly are 'primaries'?

B: Primaries are elections in which a party's candidates for public office are nominated. The winners of the primary run in the general election.

A: Nominated by whom? By the electorate as a whole?

B: That depends. Because we have a federal system, regulations vary from state to state. Most states have a "closed primary" system – only party members can vote in that party's primary. But some states have "open primaries": anyone who is on the electoral register may vote in any primary. Others again have a caucus system, in which party leaders and activists nominate the candidates.

A: So, a Republican supporter in an open primary could cast a vote for the weakest Democratic candidate, because he or she would be easier to defeat in the general election?

B: That's right. But in most states, you are only eligible to vote in *one* primary. So your Republican would forfeit the right to vote in his own party's primary.

A: I see ... Are presidential candidates nominated in the same way?

B: Not exactly. They're nominated by a national convention of their party. But the delegates to these conventions are picked in primaries – presidential primaries.

A: So the presidential hopefuls just sit around in Washington waiting to be nominated?

B: You've got to be joking! The presidential primaries are spread over several months, and the candidates travel from state to state campaigning.

A: That sounds expensive and time-consuming. Where does the money come from?

B: A large proportion of the campaign funds are contributed by special-interest groups.

A: Surely that must give them unfair political influence?

B: That's one of the criticisms levelled at the system. Another is that presidential primaries become huge media circuses, focusing on personalities instead of serious issues. A third is that the candidates aren't really accountable to their parties. But no system is perfect!

A: Do most people vote in the primaries?

B: No, they usually attract a low turnout. That means that an active minority can distort the result. Also, the early primaries are disproportionately important, as they can establish – or destroy – a candidate's reputation and sway voters in later primaries.

election	Wahl	VT	*to elect*
electoral system	Wahlsystem		
primary	Vorwahl		
candidate ['kændɪdət]	Kandidat/in	vgl.	*candidacy – Kandidatur*
public office	öffentliches Amt		
to nominate	nominieren	N	*nomination*
to run	kandidieren	≈	*to stand*
general election	Parlamentswahlen		
electorate [ɪ'lektərət]	Wählerschaft		
federal	föderalistisch	N	*federalism*
regulations	Vorschriften	≈	*rules*
party member	Parteimitglied		
to vote	wählen, seine Stimme abgeben	N	*vote – Stimme; Abstimmung*
electoral register [ɪ'lektərəl]	Wählerverzeichnis	VTI	*to register*
caucus	Ausschuss-		
supporter	Anhänger/in	VT	*to support*
to cast a vote	eine Stimme abgeben	≈	*to vote*
to defeat	besiegen	N	*defeat*
eligible ['elɪdʒəbl]	berechtigt	ADJ	*ineligible*
to forfeit ['fɔːfɪt]	verwirken	ADJ	*forfeit*
presidential candidate	Präsidentschafts-kandidat/in		
national convention	Nationalversammlung	VTI	*to convene*
delegate to ['deləgət]	Delegierte/r für		
presidential primary	Vorwahl für die Präsidentschaft	vgl.	*president – Präsident/in*
presidential hopeful	Präsidentschafts-anwärter/in	vgl.	*hopeful – hoffnungsvoll*
to campaign [kæm'peɪn]	den Wahlkampf führen	N	*campaign*
funds	Mittel, Gelder	VT	*to fund*
to contribute	spenden, beisteuern	N	*contribution*
special-interest group	Interessengruppe	≈	*lobby*
to level a criticism at	eine Kritik erheben gegen	≈	*to criticize*
media circus	Medienzirkus		
to focus on	sich konzentrieren auf	≈	*to concentrate on*
issue	Frage, Angelegenheit	≈	*question, topic*
accountable to	verantwortlich + *Dat.*	N	*accountability*
turnout	Wahlbeteiligung		
minority	Minderheit	<>	*majority*
to distort	verzerren	N	*distortion*
disproportionately	unverhältnismäßig	<>	*proportionately*
reputation	Ruf		
to sway	beeinflussen	≈	*to influence*

The United Kingdom: Central Government

THE UNITED KINGDOM is a monarchy and a parliamentary democracy. Its constitution is partly unwritten, with legislation and the decisions of the law courts as its main sources. The proponents of this system point out that it is flexible and adaptable, but its critics argue that a formal constitution would be a better safeguard of democracy and civil liberties.

Parliament is the country's legislative assembly and comprises two chambers: the elected House of Commons and the appointed House of Lords. The House of Commons consists of approximately 650 Members of Parliament (MPs), who are elected by local constituencies, either in a general election (every four to five years) or in occasional by-elections (when an MP stands down or dies). The House of Lords can initiate amendments to bills, but it cannot veto them.

The head of state is the sovereign, the reigning king or queen. He or she appoints as head of government (the Prime Minister) the leader of the party with most seats in the House of Commons. The Prime Minister appoints an advisory council of around 20 senior ministers, called the Cabinet. Most – but not all – of the cabinet ministers are in charge of government departments, whose permanent staff is provided by the civil service.

Because the sovereign's power is almost entirely symbolic, and the House of Lords has only a consultative function and the constitution is flexible, the Prime Minister and his or her cabinet have a great deal of power. This enabled the Labour Party under Tony Blair to implement sweeping and fundamental changes in the last years of the twentieth century – reforming the House of Lords and devolving power to new regional assemblies in Scotland, Wales and Northern Ireland.

government	Regierung	VTI	*to govern*
monarchy ['mɒnəki]	Monarchie	vgl.	*monarch* ['mɒnək]
parliamentary	parlamentarisch	N	*parliament*
democracy	Demokratie	ADJ	*democratic*
constitution	Verfassung	ADJ	*constitutional*
legislation	Gesetzgebung, Gesetze	VI	*to legislate*
law court [kɔːt]	Gericht(shof)	vgl.	*judge* – *Richter/in*
proponent	Befürworter/in	≈	*supporter*
adaptable	anpassungsfähig	VTI	*to adapt*
critic	Kritiker/in	VTI	*to criticize*
safeguard	Schutz	VT	*to safeguard*
civil liberties	Bürgerrechte	vgl.	*liberty* – *Freiheit*
legislative assembly ['ledʒɪslətɪv]	gesetzgebende Versammlung		
chamber	Kammer		
to elect	wählen	N	*election*
House of Commons	Unterhaus		
to appoint	berufen, ernennen	N	*appointment*
House of Lords	Oberhaus		
Member of Parliament	Abgeordnete/r	ABK	*MP*
constituency [kən'stɪtjʊənsɪ]	Wahlkreis	vgl.	*constituent* – *Wähler/in*
by-election	Nachwahl		
to stand down	zurücktreten	≈	*to resign*
to initiate [ɪ'nɪʃieɪt]	initiieren, einleiten	≈	*to introduce*
amendment to	Änderung an	VT	*to amend*
bill	Gesetzesvorlage	vgl.	*act* – *Gesetz*
to veto	sein Veto einlegen gegen	N	*veto*
head of state	Staatsoberhaupt		
sovereign ['sɒvrɪn]	Souverän, Herrscher/in	ADJ	*sovereign*
to reign [reɪn]	herrschen	≈	*to rule*
head of government	Regierungschef/in	VTI	*to govern*
Prime Minister	Premierminister/in	ABK	*PM*
advisory council	Beirat	VTI	*to advise*
senior minister	Staatsminister/in	vgl.	*junior minister* – *Staatssekretär/in*
Cabinet	Kabinett		
staff	Mitarbeiter/innen		
civil service	Staatsdienst	–	*ohne Lehrer u. Richter*
consultative [kən'sʌltətɪv]	beratend	VT	*to consult*
to implement	vollziehen	N	*implementation*
sweeping	drastisch	≈	*wide-ranging*
fundamental	grundlegend	<>	*superficial*
to reform	reformieren	N	*reform*
to devolve power	Macht übertragen	N	*devolution*
regional assembly	Landesversammlung		

Main institutions of the European Union

The **European Parliament** has more than 600 members (MEPs), elected directly by the citizens of the EU. All of the EU's major political parties are represented. The Parliament supervises the way the Union's policies are implemented by the other EU institutions.

Originally, the Parliament had only a consultative role, but now it shares the power of decision with the Council of Ministers in many areas. Parliament's assent is required for important international agreements such as the accession of new member states.

The European Commission has 20 members, chosen by the heads of state or government of the member states and approved by the European Parliament. It has sole responsibility for drafting legislation, submitting its proposals to the Council of Ministers and the European Parliament for approval. It is also responsible for ensuring that EU treaties are implemented correctly, taking action where necessary against member states and organizations which do not respect their obligations. Its third role is to implement EU policy, including the management of the EU's annual budget.

The **Council of the European Union** or **Council of Ministers** is made up of ministers of the member states. It determines the EU's overall political objectives and coordinates the national policies of the member states. It holds around 100 formal sessions a year.

The **European Summit** convenes at least twice a year and is made up of the heads of state or government of the member states, as well as the President of the Commission. It sets policies at the highest level and deals with contentious issues that the Council of Ministers has been unable to resolve.

The **European Court of Justice** ensures that the decisions taken by the European Commission and the Council of Ministers comply with EU law, and hears cases which involve disputes between member states as well as cases brought by individual citizens.

The **European Central Bank (ECB)** sets monetary policy for all the EU states that have joined the single currency. Its governing council includes the ECB president and the heads of the national central banks participating in the euro.

MEP	Abgeordnete/r des Europäischen Parlaments	–	*Member of the European Parliament*
major	bedeutend	<>	*minor*
to supervise	überwachen	N	*supervision*
policy	Politik, Grundsatz		
power of decision	Entscheidungsgewalt	VTI	*to decide*
Council of Ministers	Ministerrat		
assent	Zustimmung	<>	*dissent*
agreement	Vereinbarung	<>	*disagreement*
accession [æk'seʃn]	Beitritt	vgl.	*to join – beitreten*
to approve	billigen	N	*approval*
sole responsibility	alleinige Verantwortung		
to draft	entwerfen	N	*draft – Entwurf*
legislation	Gesetze	VI	*to legislate*
to submit	vorlegen	N	*submission*
proposal	Vorlage	VT	*to propose – vorschlagen*
to ensure	gewährleisten	≈	*to make sure*
treaty	Vertrag		
to take action	Maßnahmen ergreifen	≈	*to take measures*
to respect o.'s obligations	seinen Verpflichtungen nachkommen		
management	Verwaltung	VT	*to manage*
to determine	festlegen	≈	*to decide, to set*
overall	allgemein	≈	*general*
objective	Ziel	≈	*aim, goal*
to coordinate	koordinieren	N	*coordination*
session	Sitzung		
summit	Gipfel(konferenz)		
convene [kən'vi:n]	zusammentreten		
at the highest level	auf höchster Ebene	ADJ	*high-level*
to deal with	sich befassen mit		
contentious [kən'tenʃəs]	strittig	N	*contention*
to resolve	lösen	N	*resolution*
Court of Justice	Gerichtshof	vgl.	*justice – Gerechtigkeit*
to comply with	mit einer Sache im Einklang stehen	N	*compliance*
to hear a case	einen Fall verhandeln		
to bring a case	Klage erheben		
monetary policy ['mʌnətri]	Währungs-, Geldpolitik	vgl.	*fiscal – Finanz-*
single currency	einheitliche Währung		
governing council	Vorstand		
to participate in	sich beteiligen an	N	*participation*
		≈	*to take part in*

http://www.un.org/

THE UN IN BRIEF

Most of us have heard about United Nations peacekeeping and humanitarian assistance. But the many other ways the UN affects all our lives are not always so well known.

The United Nations is central to global efforts to solve problems which challenge humanity. Cooperating in this effort are more than 30 affiliated organizations known together as the UN system. Day in and day out, the UN and its family of organizations work to promote respect for human rights, protect the environment, fight disease, promote development and reduce poverty. The United Nations leads the international campaigns against illicit drug trafficking and terrorism. Throughout the world, the UN and its agencies assist refugees and set up programmes to clear landmines, help improve the quality of drinking water and expand food production, make loans to developing countries and help stabilize financial markets.

HOW THE UN WORKS

The United Nations was established on 24 October 1945 by 51 countries committed to preserving peace through international cooperation and collective security. Today, nearly every nation in the world belongs to the UN – 188 countries in all.

When States become Members of the United Nations, they agree to accept the obligations of the UN Charter, an international treaty which sets out basic principles of international relations. According to the Charter, the UN has four purposes: to maintain international peace and security, to develop friendly relations among nations, to cooperate in solving international problems and in promoting respect for human rights, and to be a centre for harmonizing the actions of nations.

UN Members are sovereign countries. The United Nations is not a world government, and it does not make laws. It does, however, provide the means to help resolve international conflict and formulate policies on matters affecting all of us.

The United Nations has six main organs. Five of them – the General Assembly, the Security Council, the Economic and Social Council, the Trusteeship Council and the Secretariat – are based at UN Headquarters in New York. The sixth, the International Court of Justice, is located at The Hague, Netherlands.

peacekeeping	Friedenssicherung		
humanitarian assistance	humanitäre Hilfe	≈	*humanitarian aid*
effort	Bemühung		
to challenge	herausfordern	N	*challenge*
to cooperate	kooperieren	≈	*to collaborate*
affiliated [ə'fɪlieɪtɪd]	angeschlossen	N	*affiliation*
to promote	fördern	<>	*to discourage*
human rights	Menschenrechte		
poverty	Armut	ADJ	*poor*
campaign [kæm'peɪn]	Kampagne	VI	*to campaign*
illicit	illegal	≈	*illegal*
drug trafficking	Drogenhandel	≈	*drug dealing*
terrorism	Terrorismus	vgl.	*terrorist*
to assist	helfen	vgl.	*aid – Hilfe*
refugee	Flüchtling	vgl.	*asylum – Asyl*
to set up	einrichten		
to clear landmines	Landminen räumen		
to expand	erweitern	N	*expansion*
loan	Darlehen	vgl.	*grant – Subvention*
developing country	Entwicklungsland		
to stabilize	stabilisieren	ADJ	*stable*
financial market	Finanzmarkt		
to establish	gründen	≈	*to found*
committed to	eintretend für	N	*commitment*
to preserve	erhalten	N	*preservation*
security	Sicherheit	<>	*insecurity*
obligation	Verpflichtung	ADJ	*obliged*
charter	Charta		
to set out	darlegen		
basic principle	Grundsatz		
international relations	internationale Beziehungen		
to maintain	bewahren		
to develop	entwickeln	N	*development*
to harmonize	aufeinander abstimmen		
sovereign country	souveränes Land		
to resolve	lösen	N	*resolution*
to formulate	formulieren		
General Assembly	Vollversammlung	vgl.	*Secretary General – Generalsekretär/in*
Security Council	Sicherheitsrat		
to be based at	seinen Sitz haben in		
headquarters	Zentrale		
to be located at	sich befinden in	N	*location*

talkback.com/uk_politics/immigration

talkback

Time to close the door?

At the beginning of the new millennium there were around 100,000 asylum seekers in the United Kingdom. Our social security system supports these applicants for the many months – often many years – that it takes for their cases to be processed by the Home Office. Is it time for more stringent measures to stem the tide of refugees?

Absolutely not! Under the present laws it is virtually impossible for a refugee to reach Britain legally: anyone who carries an asylum seeker into Britain is liable to a £2000 fine. The result: last year an estimated 1000 illegal immigrants drowned after being thrown overboard from European ships by crews who wished to avoid punishment for harbouring illegal immigrants. Asylum seekers who actually reach a UK port have five days to collect evidence to substantiate a claim to asylum. For applicants who do not speak English or have contacts in the UK, this is a virtually insurmountable hurdle.
Clarissa, Newcastle-upon-Tyne

Under the current bureaucratic system, it is unlikely that an asylum seeker will be deported after the right of residence in the UK has been refused – which may take years. Attempts to speed up the decision procedure simply result in more appeals. Meanwhile, the applicant either lives on benefits or joins the 'black economy', working in sweat shops without paying taxes and without any protection from exploitation. If the decision procedure were more lenient, it would also be quicker and cheaper to run. Refugees could integrate into society, get proper jobs and contribute to the national economy instead of being a burden upon it.
Sukhdev, Canterbury

We should keep all asylum seekers in detention camps until their applications have been processed. Those who are found not to be eligible should be deported swiftly and without appeal. At the moment, bogus asylum seekers – economic migrants – are living in luxury at the tax payer's expense!
Mike, Exeter

asylum seeker [ə'saɪləm]	Asylbewerber/in	vgl.	*to seek* – *suchen*
social security system	Sozialhilfesystem		
to support	unterstützen	N	*support*
applicant	Bewerber/in	VI	*to apply (for)*
to process a case	einen Fall bearbeiten		
Home Office	Innenministerium		
stringent ['strɪndʒənt]	scharf, energisch	N	*stringency*
measure ['meʒə]	Maßnahme		
to stem the tide	den Zustrom eindämmen		
refugee	Flüchtling		
to be liable	verurteilt werden können		
fine	Geldstrafe	VT	*to fine*
immigrant	Einwanderer/ Einwanderin	vgl.	*to emigrate*– *auswandern*
punishment	Strafe	VT	*to punish*
to harbour	Unterschlupf gewähren		
evidence	Beweise	vgl.	*to prove* – *beweisen*
to substantiate [səb'stænʃieɪt]	begründen		
claim to	Anspruch auf	VT	*to claim*
asylum [ə'saɪləm]	Asyl		
insurmountable hurdle	unüberwindbare Hürde		
bureaucratic [ˌbjʊərəʊ'krætɪk]	bürokratisch	N	*bureaucracy*
to deport	abschieben	N	*deportation*
right of residence	Aufenthaltsrecht	vgl.	*resident* – *Bewohner/in*
to speed up	beschleunigen	<>	*to slow down*
decision procedure	Entscheidungsverfahren	VTI	*to decide*
appeal	Einspruch, Berufung	VI	*to appeal (against)*
benefits	Sozialhilfe		
black economy	Schattenwirtschaft		
sweat shop [swet]	Ausbeuterbetrieb		
tax	Steuer		
exploitation	Ausbeutung	VT	*to exploit*
lenient ['liːniənt]	milde, nachsichtig	N	*leniency*
to integrate into	sich integrieren in	N	*integration*
to contribute to	beitragen zu	N	*contribution*
burden upon	Belastung für		
detention camp	Internierungslager	VT	*to detain*
application	Bewerbung		
to process	bearbeiten		
eligible ['elɪdʒəbl]	berechtigt	<>	*ineligible*
bogus	Schein-	<>	*genuine*
economic migrant	Wirtschaftsflüchtling		
at s.o.'s expense	auf jds Kosten		

Discussion: role of the armed forces

A: ... A new question for the panel: "Are the armed forces redundant in the 21st century?"

B: I don't think that armed forces are becoming redundant, but their role is changing. Instead of large armies composed of conscripts, we need small but highly trained rapid response forces.

C: I agree – elite troops who can take part in multinational peacekeeping forces to help resolve regional conflicts and protect civilian populations in areas threatened by civil wars.

D: Fine, but countries will always need to defend their national security. I think that the need is greater now than it was 30 years ago: although there was mutual hostility between the USA and the Soviet Union, at least we all knew where we stood. The world today is a much less predictable and more volatile place. The breakup of the Soviet Union was hugely destabilizing, and it will be decades before the full effects of that disintegration are apparent. The rise of nationalism or religious fanaticism in newly independent states is a constant danger.

C: But that fanaticism is in part a response to the perceived imperialist attitude of the developed world, particularly the USA. The Americans create suspicion by aiming to make themselves invulnerable – whilst enjoying the freedom to intervene militarily whenever and wherever they want.

B: Yes, take their proposed new anti-missile defence system. If that is developed and deployed – in violation of the 1972 ABM treaty – the result will be increased suspicion and hostility towards America and its allies. "Freedom to attack and freedom from attack" is not the foundation of a sensible foreign policy.

D: But with the likely proliferation of nuclear weapons over the next decade, surely there is a need for the US to keep the upper hand? Surely the fact that the US holds a massive nuclear arsenal must act as a deterrent against aggression?

B: That's a typical Cold War argument. It's time to end the arms race and start spending the money on something sensible – like development programmes for the Third World, for example. Decommissioning nuclear weapons and reducing offensive capability is the only sensible way forward ...

armed forces	Streitkräfte	vgl.	*armed – bewaffnet*
redundant	überflüssig	≈	*superfluous*
army	Heer	vgl.	*navy – Kriegsmarine; airforce – Luftwaffe*
conscript ['kɒnskrɪpt]	Wehrpflichtige/r	vgl.	*conscription – Wehrpflicht*
rapid response force	schnelle Eingreiftruppe	VI	*to respond (to)*
troops	Truppen	≈	*soldiers*
peacekeeping force	Friedenstruppe	vgl.	*to keep the peace*
to resolve	lösen	N	*resolution*
civilian population	Zivilbevölkerung	vgl.	*civilian – Zivilist/in*
to threaten ['θretn]	bedrohen	N	*threat*
civil war	Bürgerkrieg		
to defend	verteidigen	N	*defence,* US *defense*
national security	nationale Sicherheit	ADJ	*secure*
mutual	gegenseitig	<>	*unilateral*
hostility [hɒ'stɪləti]	Feindschaft	ADJ	*hostile*
predictable	berechenbar	N	*predictability*
volatile ['vɒlətaɪl]	unbeständig	<>	*stable*
breakup	Zusammenbruch	VTI	*to break up*
destabilizing	destabilisierend	N	*destabilization*
disintegration	Zerfall, Auflösung	VI	*to disintegrate*
nationalism	Nationalismus	ADJ	*nationalist*
religious fanaticism	religiöser Fanatismus	vgl.	*fanatic – Fanatiker/in*
independent	unabhängig	N	*independence*
imperialist	imperialistisch	N	*imperialism*
suspicion	Misstrauen	ADJ	*suspicious (of)*
invulnerable	unbezwingbar	<>	*vulnerable*
to intervene militarily	militärisch eingreifen	N	*intervention*
anti-missile defence system	Raketenabwehrsystem	N	*missile – Rakete*
to deploy	einsetzen	N	*deployment*
violation of	Verletzung + *Gen*	VT	*to violate*
treaty	Vertrag	vgl.	*alliance – Bündnis*
ally	Verbündete/r	ADJ	*allied*
sensible	vernünftig	!	*sensitive – sensibel*
foreign policy	Außenpolitik	<>	*domestic policy*
proliferation [prəˌlɪfə'reɪʃn]	Weitergabe	VI	*to proliferate*
nuclear weapon ['wepn]	Nuklearwaffe	≈	*atomic weapon*
to keep the upper hand	die Oberhand behalten	≈	*to maintain superiority*
arsenal	Waffenlager	≈	*arms stockpile*
deterrent [dɪ'terənt]	Abschreckung	VT	*to deter*
arms race	Wettrüsten		
to decommission	außer Dienst nehmen	<>	*to commission*
offensive capability	Angriffsfähigkeit	<>	*defensive capability*

Voxpop.com: Politics Forum

VOXPOP
• DISCUSSION FORUM •

With ten Central or Eastern European countries and Cyprus applying for EU membership, the enlargement of the EU seems inevitable. But is it a good thing?

As the world's largest single market, the EU is extremely powerful and influential. The larger that market grows, the more influence we will have. Already the prospective member states are reforming their economies, privatizing their industries, developing efficient banking systems and aligning their laws with the EU. **Armando, Portugal**

We're going too far and too fast. The institutions of the EU were created for a much smaller community, and are in urgent need of reform. Politically, the EU needs to be both democratically accountable and able to act decisively. At the moment, neither is true: the European Commission is unelected and unaccountable and the European Parliament has very limited power and cannot possibly represent 500 million citizens properly. **Siobhan, Eire**

The EU enables us to tackle issues which go beyond national boundaries, such as environmental protection, organized crime and international trade. It is in our interests to integrate the remaining European countries into the EU in order to create a stable and prosperous continent. **Luke, Scotland**

The EU is already bureaucratic, inefficient, undemocratic and corrupt. Its overregulation hinders growth and encourages excessive social spending. Making it bigger will just make the problems worse. **Alex, England**

What about the consequences of extending the Common Agricultural Policy to new members with large and inefficient agricultural sectors? I really don't think the EU can afford expansion right now. Having a vision of a united Europe is one thing, a practical and affordable EU policy on membership is another. **Knut, Denmark**

to apply for	sich bewerben um	N	*application*
membership	Mitgliedschaft	vgl.	*member* – *Mitglied*
enlargement	Erweiterung	VT	*to enlarge*
inevitable	unumgänglich	<>	*avoidable*
single market	Binnenmarkt		
influential	einflussreich	N	*influence*
prospective	in Frage kommend	vgl.	*prospect* – *Aussicht*
to reform	reformieren	N	*reform*
economy	Volkswirtschaft	ADJ	*economic*
to privatize	privatisieren	N	*privatization*
efficient	effizient	<>	*inefficient*
banking system	Bankensystem		
to align with	ausrichten auf	N	*alignment*
community	Gemeinschaft		
to be in urgent need of	dringend brauchen	N	*urgency*
accountable	verantwortlich	N	*accountability*
to act decisively	entschieden handeln	ADJ	*decisive*
unelected	nicht gewählt		
limited	begrenzt	N	*limit*
to represent	repräsentieren	ADJ	*representative*
citizen	Bürger/in		
to tackle	angehen	≈	*to deal with*
national boundary	Staatsgrenze	≈	*border*
environmental protection	Umweltschutz	VT	*to protect*
trade	Handel	VTI	*to trade*
to integrate into	integrieren in	N	*integration*
stable	stabil	N	*stability*
prosperous	wohlhabend	N	*prosperity*
bureaucratic	bürokratisch	N	*bureaucracy*
overregulation	Überregulierung	VT	*to regulate*
to hinder	behindern	N	*hindrance*
excessive	übermäßig	<>	*insufficient*
social spending	Sozialausgaben		
to extend	erweitern	N	*extension*
Common Agricultural Policy	gemeinsame Agrarpolitik	ABK	*CAP*
agricultural sector	Agrarsektor	N	*agriculture*
expansion	Erweiterung	VTI	*to expand*
united	vereint	N	*unity*
practical	praktikabel	N	*practicality*
affordable	bezahlbar	VT	*to afford*
policy on	Politik bezüglich + *Gen*		

LETTERS TO THE EDITOR

Scandal – does it matter?

I found your recent report ('Minister admits drug abuse', 14 July) on the resignation of Heather Jones rather judgemental. I don't see why an able politician's career should be ruined because of a private indiscretion. Ms Jones' drug and alcohol abuse occurred some years ago, before she became an MP, and has no relevance to her political career. It is naive to expect our political leaders to be whiter than white. Ms Jones has behaved honourably in resigning to protect her party's reputation – but I believe that it was an unnecessary step. There has been no hint of dishonesty in Ms Jones' conduct as a minister, which would have been a matter of legitimate public concern.

It is not the ex-minister's past mistakes which damage public confidence, but the hypocritical way the press has blown up the matter out of all proportion, producing exaggerated 'revelations' – unfounded rumour and malicious gossip – in an attempt to sell more newspapers.

The opposition are of course eager to exploit Ms Jones' admissions – in order to distract our attention from the serious allegations of corruption which led them to lose the last election and which continue to undermine their credibility.

Pamela Fearnley

Your editorial on the Heather Jones scandal (16 July) refers to 'old-fashioned notions of morality'. I for one find this attitude offensive and cynical. A lack of integrity in private life is likely to be a good indication of unreliability in public office also. A cabinet minister who lies about her past may also be untruthful to the British electorate – and to her colleagues – about matters of state. We have a right to insist on the highest standards of behaviour from the people to whom we entrust the running of the country. Moreover, secrets of this nature expose politicians to the threat of blackmail.

Geoffrey North

scandal	Skandal	ADJ	*scandalous*
resignation [ˌrezɪɡ'neɪʃn]	Rücktritt		
judgemental [dʒʌdʒ'mentl]	wertend	N	*judgement*
career	Karriere		
to ruin	ruinieren		
relevance	Relevanz	ADJ	*relevant*
honourably	ehrenhaft	N	*honour,* US *honor*
to resign [ri'zaɪn]	zurücktreten		
reputation	Ruf		
dishonesty	Unredlichkeit	ADJ	*dishonest*
conduct	Verhalten	≈	*behaviour*
legitimate [lɪ'dʒɪtɪmət]	begründet, berechtigt	N	*legitimacy*
public concern	öffentliches Interesse	VT	*to concern*
public confidence	Vertrauen der Öffentlichkeit	ADJ	*confident*
hypocritical [ˌhɪpə'krɪtɪkl]	heuchlerisch	N	*hypocrisy [hɪ'pɒkrəsi]*
to blow up out of all proportion	unverhältnismäßig aufbauschen		
exaggerated	übertrieben	N	*exaggeration*
revelation	Enthüllung	VT	*to reveal*
unfounded	aus der Luft gegriffen		
rumour	Gerücht		
malicious [mə'lɪʃəs]	bösartig, gemein	N	*malice*
gossip	Klatsch	VI	*to gossip*
to exploit	ausschlachten	N	*exploitation*
to distract s.o.'s attention	jds Aufmerksamkeit ablenken	N	*distraction*
allegation	Behauptung	VT	*to allege*
to undermine s.o.'s credibility	jds Glaubwürdigkeit untergraben		
morality	Moral	ADJ	*moral*
offensive	anstößig	VT	*to offend*
cynical ['sɪnɪkl]	zynisch	N	*cynicism*
integrity [ɪn'teɡrəti]	Integrität		
indication	Anzeichen	VT	*to indicate*
unreliability [ˌʌnrɪˌlaɪə'bɪləti]	Unzuverlässigkeit	ADJ	*unreliable*
public office	öffentliches Amt		
untruthful	unaufrichtig	N	*truth – Wahrheit*
matters of state	Staatsangelegenheiten	≈	*affairs of state*
to insist on	bestehen auf	N	*insistence*
standards of behaviour	Verhaltensmaßstäbe	VI	*to behave*
to entrust	anvertrauen	N	*trust – Vertrauen*
to expose to	aussetzen + *Dat*	N	*exposure*
threat [θret]	Bedrohung	VT	*to threaten*
blackmail	Erpressung	VT	*to blackmail*

Which way now?

What can Europe expect from the US in the 21st century?

History has given the US various foreign policy models: George Washington warned his country to avoid alliances which could drag it into foreign wars; the Monroe Doctrine claimed the American continents as the sphere of interest of the US, and not of European powers; the Truman Doctrine insisted that the US must help free countries throughout the world to resist Communist aggression.

Will the US of the early 21st century be isolationist, concentrating on domestic affairs and the defence of its own interests? Or will an interventionist United States uphold the principles of democracy? It is unlikely that we will see either ideology in its pure form: any US administration will adopt a practical approach, whatever its rhetoric.

Views offered by the main candidates for the 2000 presidential election provide evidence of current American attitudes:

George W. Bush thought we were living "in a world of terror and madmen and missiles"[1] and promised to rebuild the US military to defend America and its allies. No hint of isolationism: "The world seeks America's leadership … . Our greatest export is freedom."[2]

Al Gore also thought the United States had a moral obligation to provide leadership, including military intervention: "We're the natural leader of the world. I don't think that's a chauvinist American statement."[3]

Pat Buchanan warned that the UN was intruding on national sovereignty: "In nation after nation, the struggle between patriotism and globalism is under way"[4], on the other hand, Buchanan wanted to withdraw US troops from abroad and stop the use of sanctions against Cuba.

Alan Keyes wanted to "end the Clinton policy of interventionism" and withhold US contributions to the UN until the latter ceased its "opposition to the free enterprise approaches that could actually help countries around the world to develop."[5]

Whatever policies are adopted, other countries will criticize the US: for letting public opinion and domestic interests dictate the foreign policy agenda; for a nationalist belief in American superiority; for seeing the outside world as a place of conspiracy against the US. This criticism is the inevitable price of being the world's most powerful nation.

1 TV advert: "Dangerous World", November 1999; **2** p. 240 *A Charge to Keep*, 1999; **3** Democrat debate at Dartmouth College, 28 October 1999; **4** Associated Press "Attack World Government", 6 January 2000; **5** Republican debate at Dartmouth College, 29 October 1999

foreign policy	Außenpolitik	<>	*domestic policy*
alliance [ə'laɪəns]	Allianz, Bündnis		
drag into	hineinziehen in		
to claim	beanspruchen	N	*claim*
sphere of interest [sfɪə]	Interessensphäre		
to resist	sich wehren gegen	N	*resistance*
isolationist	isolationistisch	VT	*to isolate*
domestic affairs	innere Angelegenheiten	<>	*foreign affairs*
defence	Verteidigung	VT	*to defend*
interventionist	interventionistisch	VI	*to intervene*
to uphold a principle	ein Prinzip wahren		
democracy	Demokratie	ADJ	*democratic*
ideology [ˌaɪdi'ɒlədʒi]	Ideologie	ADJ	*ideological*
administration	Regierung	≈	*government*
to adopt an approach	eine Herangehens-weise wählen		
practical	praktisch	≈	*pragmatic*
evidence	Anhaltspunkt	≈	*indication*
current	gegenwärtig	≈	*present*
madman	Verrückter	ADJ	*mad*
missile ['mɪsaɪl/US 'mɪsl]	Rakete	!	*rocket* – Rakete *(als Triebwerk od. Fahrzeug)*
military	Militär	≈	*armed forces*
ally ['ælaɪ]	Verbündete/r	<>	*enemy*
leadership	Führung	VT	*to lead*
freedom	Freiheit	≈	*liberty*
moral obligation	moralische Verpflichtung		
military	militärisch	<>	*civilian*
chauvinist ['ʃəʊvɪnɪst]	chauvinistisch	N	*chauvinism*
to intrude on	verletzen	N	*intrusion*
national sovereignty ['sɒvrənti]	Staatshoheit	ADJ	*sovereign*
patriotism	Patriotismus	ADJ	*patriotic*
globalism	Globalismus	vgl.	*globalization*
to withdraw	abziehen	<>	*to deploy*
to withhold	verweigern		
contribution	Beitragszahlung		
opposition to	Widerstand gegen	VT	*to oppose*
free enterprise	freies Unternehmertum		
to criticize	kritisieren	N	*criticism*
nationalist	nationalistisch	N	*nationalism*
superiority [suːˌpɪəri'ɒrəti]	Überlegenheit	<>	*inferiority*
conspiracy [kən'spɪrəsi]	Verschwörung	VI	*to conspire*
inevitable	unvermeidlich	N	*inevitability*

talkback.com/us_politics/crime

talkback

Is the death penalty a just and humane punishment?

In 1999, 98 criminals were executed in the USA, making a total of 598 since the death penalty was reinstated in 1977. At present, over 3,600 prisoners are on death row.

Each year there are tens of thousands of homicides across the USA. If we abolish the death penalty, the problem will get worse – surely the possibility that you will lose your life if you are caught must be the ultimate deterrent? A murderer who is given a life sentence knows that there's a good chance he will be freed on parole within ten years. **Julia, California**

Crime statistics from countries which have abolished capital punishment show that the death penalty has little deterrent effect. Here in Canada the death penalty was abolished in 1975: the homicide rate fell, and has remained at a lower level ever since. **Ed, Toronto**

Society has to be protected against psychopaths and callous killers who have no respect for human life, no pity for their victims and no remorse for the suffering they inflict. The death penalty is cheaper and safer than keeping these people in prison. Why should we as tax-payers support these criminals for the rest of their lives? **Carlos, New York**

Capital punishment is the sign of a society which has no respect for the sanctity of life. Sentencing a fellow human being to death sends out the wrong message, leading to a more violent society. Killing is immoral, whether it is carried out by an individual or the state, and cannot be condoned. **Grant, New York**

We are executing innocent people along with the guilty. Twenty states have reversed capital punishment decisions since 1975, and there have been at least 85 misconvictions which were discovered before it was too late. How many innocent people have been hanged, electrocuted, killed by lethal injection, and shot by firing squad in the name of justice? As long as there is police misconduct, unreliable testimony of witnesses and inadequate legal representation of defendants, we cannot risk a single execution. **Grace, Idaho**

death penalty	Todesstrafe	VT	*to penalize – bestrafen*
just	gerecht	<>	*unjust*
humane [hjuː'meɪn]	human	!	*human – menschlich*
punishment	Strafe	VT	*to punish*
to execute	hinrichten	N	*execution*
to reinstate [ˌriːɪn'steɪt]	wieder einsetzen	≈	*to bring back*
on death row	im Todestrakt		
homicide ['hɒmɪsaɪd]	Mord, Totschlag	≈	*murder*
to abolish	abschaffen	N	*abolition*
ultimate	äußerste(r, s)		
deterrent [dɪ'terənt]	Abschreckung	VT	*to deter*
life sentence	lebenslängliche Freiheitsstrafe	≈	*life imprisonment*
to free on parole	auf Bewährung entlassen		
capital punishment	Todesstrafe		
callous ['kæləs]	gefühllos	N	*callousness*
pity	Mitgefühl	≈	*compassion*
victim	Opfer		
remorse	Reue	ADJ	*remorseful*
suffering	Leid	VTI	*to suffer*
to inflict	zufügen		
to support	unterhalten		
sanctity	Unantastbarkeit		
to sentence to death	zum Tode verurteilen	N	*sentence – Strafe*
immoral	unmoralisch	N	*immorality*
to condone	dulden	≈	*to tolerate*
innocent	unschuldig	N	*innocence*
guilty	schuldig	N	*guilt*
to reverse	rückgängig machen	N	*reversal*
misconviction	Fehlurteil	VT	*to misconvict*
to hang	hängen		
to electrocute	auf dem elektrischen Stuhl hinrichten	vgl.	*electric chair*
lethal	tödlich		
firing squad	Exekutionskommando		
justice	Gerechtigkeit	<>	*injustice*
misconduct	Berufsvergehen	vgl.	*conduct – Verhalten*
unreliable	unzuverlässig	N	*unreliability*
testimony	Aussage(n)	vgl.	*to give testimony*
witness	Zeuge, Zeugin	VT	*to witness*
inadequate [ɪn'ædɪkwət]	unzulänglich	N	*inadequacy*
legal representation	rechtliche Vertretung	vgl.	*lawyer – Rechtsanwalt/wältin*
defendant	Angeklagte/r	<>	*plaintiff*

Greenpeace Mission Statement

Greenpeace is an independent, campaigning organisation which uses non-violent, creative confrontation to expose global environmental problems, and to force the solutions which are essential to a green and peaceful future.

Greenpeace's goal is to ensure the ability of the earth to nurture life in all its diversity. Therefore Greenpeace seeks to:

- protect biodiversity in all its forms;
- prevent pollution and abuse of the earth's ocean, land, air and fresh water;
- end all nuclear threats;
- promote peace, global disarmament and non-violence.

Introduction to Greenpeace

Greenpeace was conceived in 1971 when members of the Don't Make A Wave Committee in Vancouver, Canada, renamed their organization the better to proclaim their purpose: to create a green and peaceful world.

Greenpeace today adheres to the same principle as in 1971: that determined individuals can alter the actions and purposes of even the most powerful by drawing attention to an abuse of the environment through their unwavering presence at the scene, whatever the risk.

Policies

Greenpeace is concerned only to protect the environment. It allies itself with no political party and takes no political stance. Greenpeace is independent of the influence – financial or otherwise – of any government, group or individual. Greenpeace embraces the principle of non-violence, rejecting attacks on either people or property.

Structure of Greenpeace International

Greenpeace is a closely-knit network of national and regional offices, coordinated from the headquarters in Amsterdam. More than 1,330 people currently staff 43 offices in 30 countries. Greenpeace's boats carry out high-profile actions, and visit regions and countries, highlighting local and regional environmental problems.

Where does the money come from?

Greenpeace International is funded by the national offices. These, in turn, are financed almost entirely by small contributions from 5 million supporters in 158 countries, and by sales of merchandise.

mission statement	Grundsatzprogramm		
independent	unabhängig	N	*independence*
to campaign [kæm'peɪn]	agitieren	N	*campaign*
non-violent	gewaltfrei	N	*non-violence*
to expose	aufdecken	≈	*to reveal*
to force	erzwingen		
essential to	notwendig für	≈	*vital to*
goal	Ziel	≈	*aim*
to ensure	sicherstellen		
to protect	(be)schützen	N	*protection*
to prevent	verhindern	N	*prevention*
threat	Bedrohung	VT	*to threaten*
to promote	fördern	≈	*to encourage*
disarmament	Abrüstung	VTI	*to disarm*
to proclaim	erklären	N	*proclamation*
purpose	Absicht	≈	*intention*
to adhere to	festhalten an	<>	*to depart from*
principle	Prinzip, Grundsatz	!	*principal* – Haupt-
determined	entschlossen	N	*determination*
to draw attention to s.th.	die Aufmerksamkeit auf etw. lenken		
abuse	Missbrauch	VT	*to abuse*
risk	Risiko	VT	*to risk*
policy	Grundsätze		
to be concerned to	interessiert sein an		
to ally o.s. with s.o. [ə'laɪ]	sich mit jdm verbünden	N	*ally* ['ælaɪ] – Verbündete/r
to take a political stance	politisch Stellung beziehen		
influence	Einfluss	ADJ	*influential*
to embrace a principle	sich ein Prinzip zu Eigen machen		
to reject	ablehnen	<>	*to accept, to endorse*
attack	Angriff	VT	*to attack*
closely-knit	eng geknüpft	<>	*loose-knit*
network	Netz(werk)		
to coordinate	koordinieren	N	*coordination*
headquarters	Zentrale		
high-profile	medienwirksam	<>	*low-profile*
to highlight	ein Schlaglicht werfen auf		
to fund	finanzieren	N	*funds* PL
to finance	finanzieren	N	*finances* PL
contribution	Spende, Beitrag	VTI	*to contribute (to)*
supporter	Anhänger/in	<>	*opponent*

News Archive: 1999

WTO Conference in Seattle:

Eyewitness Reports from the Demonstrations

"There are around 50,000 citizens protesting peacefully here. Sure, there are a few extremists and trouble-makers among them, but the police have been very heavy-handed. There was no need to use tear gas and rubber bullets to break up the demonstrations, or to arrest hundreds of people. After all, intolerance of dissent is a characteristic of dictatorship, not of democracy."
– Local student

"The police have done a great job in difficult circumstances, showing restraint under extreme provocation. We have seen rioting and destruction of property on a shocking scale. The authorities were right to declare a state of emergency and impose a curfew. The moderate protesters have a legitimate message, but there is no excuse for resorting to violence and rampaging through our city intimidating local residents and looting stores."
– Seattle resident

"The activists and ordinary citizens on the streets of Seattle are defending the common rights of all people, upholding the principles of justice and sustainability. Citizens from all walks of life and all parts of the world are united here in rejecting the economic dictatorship of the World Trade Organization. Petitions, marches and rallies around the globe show that we have a broad base of support."
– Environmental protester

"We respect that the protesters are standing up for their rights, but the talks must go on. We must be able to voice our legitimate concerns to the rich countries, and this is the best place for us to do so. The protesters are well-intentioned, but they're doing more harm than good."
– African delegate to the talks

citizen	Bürger/in		
to protest [prə'test]	protestieren	N	*protest* ['prəʊtest]
peacefully	friedlich	N	*peace*
trouble-maker	Unruhestifter/in	vgl.	*to make trouble*
heavy-handed	hart durchgreifend	<>	*restrained*
tear gas [tɪə]	Tränengas		
rubber bullet	Gummigeschoss	vgl.	*baton* – Schlagstock
to break up	auflösen		
to arrest	verhaften	N	*arrest*
intolerance of	Intoleranz gegenüber	ADJ	*intolerant*
dissent	abweichende Meinung	VI	*to dissent*
dictatorship	Diktatur		
democracy	Demokratie	ADJ	*democratic*
restraint	Zurückhaltung	VT	*to restrain*
provocation	Provokation	VT	*to provoke*
rioting	Randale	N	*riot* – Aufstand
destruction	Zerstörung	VT	*to destroy*
property	Eigentum		
authorities [ɔː'θɒrətiːz]	Behörden	vgl.	*authority* – Autorität
to declare a state of emergency	den Notstand ausrufen		
to impose a curfew ['kɜːfjuː]	eine Ausgangssperre verhängen		
moderate ['mɒdərət]	gemäßigt	<>	*extreme, radical*
legitimate [lɪ'dʒɪtɪmət]	berechtigt, begründet	N	*legitimacy*
message	Botschaft	vgl.	*statement* – Aussage
to resort to violence	gewalttätig werden		
to rampage	Krawalle machen	≈	*to go on the rampage*
to intimidate	einschüchtern	N	*intimidation*
to loot	plündern	N	*looting*
to defend	verteidigen	N	*defence*, US *defense*
to uphold	(unter)stützen		
justice	Gerechtigkeit	ADJ	*just*
sustainability [səˌsteɪnə'bɪləti]	Nachhaltigkeit	ADJ	*sustainable*
to unite	vereinen	N	*unity*
march	Marsch	VI	*to march*
rally	Versammlung		
broad base of support	breite Basis der Unterstützung		
to stand up for	sich einsetzen für		
talks	Gespräche	!	*speech* – Rede
to voice a concern	einer Sorge Ausdruck verleihen		
well-intentioned	guter Absicht		
delegate ['delɪgət]	Delegierte/r	VTI	*to delegate* ['delɪgeɪt]

News Archive: 1999

THE CRISIS IN KOSOVO

Background

After the disintegration of Yugoslavia, Kosovo remains a province of Serbia. Long-standing ethnic tensions between Serbs and Kosovans reach crisis point, with repression of Kosovans by Serb security forces and Kosovan demands for independence. From 1998 onwards, Serbia uses the activities of the KLA (Kosovo Liberation Army) rebels as a pretext for ethnic cleansing.

The war

After attempts to negotiate the ending of ethnic cleansing have failed, NATO declares war on Serbia and from 24 March 1999 onwards conducts a ten-week series of air strikes on Serbia and Kosovo, with the objective of forcing Serbia to submit to its demands. Both civilian and military targets are attacked in an attempt to cut lines of communication within Serbia and kill and demoralize Serb troops in Kosovo. Refugees leave Kosovo in increasing numbers – around 850,000 between March and June 1999.
Despite claims that a ground invasion of Kosovo is the only way to end the conflict successfully, NATO refuses to deploy troops on the ground. As well as being difficult for diplomatic reasons (relations with the countries bordering on Serbia), a ground invasion is considered too dangerous in terms of likely NATO casualties. Instead, NATO relies on its superiority in the air and its sophisticated weaponry to attack targets from a safe distance.

The ceasefire

On 3 June 1999 the Serbian President Slobodan Milosevic agrees to a peace plan prepared by the European Union, the USA and Russia, and NATO air strikes cease on 10 June. The conditions of the ceasefire include the immediate ending of persecution in Kosovo, the withdrawal of all Serb military and security forces and the stationing of a multinational UN peacekeeping force in the province.

Evaluation

Opinions differ widely about how successful the NATO campaign actually was. An estimated 10,000 Serb troops were killed or injured, but at the cost of appalling civilian casualties, including hundreds of Kosovan refugees mistaken for Serbian troops by NATO bombers.

crisis ['kraɪsɪs]	Krise	!	PL *crises ['kraɪsiːz]*
disintegration	Zerfall	VI	*to disintegrate*
ethnic tensions	ethnische Spannungen	ADJ	*tense*
to reach crisis point	sich zu einer Krise zuspitzen		
security forces	Sicherheitskräfte		
demand	Forderung	VT	*to demand*
independence	Unabhängigkeit	ADJ	*independent*
liberation	Befreiung	VT	*to liberate*
rebel ['rebl]	Rebell/in	VI	*to rebel [rɪ'bel]*
pretext for ['priːtekst]	Vorwand für	VI	*to pretend*
ethnic cleansing ['klenzɪŋ]	ethnische Säuberung	vgl.	*genocide – Genozid*
to negotiate [nɪ'gəʊʃieɪt]	verhandeln über	N	*negotiation(s)*
to declare war on s.o.	jdm den Krieg erklären	N	*declaration*
to conduct [kən'dʌkt]	durchführen	≈	*to carry out*
air strike	Luftangriff	VTI	*to strike*
objective	Ziel	≈	*aim*
to force	zwingen	N	*force*
to submit	unterwerfen	N	*submission*
military	militärisch		
target	Ziel	VT	*to target*
lines of communication	Verbindungswege	VI	*to communicate*
to demoralize	demoralisieren	vgl.	*morale – Moral*
troops	Truppen	≈	*soldiers*
refugee	Flüchtling	vgl.	*to flee – fliehen*
ground invasion	Invasion von Bodentruppen	VTI	*to invade*
to deploy	einsetzen	N	*deployment*
diplomatic	diplomatisch	N	*diplomacy*
to border on	grenzen an	N	*border*
casualty ['kæʒuəlti]	Opfer		
superiority [suːˌpɪəri'ɒrəti]	Überlegenheit	ADJ	*superior*
sophisticated	hoch entwickelt	<>	*crude*
weaponry ['wepənri]	Waffen	≈	*weapons*
ceasefire ['siːsfaɪə]	Waffenruhe	vgl.	*to cease fire*
peace plan	Friedensplan		
condition	Bedingung	ADJ	*conditional*
withdrawal [wɪð'drɔːəl]	Rückzug	VTI	*to withdraw*
to station	stationieren		
peacekeeping force	Friedenstruppe		
evaluation	Einschätzung	VT	*to evaluate*
campaign	Feldzug		
appalling [ə'pɔːlɪŋ]	entsetzlich	≈	*horrific, horrifying*

DIALOGUE: HUMAN RIGHTS

Mel: I was pretty shocked by the news last night about the latest human rights violations in Afghanistan. I gather that the UN has imposed sanctions – but when have sanctions and embargos ever had any effect on totalitarian governments?

James: I think that sometimes diplomatic pressure and sanctions have more effect behind the scenes than we realize, although I don't know that's true in this case. Afghanistan is just one instance among many, though. Did you know that there were reliable reports of torture and ill-treatment by security forces in 130 countries last year? Or that people were executed without a fair trial in 40 countries?

Mel: That's awful ... But I guess there's not a lot we can do about it – as individuals, I mean.

James: As individuals, no. On the other hand, I joined Amnesty International recently.

Mel: Oh ... I don't get involved with political organizations like that.

James: But Amnesty is completely non-political! It simply promotes human rights around the world. It campaigns to free prisoners of conscience, ensure fair trials, abolish the death penalty and torture – things like that.

Mel: I see. So it "promotes" and "campaigns" ... What does that mean, exactly?

James: Well, for example, Amnesty delegates visit countries worldwide to observe trials, talk with victims of human rights abuses, and interview local activists and officials. It gathers information, being careful not to just pass on unsubstantiated rumours and allegations. Then it raises public awareness and mobilizes public opinion, publicizing its concerns in posters, newsletters, ads and on the internet. Equally, it confronts the offending governments with its findings directly in detailed reports, and it lobbies other governments and the UN to take effective action.

Mel: What's your contribution to all of this?

James: I write letters to prisoners of conscience – letting them know that they have not been forgotten – and also to governments expressing my concern about their human rights violations. And I get involved in fundraising events.

Mel: And do you think it makes a difference, or does it just ease your conscience?

James: It's difficult to be sure how much difference we make, but I'm sure that Amnesty raises public awareness. After all, I've just raised your awareness, haven't I?

human rights	Menschenrechte	vgl.	*humane* – menschlich
to shock	erschüttern	ADJ	*shocking*
violation	Verletzung	VT	*to violate*
to impose sanctions	Sanktionen verhängen		
embargo	Embargo		
totalitarian	totalitär	<>	*democratic*
diplomatic	diplomatisch	N	*diplomacy*
pressure	Druck		
behind the scenes	hinter den Kulissen		
torture	Folter	VT	*to torture*
ill-treatment	Misshandlung	VT	*to ill-treat*
security forces	Sicherheitskräfte		
to execute	hinrichten	N	*execution*
trial	Verhandlung	VT	*to try*
to promote	fördern	N	*promotion*
to campaign	sich einsetzen für	N	*campaign*
prisoner of conscience	aus politischen oder religiösen Gründen Inhaftierte/r		
to ensure	sicherstellen		
to abolish	abschaffen	N	*abolition*
death penalty	Todesstrafe	≈	*capital punishment*
delegate	Beauftragte/r	VTI	*to delegate*
to observe	beobachten	N	*observation*
victim	Opfer	VT	*to victimize*
abuse [ə'bju:s]	Verletzung, Missbrauch	VT	*to abuse [ə'bju:s]*
official	Funktionär/in		
to pass on	weitergeben		
unsubstantiated	unbewiesen		
rumour	Gerücht		
allegation	Behauptung	VT	*to allege*
to raise public awareness	ein öffentliches Bewusstsein schaffen		
to mobilize public opinion	die öffentliche Meinung mobilisieren		
to publicize	bekannt machen	N	*publicity*
concern	Anliegen	ADJ	*concerned*
to confront with	konfrontieren mit	N	*confrontation*
to offend	ein Unrecht tun	ADJ	*offensive*
findings	Feststellungen		
to lobby	Einfluss nehmen auf		
to take effective action	wirksame Schritte unternehmen		
contribution	Beitrag	VTI	*to contribute*
fundraising event	Benefizveranstaltung		
to ease o.'s conscience	jds Gewissen beruhigen		

G Science and Technology

1 Information Technology

2 Energy Technology

3 Space Exploration

4 Biotechnology and Medicine

talkback.com/IT

talkback

Are we too dependent on computers?

Information technology has revolutionized the way we live and work, but when computer systems crash, the result can be millions of dollars of lost business. That was the case on April 11 2000, when the London Stock Exchange went offline for eight hours and workers stared at blank screens.

Large computer networks will always be more vulnerable to catastrophic failure, or malicious hacking and viruses, than small, simple systems like the PC in your study at home. The solution lies in safeguards, maintenance and backups. There's nothing wrong with the technology itself. As always, the fault lies in the human beings who implement the technology. **Andrea Scott, UK**

In the last decades of the 20th century, many organizations rushed into computerization too quickly, without a proper IT strategy and with poorly trained programmers. The result was lots of bad code, some of which is still in use in large and complex systems. Reliance on these flawed systems is dangerous, and more high-profile crashes are inevitable. **Wayne Mitchell, California**

A pointless question! Our civilization is absolutely dependent on microprocessor technology, and we really have no choice but to rely on it. We can't reverse the IT Revolution, any more than we can reverse the Industrial Revolution. **Selina Duncan, UK**

The most important thing in software marketing is to beat your competitor in the race to get the latest, greatest feature into your product. Software is released onto the market without being tested thoroughly for errors – or for compatibility with other software which will run on the same systems. As long as technology continues to develop at this pace, failures will occur. There should be more investment in making systems stable and reliable, rather than boosting performance in terms of processing power and storage capacity. But of course, reliability isn't glamorous. **Zaki C, S.Africa**

If a tool is useful, people will rely on it. But technology has become more than a tool for us – a way of life. I couldn't live or work without my laptop, the Internet and so on. Without them, I might even be forced to talk to my girlfriend instead of emailing her!
Mike Campbell, Holland

dependent on	abhängig von	N	*dependence, dependency*
information technology	Informationstechnologie	ABK	*IT*
to revolutionize	revolutionieren		
to crash	abstürzen	N	*crash*
stock exchange	Börse	≈	*stock market*
screen	Bildschirm	≈	*monitor*
vulnerable to	anfällig für	N	*vulnerability*
catastrophic [ˌkætəˈstrɒfɪk]	katastrophal	N	*catastrophe [kəˈtæstrəfi]*
failure [ˈfeɪljə]	Ausfall	VI	*to fail*
malicious	böswillig	N	*malice*
safeguard	Schutz(vorrichtung)	VT	*to safeguard*
maintenance [ˈmeɪntənəns]	Instandhaltung, Pflege	VT	*to maintain*
fault	Fehler	≈	*bug*
		vgl.	*to debug – entwanzen*
to implement	einsetzen	N	*implementation*
computerization	Computerisierung	VT	*to computerize*
programmer	Programmierer/in	VTI	*to program*
reliance on	Vertrauen in	VT	*to rely on*
flawed	fehlerhaft	≈	*faulty*
high-profile	Aufsehen erregend		
inevitable	unvermeidlich	≈	*unavoidable*
microprocessor	Mikroprozessor	vgl.	*to process – verarbeiten*
pointless	sinnlos		
to reverse	rückgängig machen	N	*reversal*
competitor [kəmˈpetɪtə]	Konkurrent/in	ADJ	*competitive*
feature	Neuheit, Besonderheit		
to release onto the market	auf den Markt bringen	vgl.	*to market – vertreiben*
compatibility [kəmˌpætəˈbɪləti]	Kompatibilität	ADJ	*compatible*
investment	Investition(en)	VTI	*to invest*
stable	stabil	N	*stability*
reliable [rɪˈlaɪəbl]	zuverlässig	≈	*robust*
to boost	verstärken	≈	*to increase*
performance	Leistung	VTI	*to perform*
processing power	Arbeitsleistung	ADJ	*powerful*
storage capacity	Speicherkapazität	≈	*memory*
reliability [rɪˌlaɪəˈbɪləti]	Zuverlässigkeit	<>	*unreliability*
glamorous	glamourös	N	*glamour,* US *glamor*
tool	Werkzeug		
way of life	Lebensweise		
to email	E-Mails schicken an		

INTERVIEW: ARTIFICIAL INTELLIGENCE

Interviewer: ... Dr Franklin, what exactly *is* artificial intelligence?

Franklin: A branch of science concerned with creating computers which "think". Finding solutions to that problem involves computer science and robotics – but also psychology, linguistics and so on. Different research teams around the world have adopted different approaches – and different definitions of the goal.

Interviewer: Why is that?

Franklin: Well, we frankly can't agree on a universal definition of intelligence. The British scientist Alan Turing considered that a computer is intelligent if its behaviour is indistinguishable from that of a human. But is that just the *simulation* of intelligence?

Interviewer: What's your definition?

Franklin: Personally, I don't think it matters in the short term. What we are aiming for is a computer which is able to *learn* – that is, which is able to experiment with ways of achieving a goal, and come up with more and more efficient solutions. That requires making decisions, gathering, analysing and comparing data and making deductions – which lead to improved decisions. At first, its decisions will be made randomly and it will proceed by pure trial and error; as it acquires more knowledge, it will be able to reason.

Interviewer: And in the longer term?

Franklin: We *may* have to address more difficult issues. Does true intelligence require personality? Do we need to create a synthetic life form which has emotions and opinions? Which has self-awareness?

Interviewer: Why do you say that you *may* have to address these issues?

Franklin: It depends on what we want. Will we be satisfied with practical applications of artificial intelligence – such as computers which can interact with us in natural language and robots which can perform intricate tasks like surgery without supervision? Or must we push back the boundaries until we create computers with superhuman intelligence – which could evolve into god-like beings?

Interviewer: That sounds a terrifying prospect!

Franklin: Yes, but an interesting challenge, don't you think?

artificial intelligence	künstliche Intelligenz		
branch	Zweig		
science ['saɪəns]	Wissenschaft	ADJ	*scientific*
computer science	Informatik	vgl.	*computer scientist*
robotics	Robotertechnik	vgl.	*robot* – Roboter
linguistics	Linguistik	ADJ	*linguistic*
research team	Forschungsteam	VT	*to research*
to adopt an approach	einen Ansatz übernehmen	VT	*to approach*
goal	Ziel	≈	*objective*
universal	universell	N	*universality*
scientist ['saɪətɪst]	Wissenschaftler/in		
indistinguishable [ˌɪndɪ'stɪŋgwɪʃəbl]	nicht unterscheidbar	VT	*to distinguish* – unterscheiden
in the short term	vorläufig, kurzfristig	ADJ	*short-term*
to experiment	experimentieren	N	*experiment*
to achieve	erreichen	N	*achievement*
to gather	sammeln	≈	*to collect*
to analyse ['ænəlaɪz]	analysieren	N	*analysis*
data	Daten		
to make a deduction	eine Schlussfolgerung ziehen	ADJ	*deductive*
randomly	zufällig	≈	*at random*
to proceed	vorgehen		
trial and error	Ausprobieren		
to acquire	sich aneignen	N	*acquisition*
knowledge	Wissen	ADJ	*knowledgeable*
to reason	logisch denken	N	*reasoning*
personality	Persönlichkeit		
synthetic [sɪn'θetɪk]	synthetisch, künstlich	≈	*artificial*
life form	Lebensform	≈	*form of life*
self-awareness	Selbstbewusstsein	ADJ	*self-aware*
practical	praktisch		
application	Anwendung	VT	*to apply*
to interact with	interagieren mit	N	*interaction*
to perform a task	eine Aufgabe ausführen	≈	*to carry out a task*
intricate ['ɪntrɪkət]	kompliziert	N	*intricacy*
surgery	Chirurgie	vgl.	*surgeon* – Chirurg/in
supervision	Aufsicht	VT	*to supervise*
to push back the boundaries	die Grenzen zurückversetzen		
superhuman	übermenschlich		
to evolve into	sich entwickeln zu	N	*evolution*
prospect	Aussicht		
challenge	Herausforderung	VT	*to challenge*

Renewable energy – Options for the UK

Renewable energy is generated through the exploitation of natural energy resources which are constantly replenished and thus cannot be exhausted. The UK is fortunate in having some of the world's richest renewable energy resources, yet we currently obtain only 2% of our energy from them, mainly in the form of large hydroelectric plants. By contrast, more than 50% of our generating capacity consists of coal-fired power stations, with nuclear power providing a further 20%.

Whilst no technology is completely benign, energy generation from renewable resources tends to have far less impact on the environment than conventional generation from fossil fuels or nuclear fission. Also, the negative consequences are usually localized, as opposed to the global problems created by the emission of carbon dioxide and the production of high-level radioactive waste.

Here are some realistic renewable energy options for the UK:

1 Hydroelectric power currently supplies around 20% of the world's electricity. Water flows through a turbine, producing electricity in a manner which is clean, cheap (once the initial cost of construction has been recouped) and infinitely renewable. However, the local environmental impact of huge dams blocking and inundating river valleys and interfering with the natural flow of streams and rivers is often unacceptable. Small-scale plants are less obtrusive, but also damage local ecosystems.

2 Wave power can be harnessed by floating devices which convert the kinetic energy of the waves into electricity. Perhaps 20% of the UK's energy requirement could be met by this technology if developed and deployed to its full potential.

3 Tidal power is a promising option for the UK, whose coastal waters experience some of the most powerful tides on Earth. Barrages or turbines in suitable sites (e.g. in estuaries or narrow channels) could have huge outputs. A scheme proposed for the Severn Estuary could alone supply 6% of our electricity requirement. Here again, there would be environmental problems, as estuaries tend also to be ecologically sensitive areas, providing food for large numbers of migratory birds and many other species.

>> FORTSETZUNG SEITE 162

renewable	erneuerbar	<>	*non-renewable*
to generate	erzeugen	N	*generation*
exploitation [ˌeksplɔɪ'teɪʃn]	Nutzung	VT	*to exploit*
resource	Ressource		
to exhaust [ɪg'zɔːst]	erschöpfen	N	*exhaustion*
hydroelectric plant	Wasserkraftwerk	vgl.	*hydroelectric power* – Wasserkraft
generating capacity	Stromerzeugungskapazität		
coal-fired power station	Kohlekraftwerk		
nuclear power	Atomkraft	≈	*atomic power*
benign [bə'naɪn]	*hier:* umweltfreundlich		
conventional	konventionell		
nuclear fission	Kernspaltung	vgl.	*nuclear fusion* – Kernverschmelzung
consequence	Folge		
localized	lokal begrenzt	<>	*widespread*
high-level radioactive waste	hoch radioaktiver Abfall		
initial	anfänglich	<>	*final*
construction	Bau	VT	*to construct*
to recoup	wieder einbringen		
infinitely	unendlich		
dam	Damm	VT	*to dam*
to block	blockieren	N	*blockage*
to inundate ['ɪnəndeɪt]	überfluten	≈	*to flood*
to interfere with	stören	N	*interference*
small-scale	kleiner ausgelegt	<>	*large-scale*
obtrusive	auffällig		
to harness	nutzbar machen	≈	*to exploit, to use*
to convert into	(um)wandeln in	N	*conversion*
requirement	Bedarf	VT	*to require*
to deploy	einsetzen	N	*deployment*
tidal power	Gezeitenenergie	vgl.	*tides* – Gezeiten
promising	viel versprechend		
coastal waters	Küstengewässer	vgl.	*coast* – Küste
barrage ['bærɑːʒ/US bə'rɑːʒ]	Staudamm		
site	Standort	≈	*location*
estuary ['estʃuəri]	Mündung	≈	*river mouth*
output	Erzeugungsleistung	VT	*to output*
scheme [skiːm]	Projekt	≈	*project*
ecologically sensitive	ökologisch empfindlich	N	*sensitivity*
migratory bird	Zugvogel	VI	*to migrate*

>> Fortsetzung Seite 163

One disadvantage of both wave and tidal power is the considerable cost of large off-shore installations. This has discouraged investment in these fields.

4 Wind power is a realistic option: Scotland has more of this resource than the rest of Europe put together. Wind turbines are sustainable, cost-effective and cause minimal disturbance to local ecosystems. In principle, they could provide 20% of our energy requirement – the same amount provided by all of our nuclear power stations. However, in our densely populated country, the siting of new wind farms needs to be negotiated through sensitive consultation with local communities, who may be opposed on the grounds of noise pollution or visual intrusion.

5 Solar power is becoming more viable in the UK as photovoltaic cell technology improves. Unfortunately, this technology has yet to attract much investment in our country, as it has had to compete against heavily subsidized power from conventional sources. Surprisingly (given our short and cloudy summers), the potential is vast. If all of the suitable south-facing surfaces (rooftops and walls) in the UK were utilized, the resulting power would probably exceed our total national electricity requirement.

6 Energy crops are plants which are grown as fuel rather than food. For example, oil seed rape can be processed into biodiesel, and fast-growing trees such as willow or poplar can be grown as biomass for combustion in power plants. Growing and burning energy crops is neutral as far as greenhouse gases are concerned, because the amount of CO2 released by combustion is the same as that absorbed during the growth of the crop. Given our agricultural overcapacity, and the European Union's set aside policy, energy crops represent an attractive new market for the UK's farmers.

Clearly, each of the renewable energy sources has its advantages and disadvantages. There is a need to strike a balance between the various supply options as part of an integrated national policy. A further important issue is energy conservation: more efficient insulation of buildings and the introduction of more energy-efficient technology can drastically reduce energy wastage.

installation	Anlage	≈	*plant*
to discourage	abhalten	<>	*to encourage*
investment	Investition	VTI	*to invest*
cost-effective	kosteneffizient, rentabel	N	*cost-effectiveness*
disturbance	Störung	VT	*to disturb*
densely populated	dicht besiedelt	<>	*thinly/sparsely populated*
siting	Standortbestimmung		
to negotiate [nɪ'gəʊʃieɪt]	verhandeln	N	*negotiation*
consultation with	Beratung mit	VT	*to consult (with)*
local community	örtliche Gemeinde		
noise pollution	Lärmbelästigung		
visual intrusion	visuelle Belästigung		
viable	rentabel	N	*viability*
photovoltaic cell	photovoltaische Zelle		
to compete against	konkurrieren mit	N	*competition*
heavily subsidized	hoch subventioniert	N	*subsidy* – Subvention
surface	Oberfläche		
to utilize	nutzen	≈	*to use, to make use of*
to exceed	hinausgehen über	N	*excess*
energy crop	energieliefernde Pflanze		
fuel	Kraft-, Brennstoff	VT	*to fuel*
oil seed rape	Raps		
to process into	verarbeiten zu		
biomass	Biomasse		
combustion	Verbrennung		
greenhouse gas	Treibhausgas		
to release	freisetzen	N	*release*
to absorb	aufnehmen, absorbieren	N	*absorption*
agricultural	landwirtschaftlich	N	*agriculture*
overcapacity	Überkapazität		
set aside policy	Politik der Stilllegung von Ackerflächen	VT	*to set aside*
to strike a balance	das richtige Verhältnis finden	≈	*to balance*
supply	Versorgung	VT	*to supply*
integrated	integriert	N	*integration*
energy conservation	Energieeinsparung	VT	*to conserve*
insulation	isolierung	VT	*to insulate*
energy-efficient	energieeffizient	N	*energy-efficiency*
drastically	drastisch	ADJ	*drastic*
wastage ['weɪstɪdʒ]	Verschwendung	VT	*to waste*

SPACE EXPLORATION– Lemisse Al-Hafidh

Space – a distraction from more important issues?

I WAS RECENTLY discussing the latest advances in space exploration, in particular the International Space Station (ISS), with a colleague. After listening for a while, she commented: "I could think of a lot more important things we could do with that money."

That set me to thinking. When the Earth is beset with so many problems, is the space programme an expensive extravagance? Having weighed up the arguments, my answer is still an emphatic no. The ISS enables us to conduct research which would be impossible under the constraints of gravity, experiments which will have real benefits for the earthbound majority, rather than just satisfying the curiosity of a few scientists or demonstrating to the world our technological superiority.

It's true that the space programme is horribly expensive, but look at the benefits we already take for granted. Satellite telecommunication, improved weather forecasting, reliable navigation via GPS, non-stick frying pans ... Satellite imaging is giving us a better understanding of the ecology of our planet and the impacts of our actions – for example, on the ozone layer. None of this would have happened without the space pioneers' spirit of discovery and adventure, and without political leaders with the vision and foresight to finance that quest.

Whereas our activities in orbit around the Earth have had tangible benefits, deep space missions, sending unmanned probes to the farthest reaches of the solar system – and beyond into interstellar space – may seem an extravagance. Cash-starved oceanographers complain that we already know more about the surfaces of Venus and Mars than we do about our own deep oceans.

However, what seems like fascinating but useless knowledge, bought at an exorbitant price, may prove to be of incalculable benefit to humanity. The study of Venus and Mars is helping us to understand how our own planet was formed – and what might happen to it in the future. We have reached the point where eminent scientists can seriously discuss the viability of colonies on Mars within the next 50 years.

space	Weltraum		
distraction	Ablenkung	VT	*to distract*
advance	Fortschritt	VI	*to advance*
space exploration	Weltraumerforschung	VTI	*to explore*
space station	Raumfahrtstation		
to be beset with problems	voller Probleme sein	≈	*to be plagued by problems*
extravagance [ɪk'strævəgəns]	Extravaganz	ADJ	*extravagant*
to conduct research	Forschungen durchführen	VT	*to research*
constraint	Beschränkung	VT	*to constrain*
gravity	Schwerkraft		
benefit	Vorteil	ADJ	*beneficial*
earth-bound	erdgebunden		
to demonstrate	demonstrieren	vgl.	*to prove* – beweisen
technological	technologisch	N	*technology*
superiority [su:ˌpɪəri'ɒrəti]	Überlegenheit	ADJ	*superior*
to take for granted	als selbstverständlich hinnehmen		
weather forecasting	Wettervorhersagen	vgl.	*forecast* – Vorhersage
ecology [i:kɒlədʒi]	Ökologie	ADJ	*ecological [ˌi:kə'lɒdʒɪkl]*
impact	Auswirkung	vgl.	*consequence* – Folge
ozone layer	Ozonschicht		
pioneer	Pionier/in	VT	*to pioneer*
spirit of discovery/ adventure	Entdecker-/ Abenteuergeist	VT	*to discover*
foresight	Weitblick		
quest	Suche, Streben		
orbit	Umlaufbahn	VTI	*to orbit*
tangible ['tændʒəbl]	handfest	<>	*intangible*
deep space	der äußere Weltraum		
unmanned	unbemannt	vgl.	*crew* – Besatzung
probe	Sonde	!	*test, sample* – Probe
the farthest reaches	die entferntesten Bereiche		
cash-starved	an akutem Geldmangel leidend		
oceanographer	Ozeanograph/in	vgl.	*oceanography*
fascinating ['fæsəneɪtɪŋ]	faszinierend	N	*fascination*
exorbitant [ɪg'zɔ:bɪtənt]	überhöht	≈	*excessive*
incalculable [ɪn'kælkjələbl]	unermeßlich	VT	*to calculate*
humanity	Menschheit	ADJ	*human*
eminent	hoch angesehen	N	*eminence*
viability	Realisierbarkeit	ADJ	*viable*
colony	Kolonie	VT	*to colonize*

SCIENCE

THERE'S GOLD (AND WATER) IN THEM THERE ASTEROIDS

Entrepreneurs are joining the space race – with lucrative mining rights as an incentive.

INCREASINGLY, space exploration is coming within the reach of commercial organizations, not just government agencies. San Diego-based company SpaceDev plans to send its unmanned spacecraft Neap (Near Earth Asteroid Prospector) to rendezvous with the asteroid Nereus in 2001. There it will gather data for scientists who have paid to put their instruments on board, and send a probe to the surface to search for traces of minerals and water. Meanwhile another US company, LunaCorp of Arlington, VA, plans to send robots to the lunar surface from 2003 onwards to prospect for water and prepare the way for human colonies. Its Icebreaker Moon Rover will be financed by corporate sponsors and the sale of exclusive television rights.

Ironically, water is set to become one of the most valuable commodities in space. Its uses go far beyond drinking, washing and growing food. Splitting it into its constituents will provide oxygen to breathe, and hydrogen as the propellant for the ion drive engines which may power the next generation of interplanetary vehicles. However, the costs of freighting water in large quantities from Earth are prohibitive, because of the huge escape velocity needed to counteract the Earth's strong gravity.

Scientists believe that Nereus may be the core of a comet – in other words, a huge chunk of ice coated with dust. Other asteroids seem to have mineral cores, possibly including precious metals. Closer to home, substantial amounts of ice have been detected at the lunar poles – believed to be the debris of comet and meteor impacts.

The Neap mission raises the contentious issue of private property rights in space – SpaceDev's founder Jim Benson plans to claim Nereus as his own, which would set a precedent. Whilst the incentive of private ownership would boost the commercial exploitation of space, there is a strong feeling in the international community that extraterrestrial objects such as planets, moons and asteroids should belong to everyone.

JILL CARVER

entrepreneur [,ɒntrəprə'nɜː]	Unternehmer/in	ADJ	*entrepreneurial*
space race	Wettlauf um das All	VTI	*to race*
lucrative	Gewinn bringend		
to mine	fördern, abbauen	N	*mine – Bergwerk*
incentive	Anreiz		
to come within s.o.'s reach	in jds Reichweite kommen	<>	*to be out of s.o.'s reach*
commercial [kə'mɜːʃl]	kommerziell	N	*commerce – Handel*
government agency	Regierungsstelle		
spacecraft	Raumfahrzeug	vgl.	*rocket – Rakete*
to rendezvous ['rɒndɪvuː]	sich treffen	N	*rendezvous*
to gather data	Daten sammeln	≈	*to collect data*
instrument	(Mess)Gerät	vgl.	*equipment – Geräte*
on board	an Bord		
trace	Spur	≈	*sign*
to prospect for [prə'spekt]	suchen nach		
to prepare the way	den Weg bereiten	N	*preparation*
corporate sponsor ['kɔːpərət]	Firmensponsor	VT	*to sponsor*
commodity	Grundstoff		
constituent	Bestandteil	≈	*component*
oxygen	Sauerstoff		
hydrogen	Wasserstoff		
propellant	Treibstoff	VT	*to propel*
to power	antreiben		
interplanetary	interplanetarisch		
vehicle ['viːəkl]	Fahrzeug	≈	*craft*
to freight [freɪt]	befördern	N	*freight – Fracht*
prohibitive	unerschwinglich	VT	*to prohibit – verbieten*
escape velocity	Fluchtgeschwindigkeit		
to counteract	neutralisieren		
core	Kern	<>	*surface – Oberfläche*
precious metal	Edelmetall		
debris ['debri]	Trümmer		
impact	Einschlag		
to raise an issue	eine Frage aufwerfen		
contentious [kən'tenʃəs]	umstritten	≈	*controversial*
private property rights	Privateigentumsrechte		
to set a precedent ['presədənt]	einen Präzedenzfall schaffen		
ownership	Eigentum	vgl.	*owner – Eigentümer/in*
to boost	ankurbeln		
exploitation	Nutzung	VT	*to exploit*
extraterrestrial [,ekstrətə'restriəl]	außerirdisch	<>	*terrestrial*

Benefits of Genetic Modification

Genetic modification (GM) is the name given to techniques used to alter the genetic composition of living organisms. The process basically involves isolating a gene in one organism, extracting it and inserting it into another organism. The genes may be provided by (1) a different individual of the same species, (2) a closely related species, or (3) a completely different type of organism, e.g. genes from humans can be transferred to plants. The first two possibilities duplicate traditional selective breeding techniques, but with greater precision; the third possibility can create new types of organism which could not be produced by traditional means.

Organisms which have been altered in this way are called 'genetically modified'. However, there is no special 'GM' characteristic about these organisms: their genes are not unstable in some way. Their characteristics depend on which genes have been inserted into them.

Uses of genetic modification in agriculture

GM can be used to produce new varieties of a crop which have a range of desirable characteristics. For instance: they may have a higher resistance to pests; be more tolerant of arid conditions or extremes of temperature; they may not exhaust soil fertility by removing nutrients; they may be more nutritious or produce greater yields. This could have ecological benefits such as less use of agrochemicals.

Uses of genetic modification in medicine

GM can be used to produce larger quantities of a medicine than could be produced from natural sources (e.g. from rare plants), so that more people can be treated at less cost.

GM can also be used to produce drugs more safely than traditional techniques. For example, human growth hormone used to be extracted from corpses – with the risk that diseases would also be transferred to the recipient. Now it is produced by cloning human genes into bacteria. Plants are being used to produce vaccines for a variety of animal and human diseases.

benefit	Vorteil, Nutzen	VT	*to benefit*
genetic modification	gentechnische Veränderung		
technique [tek'ni:k]	Verfahren, Technik	≈	*process*
to alter	verändern	≈	*to modify*
genetic composition	genetische Zusammensetzung		
organism	Organismus	vgl.	*organic – organisch*
to isolate	isolieren	N	*isolation*
gene [dʒi:n]	Gen	ADJ	*genetic*
to extract	entnehmen	N	*extraction*
to insert	einführen	N	*insertion*
species ['spi:ʃi:z]	Art, Spezies		
to transfer to	übertragen auf	N	*transfer(ence)*
to duplicate	wiederholen	N	*duplication*
to breed	züchten		
precision	Präzision	ADJ	*precise*
genetically modified	gentechnisch verändert		
characteristic	Eigenschaft	≈	*property*
unstable	instabil	N	*instability*
agriculture	Landwirtschaft	ADJ	*agricultural*
crop	Nutzpflanze		
desirable	wünschenswert	<>	*undesirable*
resistance to	Widerstandskraft gegen	VTI	*to resist*
pest	Schädling		
arid	trocken	N	*aridity*
to exhaust [ɪg'zɔ:st]	erschöpfen	<>	*to replenish*
soil fertility	Bodenfruchtbarkeit	ADJ	*fertile*
nutrient ['nju:trient/US 'nu:-]	Nährstoff		
nutritious [nju:'trɪʃəs/US nu:-]	nährstoffreich		
yield	Ertrag	vgl.	*harvest – Ernte*
ecological	ökologisch	N	*ecology*
agrochemical	Agrochemikalie		
medicine ['medɪsn]	Medizin	ADJ	*medical*
quantity	Menge	≈	*amount*
medicine ['medɪsn]	Medikament	ADJ	*medicinal*
source	Quelle		
to treat	behandeln	N	*treatment*
growth hormone	Wachstumshormon		
disease	Krankheit		
to clone	klonen	N	*clone*
bacteria	Bakterien	SG	*bacterium*
vaccine ['væksɪn]	Impfstoff	VT	*to vaccinate*

Voxpop.com: Science Forum

VOXPOP
• DISCUSSION FORUM •

GM agriculture – good or bad?

The ecological consequences of GM are unpredictable and could be devastating. For example, if crops are genetically modified to compete more successfully with weed species – to grow faster, stronger – they themselves could become 'superweeds' when they spread into the wild. Field trials of genetically modified plants are dangerous: how can you guarantee that their pollen or seeds won't spread over a wider area? **Brian D, Australia**

Despite the hysteria created by the media and some pressure groups, I don't think GM is inherently good or bad, hazardous or beneficial. It depends on the uses to which it's put, and how thoroughly the potential dangers are researched. Genetics is a relatively new science, and we actually know very little about the functions of genes. It's foolish to rush into the widespread application of GM to food production. I think the public is right to be suspicious of GM – but not to reject it because of emotional reasons. **Andrew Mossop, England**

Herbicide-resistant crops are being developed so that more and more toxic herbicides can be used to eradicate weeds on agricultural land. The results: barren agricultural 'deserts' and more toxins in the soil, the groundwater and the foodchain. Pest-resistant crops sound a better idea on the face of it, but they will remove important food sources for wildlife. Agricultural 'inefficiency' leads to greater biodiversity. **Benjamin, Jersey**

We are creating new forms of life which could never have existed naturally. How can we possibly foresee all the potential repercussions of interfering with nature in this way? I can accept the use of GM for medical reasons, but to tamper with our food and the balance of nature purely for the sake of profit is stupid. **M. Blayney, Eire**

Fact 1: the world's human population is growing rapidly and needs to be fed. Fact 2: 700 million people are already chronically undernourished. Fact 3: intensive agriculture is not sustainable in the long term – it will exhaust and degrade the soil, as well as polluting the environment with chemicals. Put these facts together, and ask yourself: how can we afford NOT to research GM solutions? **Trudi Botha, South Africa**

consequence	Folge	≈	*result*
unpredictable	unvorhersehbar		
devastating ['devəsteɪtɪŋ]	verheerend	N	*devastation*
to compete	konkurrieren	N	*competition*
weed	Unkraut		
to spread into the wild	sich in der freien Natur verbreiten		
field trial	Feldversuch	VT	*to trial*
to guarantee [ˌɡærən'tiː]	gewährleisten	N	*guarantee*
seed	Same		
hysteria [hɪ'stɪəriə]	Hysterie	ADJ	*hysterical* [hɪ'sterɪkl]
inherently [ɪn'hɪərəntli]	von Natur aus		
hazardous ['hæzədəs]	gefährlich	N	*hazard*
beneficial	nützlich	<>	*harmful*
thoroughly ['θʌrəli]	sorgfältig	N	*thoroughness*
to research	erforschen	≈	*to investigate*
foolish	töricht	<>	*sensible* – vernünftig
application	Anwendung	VT	*to apply*
suspicious of [sə'spɪʃəs]	argwöhnisch gegenüber	N	*suspicion*
to reject	ablehnen	<>	*to accept*
herbicide	Unkrautvernichtungs-mittel		
toxic	giftig	≈	*poisonous*
to eradicate	ausrotten	≈	*to wipe out*
barren	unfruchtbar, karg	<>	*fertile*
toxin	Giftstoff	≈	*poison*
groundwater	Grundwasser		
foodchain	Nahrungskette		
on the face of it	so, wie es aussieht		
wildlife	die Tierwelt		
inefficiency	Ineffizienz	ADJ	*inefficient*
biodiversity	Artenvielfalt	vgl.	*diverse – vielfältig*
to foresee	vorhersehen	ADJ	*foreseeable*
repercussion [ˌriːpə'kʌʃn]	Auswirkung		
to interfere with	eingreifen in	N	*interference*
to tamper with	herumdoktern an	≈	*to meddle with*
balance of nature	Gleichgewicht der Natur	ADJ	*balanced*
chronically	chronisch		
undernourished	unterernährt	≈	*malnourished*
sustainable	tragbar	N	*sustainability*
to degrade	verderben	N	*degradation*
to pollute	verschmutzen	N	*pollution*
chemical	Chemikalie	ADJ	*chemical*

LETTERS TO THE EDITOR

Laboratory tests on animals

I would like to thank Polly Nelson for exposing vivisectionists and their dubious practices ('Under the knife', June 23). It is high time that this torture of animals in the name of progress was abolished. Supporters of vivisection try to justify animal trials on the grounds of human welfare, but there are too many vested interests, including researchers' pride and financial interests. Vivisectionists are too ready to take the credit for every new medical breakthrough: just because a drug was tested on animals doesn't mean that the tests were relevant, useful or valid. In fact, animal tests can be dangerously misleading in predicting the effects of drugs on human patients.

Dr Jean Simons, Princeton

Like so many animal rights campaigners, Polly Nelson fails to check her facts properly. She writes that 'conducting medical experiments on animals and extrapolating the results to humans is scientifically unsound.' This is not true: biological similarities between humans and other mammals mean that animal tests can produce conclusive and reliable results – if the animal is well chosen. Research with animals has led to many important discoveries and has greatly reduced human suffering.

Secondly, I must refute Ms Nelson's allegation that laboratory animals are kept in unsuitable conditions and generally maltreated. Any research scientist knows that a well-treated animal gives more reliable results than one subjected to stress or pain. Moreover, federal laws such as the Animal Welfare Act impose strict controls on how animals are treated in the laboratory.

Dr Stan Howard, Harvard

laboratory test [lə'bɒrətri]	Laborversuch	VT	*to test*
to expose	aufdecken, enthüllen	<>	*to conceal*
vivisectionist [vɪvɪ'sekʃənɪst]	jd, der Eingriffe am lebenden Tier vornimmt		
dubious	fragwürdig	≈	*questionable*
practice	Praktik		
torture	Folter, Qual	VT	*to torture*
progress	Fortschritt		
to abolish	abschaffen	N	*abolition*
supporter	Befürworter/in	VT	*to support*
to justify	rechtfertigen	N	*justification*
trial	Versuch(sreihe)	VT	*to trial*
on the grounds of	aufgrund + *Gen*		
welfare	Wohl		
vested interest	persönliches Interesse		
researcher	Forscher/in	VT	*to research*
pride	Stolz	ADJ	*proud*
to take the credit for s.th.	das Verdienst für etw. in Anspruch nehmen		
breakthrough	Durchbruch		
valid	gültig	N	*validity*
misleading	irreführend		
to predict	vorhersagen	N	*prediction*
effect	Wirkung	VT	*to affect* – *sich auswirken auf*
animal rights campaigner	Tierschützer/in	vgl.	*animal rights* – *Tierschutz*
to conduct	durchführen	≈	*to carry out*
to extrapolate	extrapolieren		
result	Ergebnis		
scientifically unsound	wissenschaftlich anfechtbar		
biological	biologisch	N	*biology*
similarity	Ähnlichkeit	<>	*dissimilarity*
mammal	Säuger, Säugetier		
conclusive	schlüssig	VTI	*to conclude*
reliable	zuverlässig	N	*reliability*
discovery	Entdeckung	VT	*to discover*
suffering	Leiden	VTI	*to suffer*
to refute	widerlegen	N	*refutation*
allegation	Behauptung	VT	*to allege*
to maltreat	misshandeln	N	*maltreatment*
well-treated	gut behandelt	vgl.	*to treat* – *behandeln*
to subject to	aussetzen		
to impose	auferlegen		

Useful Expressions for Essay Writing

1 Introducing the topic

- **Stating the opening proposition:**
  It is often claimed/said/asserted/stated that …
  Today we are often confronted with the problem of …
  We often read in the newspapers that …
  X made the assertion that …

- **Calling the proposition into question:**
  One must ask oneself whether/why/how …
  This assertion raises a fundamental question/issue: …
  We must examine the truth of this assertion.

2 Developing the argument

- **Enumerating the elements:**
  Firstly … secondly … thirdly
  On the one hand … and on the other …

- **Adding another point:**
  Furthermore, …
  In addition to this, …
  It must also be said that …
  We must also consider …

- **Introducing an example:**
  For example, …
  Take for example …
  To illustrate this, …
  … illustrates this point perfectly.

- **Introducing a quotation:**
  As X said/wrote, …
  In the words of …
  To quote X, …

- **Introducing a hypothesis:**
  It is quite possible that …
  … leads one to believe that …
  … may well be/have …

- **Expressing certainty:**
  All the indications are that ...
  It is certainly true that ...
  It is clear/certain that ...
  It is very clear that ...
  The truth is that ...
  ... as everyone knows.

- **Expressing uncertainty:**
  It is difficult to believe that ...
  It is uncertain whether ...
  This may be true, but ...
  ... seems likely/unlikely/probable/possible.

- **Emphasizing a point:**
  It is important/vital/essential to realize that ...
  We must remember that ...
  ... is an important/vital/essential point.

3 Considering counter-arguments

- **Signalling a change of viewpoint:**
  However, there are other issues to consider.
  However, this is just one side of the matter.
  However, we must not forget that ...
  In X's view, however, ...
  Let us now consider ...
  Let us now turn to ...
  On the other hand, ...
  Turning to ...

- **Conceding a point:**
  It must be admitted/conceded that ...
  There is no denying that ...

- **Denying a point:**
  It would be ridiculous to maintain that ...
  On the contrary, ...
  One cannot accept that ...
  This completely contradicts/disproves ...

4 Ending the essay

- **Summarizing the arguments:**
  Let us remind ourselves of the main arguments: …
  To summarize: …
  We have seen/established that …
- **Drawing conclusions:**
  All in all …
  All of these facts lead me to the conclusion that …
  From this I must conclude that …
  Having considered all these issues …
  Having outlined the main arguments …
  Having taken all these factors into account …
  What conclusions can be drawn from this analysis?
- **Stating one's own point of view:**
  I am convinced that …
  I personally believe that …
  In my opinion …
  It seems to me that …
  My own point of view is that …

Index

to abide by 121
ability 97
level of ~ 15
to abolish 145, 153, 173
absenteeism 3, 73
to absorb 43, 49, 163
abstract 81
absurdity 95
abundant 55
abuse 147, 153
drug ~ 29
academic 15
academic institution 111
academic performance 17
academic staff 19
to accelerate 49
acceptable 103, 115
access 51, 103, 115
to access 115
accessible 87, 93, 115
accession 131
accidental 27
accompanied by 11
according to 91
account
travel ~ 83
to account for 41
accountable 127, 139
democratically ~ 117
accurate 93
to achieve 159
achievement 17, 69
to acquire 159
acquisition 65, 69
act
to commit a violent ~ 119
to act decisively 139
acting 105
action 85
external ~ 89
to take ~ 131
to take effective ~ 153
unities of time, place and ~ 97
activity 111
actor 83
to adapt to 35, 39, 113
adaptable 113, 129
addicted
to be ~ to drugs 11
addiction 7, 11, 29
to break an ~ 7
additional 5
additive 41
to address 21, 29
adequate 103
to adhere to 97, 147
adherent 25
adjustment
structural ~ 67
administration 143
administrative 71
administrative support staff 71
admirable 97
to admire 93
adolescence 7
adolescent 7
to adopt a policy 117
to adopt an approach 143, 159
advance 63, 165
advanced 15
adventure
spirit of ~ 165
advisory council 129
aerospace industry 63
affairs
current ~ 109
current ~ programme 105
domestic ~ 143
economic ~ 77
affiliated 133
affordable 139
Afro-American 21
agency
government ~ 15, 167
law enforcement ~ 115
agitation 11
agrarian economy 61
agreement 131
agricultural 55, 163
agricultural sector 139
agriculturally 37
agriculture 53, 169
agrochemical 169
aid
development ~ 67
legal ~ 3
air current 41
air strike 151
to alarm 43
alienated 17
alienation 9
to align with 139
allegation 23, 25, 141, 153, 173
allegorical 87
allegory 87
all-female 17
alliance 143
alliteration 91
to allude to 81
ally 137, 143
to ally o.s. with s.o. 147
to alter 169
alteration 89
altitude 35
ambiguity 99
ambition 97
to amend 27
amendment 27, 129
amphibian 37
to analyse 17, 159
analysis 107
analytical 19
ancient woodland 33
animal rights campaigner 173
animated 111
annual leave 75
anonymous 85
anorexia 7
to anticipate 113
anti-discrimination legislation 71
anti-missile defence system 137
antisocial 95
antitrust law 63

anxiety 7, 13, 21
apathy 11
appalling 151
appeal 135
emotional ~ 91
to appeal to 81, 93
appearance 111
physical ~ 23
applicant 135
job ~ 73
application 67, 135, 159, 171
application form 73
to apply for 19, 139
to apply to 15, 81
to appoint 129
approach 29, 113, 115
to adopt an ~ 143, 159
appropriate 41
to approve 131
aptitude 113
arbitrarily 91
arid 37, 47, 169
to arise from 87
armed 27
armed forces 137
arms
to bear ~ 27
arms industry 63
arms race 137
army 137
to arouse 81, 97
to arrest 149
arsenal 137
article 107
to articulate 9, 99
artificial 55, 85, 93, 95
artificial intelligence 159
artificially 123
artistic 105
arts programme 105
Asian 21
aspirations
career ~ 17
to aspire to 99
assent 131
to assist 133
assistance
humanitarian ~ 133
assistantship
teaching ~ 19
to associate with 7, 93
associated 11
association 83
assonance 91
to assume 71
assumption
to make ~s 109
asylum 135
asylum seeker 135
attack 147
attack of guilt 7
to attain 17
to attend 15
attention 111, 121
to attract s.o.'s ~ 81
to distract s.o.'s ~ 141
to draw ~ to 147
to grip s.o.'s ~ 89
attention-grabbing 107
attitude 93
to attract 61
to attract s.o.'s attention 81
attribute 81
to attribute to 71
authentic 89
authoritarian 51, 117
authoritative 107, 113
authorities 149
authorization 73
automatic weapon 27
availability 47
available 103
average 65, 71
to award compensation 73
awareness
public ~ 111
to raise public ~ 153
awe 93
background 89, 109
bacteria 53, 169
bad taste 121
bad trip 13
balance
to strike a ~ 163
to strike the right ~ 9
balance of nature 171
balance of power 65
balanced 53, 109
to ban 115
banking system 139
barrage 161
barren 35, 171
barrier 65, 71, 123
basic principle 133
basic requirement 15
to be based at 133
to be based on 15, 55
to be beset with problems 165
to be bound by 121
to be compatible with 15
to be composed of 37
to be concerned to 147
to be concerned with 83
to be entitled to 5
to be equivalent to 15
to be in demand 19
to be in urgent need of 139
to be in vogue 51
to be liable to 135
to be located at 133
to be set 89
to be subject to 37, 39
to be under strain 3
to be under threat 45
bear
black ~ 35
grizzly ~ 35
polar ~ 35
to bear arms 27
to bear in mind 17
to beat 119
beaver 33
behaviour (US -or)
pattern of ~ 7
standards of ~ 141
behavioural (US -or-) 3
belief 25, 113
believable 83
beneficial 53, 171
benefit 135, 165, 169
educational ~ 113
fringe ~ 75
to benefit 65
to benefit from 19, 65
benign 161
betrayal 21
bias
gender ~ 71
bigot 25
bill 129
to binge 7
to bioaccumulate 43
biodegradable 55
biodiversity 47, 57, 171

biological 173
biomass 163
bitter 21
black bear 35
black economy 135
blackmail 141
bland 105
blank verse 91
blatant 121
to block 161
blood pressure 11
to blow up out of all proportion 141
body image 7
body of water 43
bogus 135
to boost 69, 77, 157, 167
to border on 151
to border upon 43
bound
  to be ~ by 121
boundaries
  to push back the ~ 159
boundary
  national ~ 139
brainwashing 25
branch 159
break
  commercial ~ 103
to break an addiction 7
to break down 11, 41, 55
to break up 149
breakdown 41, 95
breaking point
  to strain to ~ 23
breakthrough 69, 173
breakup 137
to breed 169
breeding ground 35
brief
  in ~ 109
to bring a case 131
to bring about 77
broad base of support 149
broadcasting 103
to broaden 15
broadsheet 107
broken home 3
to browse 33
brutality
  physical ~ 23
to brutalize 119
budgetary 77
to build up 43, 47
to build 89
bulimia 7
bullet
  rubber ~ 149
burden of taxation 65
burden upon 135
bureaucratic 135, 139
business climate 75
business school graduate 71
bycatch 45
by-election 129
byproduct 57
Cabinet 129
cable television 103
callous 145
camerawork 105
camp
  detention ~ 135
campaign 9, 41, 133, 151
to campaign 127, 147, 153
campaigner 173
cancer 11
candidate 127
  presidential ~ 127
capability 99
  offensive ~ 137
capacity 55
  generating ~ 161
  storage ~ 157
capital plant 63
capital punishment 145
capital 65, 77
carbon dioxide 39
care
  medical ~ 5, 63
career 141
career aspirations 17
career structure 75
careers service 19
caricature 109
carnage 27
case
  to bring a ~ 131
  to hear a ~ 131
  to process a ~ 135
cash crop 47, 63
cash-starved 165
cast 105
to cast a vote 127
casual violence 119
casualty 33, 151
catastrophic 39, 97, 157
cattle ranching 49
Caucasian 21
caucus 127
cause
  underlying ~ 17, 49
ceasefire 151
celebrity 105
censorship 117
centre (US center)
  population ~ 57
centralized 15
certainty 25, 99
certificate
  film ~ 117
challenge 17, 51, 65, 75, 159
to challenge 61, 109, 123, 133
challenging 89
chamber 129
channel 103, 119
chaotic 99
character 83, 85
  stock ~ 95
character study 87
characteristic 81, 91, 169
  to display a ~ 11
characterization 83, 89
charge 5
charismatic 25
charity 25
charter 133
chauvinist 143
check
  to keep in ~ 53
check-up
  dental ~ 5
chemical 57, 171
chemical compound 41
chemical fertilizer 33
chore
  household ~ 3
Christianity 25
chronically 171
cinema release 103
circulation 107
circulatory 13
circus
  media ~ 127

citizen 139, 149
civil liberties 117, 129
civil service 129
civil war 137
civilian 27
civilian population 137
claim 135
to make a ~ to 73
to claim 143
to claim title to 49
clarity 83, 113, 115
classic 105
to clear 37, 49, 133
clearance
forest ~ 37
clear-cut 81
climate 35
business ~ 75
climate change 39
climatic variability 37
climax 89
to clone 169
closely-knit 147
coal-fired power station 161
coarse 95
coastal region 39
coastal waters 161
coastline 33
cocaine
to snort ~ 13
code of practice 121
coeducational 17
to coerce 9, 65
cohabitation 3
coherent 111
to coincide with 107
to collaborate 75
collaboration 117
collaborative 19
collapse 39
colleague 75
collection 55, 87
college 17
sixth-form ~ 15
college degree 71
college of further education 15
colonialism 67
colonization 49
to colonize 33
colony 165
colourblind (US color-) 21
column 109
to combat 23, 47, 115
combustion 163
to come to terms with 3
to come within s.o.'s reach 167
comedian
stand-up ~ 105
comedy 95
comedy drama 105
comedy of manners 95
comic 95
commentary 109
commercial 103, 111, 167
commercial break 103
to commit 119
commitment
to respect a ~ 77
committed 133
commodity 167
common 7, 33
Common Agricultural Policy 139
commonplace 93
Commons
House of ~ 129
communication
lines of ~ 151
community 21, 33, 103, 115, 139
local ~ 163
community service 29
to compare favourably with 57
compassion 119
compatibility 157
compatible 15, 25
to compensate for 53
compensation
to award ~ 73
to compete 99, 163, 171
competition 21, 51, 63
competitive 77, 107
competitor 65, 69, 157
complacency 51
complacent 71, 103
complaint
skin ~ 13
to complement 69
complement 77
complementary 75
complex 81
to comply with 131
to compose 123
composed
to be ~ of 37
composition
genetic ~ 169
to compost 53
compound
chemical ~ 41
comprehensive 107
comprehensive school 15
to comprise 21
to compromise 51
compulsive 7
compulsory 103
compulsory education 15
computer science 159
computerization 157
conceited 105
to concentrate 11
concentration 11
concept 81
concern 69, 153
public ~ 141
to voice a ~ 149
to concern o.s. with 93
concerned
to be ~ to 147
to be ~ with 83
concise 83, 91
conclusion 97, 113
conclusive 173
concrete 81
condition 151
to condone 145
conduct 141
to conduct 151, 165, 173
confidence 3
public ~ 141
confidential 123
confined to 35
to confirm 21
conflict
marital ~ 3
to confront with 153
confrontation 99
confused 99
coniferous forest 35
conscience
prisoner of ~ 153
to ease o.'s ~ 153
conscript 137

consequence 39, 65, 161, 171
conservation 45
energy ~ 163
conservative 39
to conserve 55
to consolidate 61
conspiracy 143
constituency 129
constituent 167
to constitute 77
constitution 27, 129
constitutional right 27
constraint 25, 165
to construct 85
construction 161
to consult 5
consultation 5, 163
consultative 129
consumer 51, 77
consumption 51, 55
to contaminate 41, 57
contemplation 89
contemporary 87, 93, 97
content
course ~ 15
contentious 131, 167
context 109
contract 75
social ~ 75
contrary
evidence to the ~ 51
contrast 93
to contribute 127, 135
contribution 143, 147, 153
to make a ~ 55
contrived 85, 105
control
parental ~ 117
pest ~ 27
to have ~ over 7
to lose ~ 7
controller 85
controversial 5, 109
convene 131
convention 43, 119
national ~ 127
conventional 85, 161
to converge 89
conversational 93
conversion
currency ~ 77
to convert 51, 161
to convey 81
convincing 93
to cooperate 133
to coordinate 77, 131, 147
to cope with 47
coral reef 49
core 167
core skill 19
core subject 15
corporate director 71
corporate hierarchy 71
corporate sponsor 167
corporation 63, 71, 123
corporation tax 65
correspondence 121
to corrupt 113
corrupting 113
cost-effective 5, 55, 163
council 77, 129
Security C~ 133
Council of Ministers 131
counselling 3
to counteract 167
courage 97, 105
course content 15
course of study 19
court:
law ~ 129
to court 121
Court of Justice 131
coverage 103, 107
to crash 157
creative 111
credibility 23, 111
to destroy s.o.'s ~ 9
to undermine s.o.'s ~ 141
credit
to take the ~ for 173
creditworthiness 67
criminal justice system 29
criminal offence 73
crisis 3, 39, 151
oil ~ 67
to reach ~ point 151
criterion 91
critic 109, 129
critical 113
criticism 69
social ~ 99
to level a ~ at 127
to criticize 143
crop 53, 169
cash ~ 47, 63
energy ~ 163
crop rotation 53
culprit 43
cult 25
cultivation 37, 47, 53
slash-and-burn ~ 49
cultural 21
curfew 29
to impose a ~ 149
curiosity 113
currency
single ~ 131
single ~ area 77
currency conversion 77
current 41, 143
current affairs 109
current affairs programme 105
to curtail 29
custodial sentence 29
to cut 65
cynical 121, 141
cynicism 9
daily 107
dairy product 63
dam 161
to damage 13, 111
damaging 3
data 159
to gather ~ 167
to date 21
dead
to shoot ~ 27
to deal with 7, 95, 131
death
to sentence to ~ 145
death penalty 145, 153
death row 145
debris 167
debt 67
to service ~s 67
deciduous forest 35
decision procedure 135
decision
power of ~ 131
decisively
to act ~ 139
to declare a state of emergency 149

to declare war on 151
decline 45
to decommission 137
deduction
to make a ~ 159
deep space 165
deeply rooted 29
deer 33
defeat 99
to defeat 89, 127
defence 137, 143
to defend 27, 137, 149
defendant 145
to define 15, 91
deforestation 47
to degenerate into 87
to degrade 47, 171
degree
college ~ 71
honours ~ course 19
to delay 9
delegate 127, 149, 153
deliberate 27
to deliver a moral message 99
delusion 13
demand 55, 151
to be in ~ 19
to demand 17
democracy 115, 129, 143, 149
democratically accountable 117
to demonstrate 165
to demoralize 151
denomination 25
dense 37
densely populated 163
dental check-up 5
dentist 5
to depart from 81
department 19
dependency
physical ~ 13
psychological ~ 11
dependent on 157
to depict 83, 95
to deplete 45
to deploy 137, 151, 161
to deport 135
to deposit 41
to deprive of 123
deranged 27, 119
derogatory 107
descriptive 93
desert 35
desertification 37, 39, 47
to deserve 119
desirable 169
desire 111
to despise 25
destabilizing 137
to destroy s.o.'s credibility 9
destruction 49, 149
destructive 39
environmentally ~ 41
to detect 115
detective story 87
detention camp 135
to deter 123
to deteriorate 53
determination 99
to determine 131
determined 147
deterrent 29, 137, 145
deterrent effect 117
to devastate 43
devastating 171
to develop 133
to develop resistance 53
developer 45
developing country 67, 133
development 45, 89, 97
sustainable ~ 51
development aid 67
device 85
rhetorical ~ 91
to devolve power 129
to diagnose 5
to dictate 75
dictatorship 149
diction 89
to diet 7
diet
a staple ~ of 119
to differentiate between 21
dignity 97
diplomatic 151, 153
director
corporate ~ 71
disability 73
to disadvantage 21
disarmament 147
disaster 97
disastrous 33
discharge 43
disciplinary 73
disconnected 99
to discourage 5, 163
discovery 173
spirit of ~ 165
to discriminate against 17, 73
discriminatory 73
disease 169
disgrace 27
to disguise 111
dishonesty 141
to disintegrate 75
disintegration 137, 151
dismissal 73
disorder
eating ~ 7
dispassionate 89
dispersed 65
to displace 49
to display 11
disposable 55
disposal 41, 55
disproportionately 127
to disrupt 65
disruption 49
disruptive 51
dissatisfaction 3
dissent 149
to dissuade from 17
distinct 21, 85
distinction 107, 115, 123
to distinguish from 13, 119
to distort 107, 127
to distract 111, 141
distraction 165
distressingly 7
to distribute 115
distribution 33, 39, 61, 115
to disturb 119
disturbance 163, 45
diverse 21, 23
diversified 63
diversity 33, 103
to divert 67
division of labour 61
divorce 3
divorcee 3

to document 41
documentary 105
dolphin 45
domestic affairs 143
domestic life 95
to dominate 37, 63
doubt 93
downfall 97
downmarket 107
to downsize 75
downstream 49
drab 33
to draft 131
drag into 143
to drain 33, 45
drama
  comedy ~ 105
drastically 163
to draw attention to 147
to draw up 121
dredging 45
to drive away 45
driving force 51
drop 63
drought 39, 47
drug
  soft ~ 9
  to be addicted to ~s 11
drug abuse 29
drug trafficking 133
dubious 173
dump 55
dumping 43
to duplicate 123, 169
duplication 123
dynamic 93
early
  in the ~ stages 3
to earn a living 75
earth-bound 165
ease
  to put at ~ 73
to ease o.'s conscience 153
eating disorder 7
ecological 169
ecologically 55
ecologically friendly 51
ecologically sensitive 161
ecology 55, 165
e-commerce 65
economic affairs 77
economic and monetary union 77
economic migrant 135
economic prospects 67
economical 55
economics 55
economist 65
economy 61, 139
  black ~ 135
  free market ~ 51
economy of scale 57, 69
ecosystem 37, 39
editor 107
education
  compulsory ~ 15
  higher ~ 15
  secondary ~ 15
  sex ~ 9
educational 3
educational benefit 113
educator 17
effect 173
  deterrent ~ 117
effective 55, 81, 121
efficiency 69
efficient 139
efficiently 61
effort 133
egalitarian 65
to elect 129
election 127
  general ~ 127
electoral register 127
electoral system 127
electorate 127
to electrocute 145
electronic tagging 29
elementary teaching 17
eligible 127, 135
to eliminate 43
to email 157
embargo 153
to embark upon 69
to embrace a principle 147
emergency
  to declare a state of ~ 149
eminent 165
emotional appeal 91
emotional support 9, 25
to empathize with 85
emphasis 29
  to place ~ on 19
employment 69, 77
employment agency 73
to encourage 9
encyclopaedia 113
to end up 41
to endanger 41
endangered 45
to endure 95
to energize 11
energy
  reserves of ~ 7
energy conservation 163
energy crop 163
energy source 49
energy-efficient 163
to enforce 67
enforcement 63, 117
enlargement 139
enquiring mind 113
enquiry 23
to enrol for 15
to ensure 77, 131, 147, 153
enterprise
  free ~ 143
entertaining 109, 111
entertainment 103
enthusiasm 111
entitled
  to be ~ to 5
entrenched attitude 23
entrepreneur 61, 167
to entrust 141
environment 17
environmental 43, 57
environmental impact 51, 57
environmental protection 139
environmentally destructive 41
environmentally friendly 55
to envy 93
epic poetry 91
epistolary 85
equal opportunities policy 73
equipment 5, 67
equivalent
  to be ~ to 15

to eradicate 37, 117, 171
to erode 47
erosion 57
erratic 11
error 95
trial and ~ 113, 159
error of judgement 97
eruption
volcanic ~ 39
escape velocity 167
escapism 83
essential 91, 111, 119, 147
to establish 9, 133
estimate 39
estuary 161
ethical 123
ethnic 21
ethnic cleansing 151
ethnic minority 23
ethnic origin 73
ethnic tensions 151
ethnically 23
euphoria 13
euphoric 13
evaluation 151
evaporation 37
event 83, 87
eventually 11
evergreen forest 35
everyday 81
evidence 135, 143
evidence to the contrary 51
evil 97
to evoke 81
to evolve 39, 47, 159
to exacerbate 17
to exaggerate 85, 107
exaggerated 93, 95, 141
examination
public ~ 15
examination syllabus 15
to examine 15
to exceed 63
excess 49
excessive 51, 93, 139
exchange
in ~ for 123
exchange rate 77
exchange student 19
to excite 81
excitement
sexual ~ 13
to exclude from 63
exclusive 107
to excuse 121
to execute 145, 153
executive 71
senior ~ 71
exempt 5
to exhaust 47, 161, 169
exhaust fumes 43
exhilarating 89
exorbitant 165
to expand 37, 63, 69, 133
expansion 139
expectation 3, 121
7 to meet an ~
expense
at s.o.'s ~ 135
to experiment 85, 113, 159
expertise 61
explicit
sexually ~ 115
to exploit 43, 61, 123, 141
exploitation 65, 135, 161, 167
exploration 95
space ~ 165
to explore 97
to export 65
exporter 63
to expose 141, 147, 173
exposition 89
to express 81, 85, 91
expressive 83
expressly 81
to extend 35, 139
external action 89
extinction 39
to extract 169
to extrapolate 173
extraterrestrial 167
extravagance 165
extreme 81, 87
eye test 5
fable 87
face
on the ~ of it 171
facetious 107
to facilitate 67
factual 83, 109
faculty 19
failure 23, 157
fair game 121
faith 25
fallacious 123
familial 3
familiar 83
famine 47
fanaticism
religious ~ 137
fantastic 87
fantasy 119
farmer
peasant ~ 49
farmland 33
fascinating 165
fashionable 111
fate 97
fault 157
favourable 61
favourably 73
to compare ~ with 57
feasible 115
feature 157
special ~ 109
to feature 17
federal 27, 127
fee
licence ~ 103
feeding ground 35
to fell 55
female high-achiever 71
fertile 47
fertility 37, 53
soil ~ 169
fertilizer 53
chemical ~ 33
fiction 83
narrative ~ 87
fictional 83, 89
field trial 171
figurative 81
figure
public ~ 109
figure of speech 81
film certificate 117
finance 63
to finance 147
finance minister 77
financial market 133
to find in s.o.'s favour 73
findings 153

fine 135
fir 35
firearms legislation 27
firing squad 145
first-person narration 85
fiscal policy 63
fishery 43, 49
fishing fleet 43
fix
quick ~ 51
flabby 7
flaw 97
flawed 157
fleet
fishing ~ 43
flexibility 113
flooding 39
to flout 121
flow 65
fluctuation 39, 47, 57
to focus on 87, 103, 127
to follow up 113
food processing 63
foodchain 43, 171
foodstuff 55
foolish 171
foothill 37
for the sake of 45
to forbid 121
force
driving ~ 51
to force 17, 147, 151
forceful 81
forecasting
weather ~ 165
forefront
to be at the ~ 63
foreign language assistant 19
foreign policy 137, 143
to foresee 171
foresight 165
forest
coniferous ~ 35
deciduous ~ 35
evergreen ~ 35
forest clearance 37
to forfeit 127
to form a relationship 21
to formulate 133
fossil fuel 39
to foster 63
foundation 113
foundation subject 15
foundation year 19
fragile 23, 37, 99
framework 77
legal ~ 115
franchise 103
frankly 9, 95
free agent 75
free enterprise 143
free market 67
free market economy 51
to free on parole 145
free speech 115
free verse 93
freedom 143
freelance 75
to go ~ 75
to freight 167
fresh water 47
fringe benefit 75
fuel 49, 55, 163
fossil ~ 39
fulfilment (US -fill-)
personal ~ 3
fumes
exhaust ~ 43
to fund 103, 147
fundamental 129
fundamentally 81, 97
funding 5
fundraising event 153
funds 127
fungicide 53
fungus 53
to further 121
further education
college of ~ 15
futuristic 87
to gain weight 7
game
panel ~ 105
garbage 55
to gather 159, 167
gender bias 71
gender stereotyping 17
gender-defined 3, 17
gene 169
General Assembly 133
general election 127
general practitioner 5
to generate 43, 63, 69, 161
generating capacity 161
generator 57
genetic composition 169
genetic modification 169
genetically modified 169
to germinate 53
to get away with 105
to get immersed 83
to get involved in 85
to get the message across 69
to give priority to 51
glacier 35
glamorous 157
global warming 39
globalism 143
globalization 65
to go freelance 75
goal 99, 147, 159
to set ~s 19
goods
manufactured ~ 61
gorgeous 7
gossip 107, 141
governing council 131
government 129
head of ~ 129
government agency 15, 167
government official 67
gradual 39
graduate 19
business school ~ 71
grammar school 15
to grant 65, 123
graphic 111
grassland 33
gratuitous 119
gravity 165
to graze 33
grazing
livestock ~ 49
grazing animal 33
greenhouse gas 39, 57, 163
to grip s.o.'s attention 89
grizzly bear 35
gross 121
gross national product 63
ground invasion 151
grounds
on the ~ of 73, 173
groundwater 57
growth hormone 169

to guarantee 171
guidance
under the ~ of 19
guide 85, 109
guideline
moral ~ 25
guilt 7
guilty 145
gutter press 107
habitat 33, 49, 57
hallucination 13
hallucinogen 13
to halt 39
hand
to keep the upper ~ 137
handgun 27
to hang 145
harassment 23
sexual ~ 17, 71
to harbour 135
hardy 35
hare 37
harm 119
harmful 41, 53, 57, 115
harmonious 33
to harmonize 117, 133
to harness 161
harsh 35
to harvest 53
has-been 105
hatred
racial ~ 115
haven 45
hazardous 41, 57, 171
to head 23
to head for 21
head of government 129
head of state 129
head start 61
headline 107
headquarters 133, 147
to heal the rift 21
health care 5
to hear a case 131
heart rate 11
heath 33
heavy-handed 149
hedgerow 33
herbicide 53, 171
herd 35
heretic 25
hero 97, 119
heroic 99
heroine 97, 119
heron 37
hierarchy
corporate ~ 71
high school 17, 71
high-achiever
female ~ 71
high-brow 105
higher education 15
high-level 161
to highlight 147
high-profile 147, 157
hilarious 109
to hinder 139
Hispanic 21
to hit 7
home improvement 105
Home Office 29, 135
home
broken ~ 3
homicidal 119
homicide 25, 27, 145
justifiable ~ 27
honesty 93
honor 25
honourably 141
honours degree course 19
hopeful
presidential ~ 127
hormone
growth ~ 169
horror 93
to host 115
hostility 137
to hound 121
House of Commons 129
House of Lords 129
household 3, 103
household chore 3
household waste 55
human nature 95
human rights 133, 153
humane 145
humanitarian assistance 133
humanity 165
humid 37
to humiliate 119
humorous 95
to hunt 33
hunter 27
hurdle 135
hurricane 39
hydroelectric plant 161
hydrogen 167
hyperactivity 11
hypocritical 93, 121, 141
hysteria 115, 171
hysterical 9
ice
polar ~ cap 39
ice age 39
ice sheet 35
to identify with 87
identity 9, 87
sense of ~ 75
ideology 55, 143
idyllic 93
ignorance 25
illicit 123, 133
ill-informed 57
ill-treatment 153
image 81, 93, 115
body ~ 7
imagery 81, 91
imagination 81
imaginative 83
imbalance 21, 51
to imitate 119
immediate 81
immersed
to get ~ 83
immigrant 135
immoral 41, 145
immune system 13
impact 3, 33, 41, 165, 167
environmental ~ 51, 57
to make an ~ 81
impartial 85
imperialist 137
implausible 105
to implement 67, 129, 157
to imply 81
import tariff 67
to impose 29, 67, 149, 153, 173
impotence 13
impressionable 119
impressive 111
improbable 95
improvement
home ~ 105

in brief 109
inability 11
inadequate 145
inadvertent 73
incalculable 165
incentive 51, 167
incident 87
incineration 43
incinerator 57
to incite 115
income 71, 123
incompetent 67
independence 151
independent 113, 137, 147
independent school 15
in-depth 109
indication 141
indigenous 37, 41, 49
indistinguishable 159
individualization 95
to induce 11
industrial tribunal 73
industrialist 45, 61
industrialization 61
industrialized country 41
industry
manufacturing ~ 57
inefficiency 171
inequality 63
inertia 51
inescapable 97
inevitable 3, 69, 139, 143, 157
inevitably 97
inexhaustible 51
inexplicable 11
infection 13
infinitely 161
inflated 123
to inflict 145
to influence 45
influence 97, 113, 147
influential 139
information technology 157
informative 83
to infringe 27
infringement 117
inherent 51
inherently 171
to inherit 33
inheritance 33
inhibition
to break down ~s 11
inhospitable 35
initial 161
to initiate 129
innocent 27, 121, 145
innocuous 57
insect pest 39
insecurity 9
to insert 169
to insist on 105, 141
insomnia 13
installation 163
oil ~ 43
instinct
parental ~ 9
institution 111
instruction 77
instrument 167
insulation 163
insurance 63
medical ~ 5
insurmountable 135
to integrate into 29, 135, 139
integrated 163
integrity 141
intellectual 85, 105
intellectual property 123
intelligence 159
intelligible 105
to intend 91
intense 39, 43, 83, 91
intensely 93
to intensify 99
intensive
labour ~ 53
intensive care 5
to interact 99, 159
interactivity 111
interest
sphere of ~ 143
vested ~ 173
to interfere 21, 161, 171
intermarriage 21
intermediate 67
internal development 89
internal recruitment 73
international relations 133
Internet traffic 115
Internet-literate 113
interplanetary 167
to interpret 99
interracial 21
to intervene 137
intervention 63
interventionist 51, 143
interviewee 105
intimate 45, 121
to intimidate 71, 149
intolerable 97
intolerance 149
intricate 159
to introduce 15
to intrude on 143
intrusion 121
visual ~ 163
intrusive 103
to inundate 7, 161
invaluable 111
invasion
ground ~ 151
invention 61
to invest in 41, 103
investigative 107
investment 69, 157, 163
involved
to get ~ in 85
invulnerable 137
ironic 93
irreversible 51
irrigation 47
to isolate 169
isolationist 143
issue 105, 107, 127
key ~ 69
moral ~ 119
to become an ~ 7
to raise an ~ 167
to jail 29
jealousy 97
jeopardy
to place in ~ 27
job applicant 73
job segregation 71
to join in 9
journalism 107
journalistic 107
judge 29
judgement 111
error of ~ 97
quality ~ 107
judgemental 99, 109, 141
just 145

justice 145, 149
Court of J~ 131
criminal ~ system 29
justifiable homicide 27
justified 65
to justify 103, 121, 173
to keep in check 53
to keep the upper hand 137
key issue 69
keyword 113
kidney 11
knowledge 159
laboratory test 173
labour (US labor) 61
division of ~ 61
labour intensive (US labor) 53
labour pool (US labor) 61
land management 47
landfill 41, 55
landmine
to clear ~s 133
language
foreign ~ assistant 19
language workshop 19
large-scale 123
lateral thinking 113
law court 129
law enforcement agency 115
law-abiding 27
to lay off 63
leadership 61, 71, 143
to leak 41
learning materials 113
leave 75
lecture 19
lecturer 19
legal aid 3
legal framework 115
legal obligation 77
legal representation 145
legal requirement 73
legend 97
legislation 71, 115, 129, 131
firearms ~ 27
legislative assembly 129
legitimate 27, 123, 141, 149
lending 67
lenient 135
lens
telephoto ~ 121
lethal 145
level 39, 83
at the highest ~ 131
level of ability 15
level of proficiency 19
to level a criticism at 127
liable 115
to be ~ to 135
libel action 121
liberalization 65
liberating 75
liberation 151
liberties
civil ~ 117, 129
licence fee 103
lie
white ~ 9
life
way of ~ 157
life form 159
life sentence 145
lifelong 113
lifestyle 75
lighthearted 95
lighting 99
limited 113, 139
line break 91
line manager 71
linear 89
lines of communication 151
linguistic skills 19
linguistics 159
listings
television ~ 109
literal 81
literary 81
lively 87
liver 11
livestock grazing 49
living
to earn a ~ 75
lizard 37
loan 67, 133
to lobby 153
local community 163
localized 161
located
to be ~ at 133
logging 49
long term
in the ~ 49, 69
over the ~ 57
long-term 11, 23, 107
long-term unemployment 29
to loot 149
Lords
House of ~ 129
to lose control 7
low-growing 35
low-lying 37
loyalty 75
lucrative 167
lynx 33
madman 143
magistrate 29
mainstream 25
to maintain 53, 133
maintenance 157
major 39, 97, 131
to major in 17
to make a claim to 73
to make a contribution 55
to make a deduction 159
to make an impact 81
to make assumptions 109
to make redundant 75
to make reparation 29
to make up o.'s own mind 85
makeup 21
male preserve 71
malicious 141, 157
malnutrition 7, 51
to maltreat 173
mammal 35, 173
marine ~ 45
to manage 3, 33
management 131
waste ~ 57
water ~ 49
manager
line ~ 71
managing director 69
mangrove swamp 49
to manipulate 85
manners 89
comedy of ~ 95
to manufacture 41, 61
manufactured goods 61

manufacturing 55
manufacturing industry 57
manufacturing technique 61
march 149
margin
 profit ~ 69
marine 43
marine mammal 45
marital breakdown 3
marital conflict 3
market share 69
market upturn 69
market
 financial ~ 133
 single ~ 77, 139
 to release onto the ~ 157
marriage 3
marshy 35
masculinity 17
mass migration 47
mass production 61
mass 39
mass redundancy 69
massacre 27
to match 99
material
 raw ~ 57, 67
matters of state 141
mature 9
meadow 33
means of production 51
measure 115, 135
measure
 security ~ 123
 to take ~s 61
mechanics 9
media circus 127
medical care 5, 63
medical insurance 5
medical treatment 5
medication 5
medicine 169
to meet
 ~ an expectation 7
 ~ needs 5
 ~ obligations 65
member
 party ~ 127
Member of Parliament 129
membership 139
mental health 3
MEP 131
merchandise 111
to merge into 37
merger 69
message 149
 to deliver a moral ~ 99
 to get the ~ across 69
metal
 precious ~ 167
metaphor 81
metaphorical 81
meteorite strike 39
methane 57
metre 91
microprocessor 157
middle class 61
migrant
 economic ~ 135
migration
 mass ~ 47
migratory bird 35, 161
militarily 137
military equipment 27
military 143, 151
mind
 enquiring ~ 113
 state of ~ 99
 to bear in ~ 17
 to make up o.'s own ~ 85
mindset 25
to mine 167
mineral extractor 45
mineral resources 63
to mingle with 87
mining 49, 63
minister
 finance ~ 77
 Prime M~ 129
 senior ~ 129
mink 37
minor 97, 115
minority interest programme 103
minority 127
 ethnic ~ 23
to mirror 97
to misappropriate 67
misconception 25
misconduct 145
misconviction 145
misleading 173
missile 143
mission statement 147
mobility 65
to mobilize public opinion 153
to mock 95
moderate 117, 149
modification
 genetic ~ 169
modified
 genetically ~ 169
modular 19
monarchy 129
monetary
 economic and ~ union 77
monetary policy 63, 131
to monitor 117
to monopolize 17
monopoly 61, 123
mood 99
mood swing 11
moose 35
moral
 to deliver a ~ message 99
moral guideline 25
moral issue 119
moral obligation 143
morale 73
morality 141
moralizing 107
morbid 93
to motivate 111
motivated 73
 racially ~ 23
motor vehicle 43
mountainous 37
mouth
 to put into s.o's ~ 85
murder 29
mutual 137
myth 25, 93
narration
 first-person ~ 85
narrative 85
narrative fiction 87
narrator 85
nasal membrane 13
national boundary 139
national convention 127
national security 137

national sovereignty 143
nationalism 137
nationalist 143
Native American 21
native speaker 19
natural resource 51, 61
nature
balance of ~ 171
human ~ 95
necessity 77
need
to be in urgent ~ of 139
to meet ~s 5
negligible 43
to negotiate 151, 163
network 147
old boy ~ 71
nightmare 119
nightmarish 13
noble 95
noise pollution 163
nomadic herding 47
to nominate 127
non-commercial 45
non-fiction 83
non-renewable 57
non-urgent 5
non-violent 147
notorious 23
to nourish 53
novel 83
novelist 87
novella 83
NRM 25
nuclear fission 161
nuclear power 161
43nuclear reprocessing plant
nuclear weapon 137
nursery school 15
nursing 5
to nurture 9
nutrient 47, 53, 169
nutrition 53
nutritious 53, 169
to object to 21
objective 77, 131, 151
obligation 133
legal ~ 77
moral ~ 143
to meet ~s 65
to respect o.'s ~s 131
obscure 83
observation 99
to observe 153
observer 85, 93
obsessed 119
obsession 11
obsessive 99
obsolete 27, 103
obstacle
to be an ~ to 95
obtrusive 161
oceanographer 165
offence 29
criminal ~ 73
to offend 153
offender 29
offensive 117, 141
offensive capability 137
office
public ~ 127, 141
official 153
official
government ~ 67
oil crisis 67
oil installation 43
oil seed rape 33, 163
oil spill 43
oil spillage 43
old boy network 71
omniscient 85
on board 167
to operate 117
operational 77
ophthalmologist 5
opiate 13
opinionated 109
opponent 89
opportunities
equal ~ policy 73
opportunity 71, 113
opposition 21, 143
oppression 99
option 19
soft ~ 29
optional 15
orbit 165
organic 55
organism 169
to organize into 91
orientation 77
origin
ethnic ~ 73
originator 123
out of date 27
outlaw 27
to outlaw 27
to outpace 61
output 161
outrageous 105
outsider 21
to outsource 75
to outwit 95
overall 131
overcapacity 163
overdose 13
to overestimate 9
overexploitation 47
overfishing 45
overgrazing 47
overheads 69
overpopulation 49
overprotective 9
overreaction 9
overregulation 139
overt 23
ownership 167
oxygen 167
ozone layer 165
pace 89
pack 35
package 103
packaging 55
paedophile 115
panel game 105
paper mill 57
paper
waste ~ 57
parable 87
paranoia 13
parental control 117
parental instinct 9
parity 71
parliament
Member of P~ 129
parliamentary 129
to parody 95
parole
to free on ~ 145
part
spare ~ 67
to participate in 119, 131
party member 127
to pass on 153
pasture 49
pathetic 99
patriotism 143

patronizing 9, 105, 109
pattern 91
pattern of behavior 7
peace plan 151
peacefully 149
peacekeeping 133
peacekeeping force 137, 151
peasant farmer 49
peatland 33
peer group pressure 9
penalty
death ~ 145, 153
pension 63
pension plan 75
per capita 63
to perceive 81
percentage 63
perception 81
perceptive 109
to perform 83, 159
performance 11, 17, 69, 157
period 7
period detail 89
to permeate 23
permission 121
to perpetuate 25, 71
persecution 25, 121
to persist 37, 71
persistent 41
person specification 73
personal fulfilment 3
personality 159
personnel 69, 71
to persuade 111
persuasive 91
perverse 45
pessimistic 87
pest 53, 169
insect ~ 39
pest control 27
pesticide 33, 53
pharmacist 5
phenomenon 75
phobia 119
photo shoot 121
photovoltaic cell 163
physical appearance 23
physical brutality 23
physical dependency 13
piece 109
pioneer 165
piracy 123
to pirate 123
pity 97, 145
place: unities of time, ~ and action 97
to place emphasis on 19
to place in jeopardy 27
placement
work ~ 19
plain 37
plant 69
capital ~ 63
plantation 49, 57
plastic 41
plausibly 85
play 83, 91
plentiful 37
plot 83, 87, 95
to plough 33
to plough up 45
poem 83
poetic 83, 91
poetry 83, 91
epic ~ 91
point of call 5
point of view 111
pointless 157
to poison 45
polar bear 35
polar ice cap 39
to polarize 21
policy 131, 139, 147
fiscal ~ 63
foreign ~ 137, 143
monetary ~ 63, 131
sentencing ~ 29
set aside ~ 163
to adopt a ~ 117
policy maker 71
political
to take a ~ stance 147
poll 21
pollutant 41, 57
to pollute 45, 53, 171
pollution 41, 55, 57
noise ~ 163
pompous 109
to pool 75
popular science programme 105
popular 109
populated
densely ~ 163
population 61
civilian ~ 137
population centre (US center) 57
populist 107
pornography 115
porpoise 45
to portray 87
portrayal 89
position of power 17
postgraduate student 19
to postpone 51
potentially 115
poverty 47, 67, 133
power
balance of ~ 65
nuclear ~ 161
position of ~ 17
processing ~ 157
tidal ~ 161
to devolve ~ 129
to power 167
power station
coal-fired ~ 161
powerfully 93
practical 139, 143, 159
practice 5, 25, 47, 173
code of ~ 121
private ~ 5
prairie 35
praise 17
to precede 3
precedent
to set a ~ 167
precious metal 167
precise 99
precision 169
precondition 67
to predict 119, 173
predictable 83, 89, 109, 137
preference
reading ~ 83
pregnancy 9
prejudice 21, 25, 109
racial ~ 23
preoccupation 93
to prepare for 19
to prepare the way 167
to prescribe 5
to present 87
presenter 105
to preserve 133

presidential candidate 127
presidential hopeful 127
presidential primary 127
press
  gutter ~ 107
pressure 43, 47, 57, 153
  blood ~ 11
  peer group ~ 9
  social ~ 17
  to put ~ on 77, 117
pretentious 85
pretext 49, 151
to prevent 41, 55, 71, 115, 147
preventative 5
prey 45
to prey on 53
pride 173
  to take ~ in 17
primary 127
  presidential ~ 127
primary school 15
Prime Minister 129
principal 17
principle 97, 133, 147
  to embrace a ~ 147
  to uphold a ~ 143
to prioritize 41
priority
  to give ~ to 51
prisoner of conscience 153
privacy 121
private practice 5
private property 167
privatization 65
to privatize 67, 139
probation order 29
probe 165
problem
  to be beset with ~s 165
  to deal with a ~ 7
procedure
  decision ~ 135
to proceed 159
to process 55, 65, 135, 163
processing power 157
to proclaim 147
production
  mass ~ 61
  means of ~ 51
productivity 3, 47, 61
proficiency
  level of ~ 19
profit margin 69
profitable 61, 123
profoundly 33
profuse 11
programme
  minority interest ~ 103
  popular science ~ 105
programmer 157
programming 103
progress 23, 173
to prohibit 43
prohibitive 167
project
  self-help ~ 67
proliferation 137
promiscuity 9
promising 71, 111, 161
to promote 27, 71, 111, 133, 147, 153
promotion 71
prompt 51
propellant 167
property 149
  intellectual ~ 123
  private ~ 167
proponent 25, 129
proportion 21
  to blow up out of all ~ 141
proposal 131
proprietor 107
prosaic 91
prose 83, 91
to prosecute 115
prosecution 23, 117
prospect 159
  economic ~s 67
to prospect for 167
prospective 139
prosperity 77
prosperous 139
to protect 147
protection
  environmental ~ 139
protectionist 65
to protest 121, 149
to provide 115
to provide for 3
provocation 149
provocative 109
prudish 9
psychological 87, 99
psychological dependency 11
puberty 7
public
  in the ~ eye 121
  in the ~ interest 121
  to raise ~ awareness 153
public awareness 111
public concern 141
public confidence 141
public examination 15
public figure 109
public office 127, 141
public opinion 153
public school 17
public spending 67
public utilities 63
to publicize 153
public-sector 103
to publish 113, 121
pun 107
punishment 29, 135, 145
  capital ~ 145
punitive 29
puppet 85
purity 13
purpose 111, 147
to pursue 77
pursuit 99
to push back the boundaries 159
to put at ease 73
to put forward 111
to put pressure on 77, 117
quality 99
quantity 169
quest 165
quick fix 51
race 73
race relations 21
racial 87
racial hatred 115
racial prejudice 23
racial tension 21
racially motivated 23
racism 23
racist 23
racist stereotyping 23

radio station 103
radioactive waste 161
radioactivity 43
rainfall 37
rainforest 35, 49
to raise an issue 167
to raise public awareness 153
to raise 73
rally 149
to rampage 149
ranching
cattle ~ 49
randomly 159
rank 97
rapid 39
rapid response force 137
rare 45
rate 49
rattlesnake 37
raw material 57, 67
reach
the farthest ~es 165
to come within s.o.'s ~ 167
to reach crisis point 151
to react 85
readership 87, 107
reading preference 83
real estate 63
realism 95
social ~ 87
to reason 159
reasonable 121
rebel 151
rebellious 9
reception 103
recession 67
recipient 67
recommendation 23
record
to have a poor ~ 9
to record 123
record company 123
to recoup 161
to recover from 47
to recruit 23, 25, 69
recruitment 5, 73
internal ~ 73
recruitment figures 23
to rectify 51
recyclable 55
recycling scheme 57
reduction 65
redundancy
mass ~ 69
voluntary ~ 69
redundant 137
to make ~ 75
reef
coral ~ 49
to reevaluate 3
to refer to 5
references
to take up ~ 73
to reflect 23, 51, 89, 99
reforestation 49
to reform 129, 139
refugee 133, 135, 151
to refute 173
regardless of 67
region
coastal ~ 39
regional assembly 129
register
electoral ~ 127
to register with 5
regular 91
to regulate 115
regulated 65
regulation 55, 63, 127
rehabilitation 29
to rehearse 105
to reign 129
to reinstate 145
to reject 69, 147, 171
to relate to 9
related 113
relations 23
relationship 87, 95
to form a ~ 21
release 29, 41
to release 39, 89, 157, 163
relentlessly 97
relevance 141
reliability 157
reliable 113, 157, 173
reliance on 157
religious fanaticism 137
reluctant 3
to rely on 117
remorse 145
to rendezvous 167
renewable 55, 161
to reoffend 29
reorganization 61
reparation
to make ~ 29
repeat 103
repercussion 171
report 107
reporting 107
to represent 95, 139
representation
legal ~ 145
reprocessing
43 nuclear ~ plant
reproduction 45
sexual ~ 9
reputation 127, 141
to require 55, 117
requirement 15, 161
legal ~ 73
rerun 103
research
to conduct ~ 165
to research 111, 113, 171
research and development 65
research team 159
researcher 173
resentment 21
reserves of energy 7
residence
right of ~ 135
resident 37
residue 53
to resign 141
resignation 141
resilient 47
to resist 143
resistance 169
to develop ~ 53
resolution 95
resolve 3
to resolve 95, 131, 133, 137
to resort to 5, 149
resource 113
mineral ~s 63
natural ~ 51, 61
to respect 77, 121, 131
to respond to 17
respondent 3
response 9
responsibility 131
to take ~ for 19

responsible 117
restraint 149
restriction 77
restrictive 85
restructuring 69
result 173
search ~ 111
retail trade 63
to reveal 87
revealing 121
revelation 141
revenue 69
to reverse 145, 157
review 89, 109
to revolutionize 157
rewarding 75
rhetorical device 91
rhyme 91
to rhyme 91
rhythm 89, 91
to ride roughshod over 45
to ridicule 95
ridiculous 93
rife 51, 123
rifle 27
rift
to heal the ~ 21
right
constitutional ~ 27
human ~s 133, 153
in o.'s own ~ 85
right of residence 135
rightful 123
riot 23
rioting 149
risk 147
robotics 159
rodent 37
role model 17, 119
role 85
romance 21
rotation
crop ~ 53
roughshod
to ride ~ over 45
routinely 43
royalty 123
rubber bullet 149
to ruin 141
to rule out 69
rumour 69, 141, 153
to run 127
run-off 43
rural community 55
ruthless 93
safeguard 57, 129, 157
safety valve 119
sake
for the ~ of 45
sanction
to impose ~s 153
sanctity 145
sanitation department 55
satire
social ~ 95
satirical 87, 95, 109
satisfactory 85
scale 49, 61
economy of ~ 57, 69
scandal 141
scare story 9
scene 99
behind the ~s 153
schedule 103
scheme 161
school
comprehensive ~ 15
grammar ~ 15
high ~ 17, 71
independent ~ 15
nursery 15
primary ~ 15
public ~ 17
secondary ~ 15
school-leaving age 15
science 159
popular ~ programme 105
scientifically unsound 173
scientist 159
scrap steel 57
screen 157
scrub 37
sea bed 45
sea level 39
seal 45
search result 111
search term 113
searching 105
secondary education 15
secondary school 15
secure 75
security 27, 75, 133
national ~ 137
Security Council 133
security forces 151, 153
security measure 123
seed 53, 171
segregation: job ~ 71
to select 15, 85
selection 73
selective 75, 113
self-awareness 159
self-confidence 113
self-conscious 93
self-defeating 123
self-defense 27
self-delusion 99
self-destructive 7
self-esteem 3, 75
self-help project 67
self-indulgent 83
selfishness 9
self-regulation 117
semidesert 35
send-up 109
senior 23
senior executive 71
senior minister 129
sensationalist 107
sense of identity 75
senses 93
sensible 137
sensitive 105
ecologically ~ 161
sentence
custodial ~ 29
life ~ 145
to serve a ~ 29
to sentence 29
to sentence to death 145
sentencing policy 29
separation 3
sequence 89, 97
series 103
to serve a sentence 29
service 77
social ~s 67
to service debts 67
session 131
set 105
stage ~ 99
to be ~ 89
to set a precedent 167
to set down 77
to set goals 19

to set out 133
to set up 133
set aside policy 163
severe 13, 39, 117
sex education 9
sexual act 115
sexual excitement 13
sexual harassment 17, 71
sexual reproduction 9
sexuality 7
sexually explicit 115
share
market ~ 69
shareholder 69
shield 7
to shield from 117
shift 51
shipping 43
to shock 153
shocking 89
to shoot dead 27
short story 87
short term
in the ~ 159
shortage 5, 49
short-lived 75
short-term 11, 45
shotgun 27
shrub 37
side effect 11
to sift 111
to sift out 73
silt 49
similarity 173
simile 81
single currency 131
single currency area 77
single market 77, 139
single-sex 17
sinister 87
sitcom 105
site 33, 161
siting 163
sixth form 15
sixth-form college 15
skilful 89
skill 73, 113
core ~ 19
linguistic ~s 19
skilled worker 61
skin complaint 13
slapstick 95
slash-and-burn cultivation 49
slick 111, 119
small-scale 67, 161
smug 105
to snort cocaine 13
soap opera 105
social contract 75
social criticism 99
social pressure 17
social realism 87
social satire 95
social security system 135
social services 67
social spending 139
socioeconomic 61, 75
soft drug 9
soft option 29
soil 47, 53
soil fertility 169
sole responsibility 131
solitary 75
solution 41
sophisticated 117, 151
to sort 55
sound 77
source 43, 169
virgin ~ 57
sovereign 129
sovereign country 133
sovereignty
national ~ 143
space 165
deep ~ 165
space exploration 165
space race 167
space station 165
spacecraft 167
spare part 67
spawning ground 45
special feature 109
special-interest group 127
specialist therapist 5
specialization 61
specialized 19, 105
species 33, 47, 169
spectator 17
speech
free ~ 115
to speed up 135
spending
public ~ 67
social ~ 139
sphere of interest 143
spirit of discovery/adventure 165
spiritual 25
spoilage 55
sponsor
corporate ~ 167
spontaneous 105
sporting tournament 103
to spray 53
to spread into the wild 171
squalor 65
squirrel 37
stability 77
to stabilize 133
stable 3, 75, 77, 139, 157
staff 19, 71, 129
stage 83
stage set 99
stance 107
to take a political ~ 147
to stand down 129
to stand up 27
to stand up for 149
standards of behaviour 141
stand-up comedian 105
stanza 91
stark 93
starvation 7
state 11, 15
head of ~ 129
matters of ~ 141
state of mind 99
statement 123
station 103
to station 151
steady 49
steel
scrap ~ 57
to stem the tide 135
stereotype 109
stereotyping
gender ~ 17
racist ~ 23
sterile 57
stilted 89

to stimulate 65
stock character 95
stock exchange 157
storage capacity 157
storyline 105
storytelling 89
straightforward 89
strain
 to be under ~ 3
to strain to breaking point 23
strand 89
to strengthen 77
strike 151
 meteorite ~ 39
to strike a balance 163
to strike the right balance 9
striking 81
stringent 135
to strip of 47
structural adjustment 67
structure 91
 career 75
to structure 113
student
 exchange ~ 19
 postgraduate ~ 19
 undergraduate ~ 19
study
 course of ~ 19
subject
 core ~ 15
 foundation ~ 15
 to be ~ to 37, 39
to subject to 173
subject matter 93, 97
subjective 83, 91
to submit 7, 131, 151
subplot 97
to subscribe to 103
subsidiary 15, 69
to subsidize 5
subsidized 163
subsidy 45, 65
to substantiate 135
subtle 81, 105
to suffer 25, 51
suffering 95, 145, 173
suicide 25, 27
suitable 47
summit 131
superficial 111
superhuman 159
superiority 95, 143, 151, 165
supernatural 87, 97
to supervise 131
supervision 73, 159
supplement 109
supply 49, 163
support 19, 71
 broad base of ~ 149
 emotional ~ 9, 25
to support 33, 47, 119, 135, 145
supporter 43, 127, 147, 173
supposition 107
surface 163
to surface 7
surgery 159
to surpass 61
surplus 63
surveillance 115
survey 3
survival 93
to suspend 119
suspicion 137
suspicious 113, 171
to sustain 61
sustainability 149
sustainable 33, 47, 171
sustainable development 51
swamp
 mangrove ~ 49
to swap 123
to sway 127
sweat shop 135
sweating 11
sweeping 129
swing
 mood ~ 11
syllable 91
syllabus
 examination ~ 15
symbolic 87
sympathetic 89
synopsis 109
synthetic 41, 53, 57, 159
syringe 13
systematically 121
tabloid 107
to tackle 29, 117, 139
tagging
 electronic ~ 29
to take action 131
to take effective action 153
to take for granted 75, 165
to take into account 55
to take its toll 45
to take measures 61
to take pride in 17
to take responsibility for 19
to take the credit for 173
to take up references 73
talks 149
to tamper with 171
tangible 165
target 151
task
 to perform a ~ 159
task force 23
taste
 in bad ~ 121
to taunt 7
tax 135
 corporation ~ 65
taxation
 burden of 65
teaching
 elementary ~ 17
teaching assistantship 19
teachings 25
tear gas 149
technical training 67
technically 115
technician 67
technique 85, 169
 manufacturing ~ 61
technological 61, 165
technology
 information ~ 157
telephoto lens 121
television listings 109
temperate 35
to tend to 9
tension 3, 89
 ethnic ~s 151
 racial ~ 21
term
 search ~ 113
terrifying 93
terrorism 133

test
laboratory ~ 173
testimony 145
theft 29, 123
therapist 5
thicket 37
thinking
lateral ~ 113
thoroughly 171
thought-provoking 109
threat 41, 141, 147
to be under ~ 45
to threaten 45, 99, 137
to thrive 33
tidal power 161
tide
to stem the ~ 135
timber 55
time
it is high ~ 121
unities of ~, place and action 97
timescale 89
title
to claim ~ to 49
tolerance 21
to tolerate 71
tone 87
tool 157
topic 87, 113
torture 153, 173
totalitarian 153
tough 29
tournament
sporting ~ 103
toxic 41, 53, 57, 171
toxics 41
toxin 171
trace 167
to trace 97
track 123
trade 41, 139
wholesale ~ 63
trade union 73
traffic
Internet ~ 115
trafficking
drug ~ 133
tragedy 95
tragic 95
tragicomedy 95
to train 17
training
technical ~ 67
to undergo ~ 27
vocational ~ 67
to transfer 65, 169
transferable 19
to transform 33
transformation 61, 75
transition 37
transitional 99
transmission 103
to transport 57
to trap 39
to traumatize 119
travel account 83
to trawl 43
to treat 169
treatment 87
medical ~ 5
treaty 77, 131, 137
trembling 11
trial 153, 173
field ~ 171
trial and error 113, 159
tribunal
industrial ~ 73
trivia 109
troops 137, 151
tropical 35
trouble-maker 149
truancy 29
trust 23
tuition 19
tune 111
turnout 127
turnover 69
tutorial 19
twist 83
ultimate 43, 145
ultimately 99
uncertainty 39, 77
unconscious 23
to undergo 27, 61
undergraduate student 19
underlying cause 17, 49
to undermine 123, 141
undernourished 171
to underpin 77
understated 93
uneasy 23
unelected 139
unemployment
long-term ~ 29
unfounded 25, 141
unified 97
union
trade ~ 73
unique 49
to unite 149
united 139
unities of time, place and action 97
unity 25, 77
universal 159
unjustified 111
unmanned 165
unnerving 7
unobtrusive 85
unprecedented 61
unpredictable 13, 99, 171
unpretentious 89
unprofitable 67, 69
unregulated 49
unreliability 141
unreliable 85, 107, 111, 145
unscrupulous 121
unsound
scientifically ~ 173
unstable 169
unsubstantiated 153
unsuitable 73, 119
untruthful 141
up to date 109
to uphold 143, 149
to upset 119
upturn
market ~ 69
urban 61
urge 7
urgent
to be in ~ need of 139
utilities
public ~ 63
to utilize 75, 163
utopian 51
vaccine 169
valid 113, 173
to value 107
variability
climatic ~ 37
variable 13, 111
vast 49
vehicle 167
motor ~ 43

velocity
escape ~ 167
versatile 83
verse 91
blank ~ 91
free ~ 93
vested interest 173
to vet 117
to veto 129
viability 123, 165
viable 163, 53
vicious circle 67
victim 17, 121, 145, 153
victimless 123
view 87
to view 115
viewer 103
viewpoint 85, 97
villain 119
violation 137, 153
violence 29, 89, 119
casual ~ 119
to resort to ~ 149
violent
to commit a ~ act 119
virgin source 57
virtue 97
visible 23
vision 93
visual intrusion 163
to visualize 83
vital 35
vivid 83, 89
vivisectionist 173
vocational 15
vocational training 67
vogue
to be in ~ 51
to voice a concern 149
volatile 75, 137
volcanic eruption 39
volition
of one's own ~ 25
volume 117
voluntary 117
voluntary redundancy 69
to vomit 7
vote
to cast a ~ 127
to vote 127
vulnerable 37, 157
vulture 37
wacky 111
wages 65
waiting list 5
war
civil ~ 137
to declare ~ on 151
warming
global ~ 39
warrior 119
wastage 163
waste 43
household ~ 55
radioactive ~ 161
waste management 57
waste paper 57
wasteful 55
water
body of ~ 43
coastal ~s 161
to water 53
water management 49
water table 47
waterlogged 47
waterway 41
way
to prepare the ~ 167
way of life 157
wealth 61
weapon 27
nuclear ~ 137
weaponry 151
weather forecasting 165
weed 53, 171
weekly 107
weight
to gain ~ 7
welfare 173
well thought-out 83
well-intentioned 23, 149
well-treated 173
wetland 33
wheat 33
white lie 9
wholesale trade 63
wicked 109
widespread 23, 39
wild
to spread into the ~ 171
wildlife 33, 41, 171
to wipe out 45
wit 105
to withdraw 143
withdrawal 11, 151
to withhold 143
to witness 119
witness 145
witty 89, 93, 109
wolf 35
woodland 33
work placement 19
workable 115
worker
skilled ~ 61
workforce 65, 69, 73
worship 25
yield 53, 169